Bag Man

Lew Frankfort
FORMER CEO, COACH
with Joanne Gordon

Bag Man

THE STORY BEHIND THE IMPROBABLE RISE OF COACH

HARVARD BUSINESS REVIEW PRESS • BOSTON, MASSACHUSETTS

Printed in the United States of America

10 9 8 7 6 5 4 3 2 1

Library of Congress Cataloging-in-Publication Data
Names: Frankfort, Lew, author.
Title: Bag man : the story behind the improbable rise of Coach / Lew Frankfort, former CEO, Coach.
Description: Boston, Massachusetts : Harvard Business Review Press, [2025] | Includes index.
Identifiers: LCCN 2025005867 (print) | LCCN 2025005868 (ebook) | ISBN 9798892790727 (hardcover) | ISBN 9798892790734 (epub)
Subjects: LCSH: Frankfort, Lew. | Coach Inc. | Handbag industry—United States—Management. | Chief executive officers—United States—Biography.
Classification: LCC HD9947.5.U64 C635 2025 (print) | LCC HD9947.5.U64 (ebook) | DDC 381/.4568520973—dc23/eng/20240219
LC record available at https://lccn.loc.gov/2025005867
LC ebook record available at https://lccn.loc.gov/2025005868

ISBN: 979-8-89279-072-7
eISBN: 979-8-89279-073-4

The paper used in this publication meets the requirements of the American National Standard for Permanence of Paper for Publications and Documents in Libraries and Archives Z39.48-1992.

This book is dedicated to my family, especially my mother and father, who always believed in me.

CONTENTS

INTRODUCTION

Magic Plus Logic

The nightmare first occurred in 2000, as I prepared for Coach's IPO. It was a recurring bad dream that always began the same way, with me walking down a busy Madison Avenue sidewalk in New York City on my way to an early-morning meeting with potential investors. I'm wearing a three-piece suit and carrying a leather briefcase, and at one point I look down and realize that I'm not wearing shoes. The only thing on my feet are bright blue woolly socks.

No one passing me notices. But I know, and I'm horrified. I can't face investors without shoes. I keep walking until I see a men's shoe store on a corner, a classic brand called Allen Edmonds. I walk toward it and peer through the window. Inside I see a man cleaning the floor. I wave to him but he doesn't see me. I knock on the glass but he doesn't respond. I walk to the door and try to open it, but it's locked. Finally the man looks up but he won't let me in. Desperate, I lift up my right leg and point emphatically to my blue-socked foot.

"I need shoes!" I plead. "I have to get to my meeting!"

The man shrugs and goes back to cleaning. My panic surges and I resume walking down the sidewalk in my blue woolly socks until I arrive at an office building with a gleaming metal facade and pass through its revolving doors into a cavernous marble lobby where I stop and stand, shoeless. That's when I wake up, my heart pounding, the T-shirt I slept in soaked with sweat.

Many people have similar nightmares. I call mine failure dreams, and I've had different ones throughout my life, a manifestation of a fear of failure that I've harbored for as long as I can remember. The shoeless dream was triggered by the stress I was feeling while preparing to take Coach public in 2000, while at the same time trying to reinvent the decades-old brand.

Both undertakings demanded much more time, expertise, and resources than I'd estimated, and their success was critical to the future of the company and the brand.

You're probably already familiar with Coach, either as a customer or as someone who knows the brand because it's been in the marketplace for so long. The company was founded in 1941, and the Coach bag first became popular in the 1970s for its distinctive look, quality craftsmanship, and accessible price. Coach bags even had a cult following. I went to work for its founder, Miles Cahn, in 1979 when it was just a $6 million manufacturer of leather goods.

My first day on the job I didn't know the difference between an invoice and a packing slip, but I made up for my lack of business experience with my facility with numbers and a boundless curiosity. *Why,* I wondered, *did so many women love Coach bags?*

I worked at Coach for six years before it was acquired by an unlikely buyer, and I became its CEO.

From the start I was an untraditional "bag man." The most successful handbag brands were European, most of them founded and led by eponymous designers like Louis Vuitton and Guccio Gucci. I grew up in the Bronx, the son of a cop, and spent 10 years in New York City government before joining Coach. I also paid zero attention to fashion. Because I wasn't a designer or a merchant, I first leaned into consumer research and data analytics to inform our products and business decisions. No accessory or fashion brand did that back in the 1980s, and taking a more logical approach to a creative business became a key component of Coach's competitive advantage. In my first 12 years as CEO we grew 2,000%, to $500 million. But when our sales hit a wall we had little choice but to reimagine the brand and try to take the company public.

Bag Man is the story of how the company and I arrived at that pivotal milestone, and what we did next to build Coach into a $5 billion business, and a beloved global brand.

• • •

Coach and I were an unlikely match whose histories and destinies became intertwined. Over the course of 35 years we endured multiple owners, shifting consumer trends, increasing competitors, management missteps, and economic headwinds. I always felt lucky to be part of Coach, but I came to work every day knowing that it takes a lot more than luck to build a successful business. One reason I wanted to write a book was to explore how Coach became the rare American brand to stand the test of time, and to describe what others could learn from that journey.

At the highest level, Coach applied a philosophy I've long called magic plus logic.

I first used the phrase in the late 1980s to describe how Coach designed and sold bags people loved. Almost everyone who worked at Coach knew the phrase, but if you asked any one of us to explain what magic plus logic meant, we each had different words to express what we all understood. Not until I began to write this book did I more fully define it.

So, what is it? Magic, the creative part of the equation, influences how you evolve products, brands, and all aspects of the business. Logic refers to the discipline, knowledge, and insight-based decision-making that govern everything you do. There is magic in logic, and logic in magic—and an inherent tension between the two. Blending them in appropriate ways at the right times maximizes the likelihood of successful innovation, seamless execution of the front and back end of the business, and the ability to create sustainable, profitable growth.

There are, as I see it, five elements of magic and five elements of logic woven throughout Coach's journey, and this book:

Five Elements of Magic—Bold Imagination: The ability to envision and design things that do not yet exist. Belief: A passion for the undertaking while honoring the past. Immersive Curiosity: A never-ending love of learning and a relentless desire to understand. Instinct: Listening to your experience and inner voice. Lateral Thinking: Seeking multiple, often antithetical paths to approach situations in unexpected ways.

Five Elements of Logic—Rigor: Executing with consistency, thoroughness, and accountability. Extreme Collaboration: Working nimbly together across functions and roles. Insights: Informing actions with knowledge, consumer research, and business analytics. Adaptability: Changing minds, plans, and strategies as situations warrant. Greater-Good Mindset: Prioritizing what's best for the whole.

TEN ELEMENTS OF MAGIC AND LOGIC

Magic

Bold Imagination

The ability to envision and design things that do not yet exist

Belief

A passion for the undertaking while honoring the past

Immersive Curiosity

A never-ending love of learning and a relentless desire to understand

Instinct

Listening to your experience and inner voice

Lateral Thinking

Seeking multiple, often antithetical paths to approach situations in unexpected ways

Logic

Rigor

Executing with consistency, thoroughness, and accountability

Extreme Collaboration

Working nimbly together across functions and roles

Insights

Informing actions with knowledge, consumer research, and business analytics

Adaptability

Changing minds, plans, and strategies as situations warrant

Greater-Good Mindset

Prioritizing what's best for the whole

I articulated these 10 elements as I reflected back on Coach's history, like trying to deconstruct the recipe of a favorite meal. They are all authentic, but they are not explicitly called out in the pages that follow as they might be in a traditional business book: I wanted Coach's story to unfold as organically as it did in real time to reveal how the elements of magic and logic evolved, as well as the lessons we learned as we applied them—and what happened when we didn't. There were times, for example, when we lacked imagination, didn't adapt fast enough, or made a decision that wasn't for the greater good. Occasionally, I ignored my instincts, and it cost us.

That said, this is a business memoir, so I have tried to focus chapters on topics with a more universal interest. For instance, you will see the role that magic and logic play in most areas and stages of a business, including how to: Design, merchandise, and market products people love, time after time. Create a performance-driven culture with investment-grade leaders. Broaden a brand's appeal while staying true to its core ethos. Leverage omni-channel models to meet consumers where they are, and where they're going. Drive overarching strategies that pair a brand's unique value with the right market opportunities. Build a global brand by capitalizing on countries' unique societal shifts, cultural norms, and consumer preferences. Achieve consistently high margins and profits. Work effectively with boards of directors and investors. Adapt to competitors and economic headwinds. And, scale and transform a business to achieve next-level organic growth.

• • •

Just as writing this book allowed me to unpack magic and logic, it also moved me to explore the fear of failure that hounded my dreams, along with my equally powerful drive for excellence. Over the years, these dual motivations—trying to reduce the likelihood of failing, while maximizing the chances of success—have manifested in ways good and bad, for Coach and for me.

Not coincidentally, my fear and drive influenced elements of magic and logic—like using consumer insights to inform decisions, insisting on rigorous execution, and holding everyone accountable to high standards. Fear and drive also inclined me to be tough on people who didn't meet those standards, sometimes too tough, or to micromanage in an attempt to control outcomes. There were also times when my need for more knowledge and understanding to reduce uncertainty made me risk averse, or slower to act.

More personally, fear and drive manifested as stress in my mind and body, which I had to find ways to relieve so they didn't get in the way of leading. I also am prone to occasional depressive episodes that I had to learn how to recognize and navigate, a lifelong pursuit. My struggles aren't unique or more challenging than anyone else's, but I share them for a few reasons. One reason is that I've counseled many leaders, entrepreneurs, and young professionals, who find it reassuring to know that their emotional ups and downs are not uncommon but part of the human condition. Second, it's important to have coping tools to manage whatever emotional disequilibrium we face at all stages of our working lives. I know firsthand that uncomfortable, even debilitating feelings like fear, self-doubt, and depression don't necessarily diminish with age or accomplishment. So I share some techniques that I've adopted over the course of my career, like how to prioritize tasks in moments we feel overwhelmed, boost energy when we're dragging, and handle dark periods.

I share some aspects of my emotional and mental well-being because people's personal and professional lives are inevitably intertwined. We bring our full selves to work every day. Without my fear and drive, the blend of magic and logic that fueled Coach's growth probably would not exist. My story is part of Coach's story.

• • •

Before we begin at the beginning, I want to thank all the talented people who built Coach over so many years. You'll meet many, and because they have their own expertise and versions of Coach's history, my writing collaborator, Joanne Gordon, and I connected with more than 75 people to help bring Coach's journey to life. I tried to be accurate in my storytelling while expressing my own truths. I also chose to leave out various events, people, and details for space limitations, and I left out some of my own opinions out of respect for people's privacy, or because I decided they didn't contribute to the book's main intent, which is to retrace my journey with an iconic brand while offering insights into business, branding, leadership, and, hopefully, personal well-being.

Finally, leading Coach and writing this book would not have been possible without my wife, Bobbie, or our children Tamara, Sam, and Alana, who encouraged me to share my full self as part of Coach's history. I don't include details about our family life in the context of Coach's story, but the two are also inextricably intertwined. We're a close-knit family, and my wife's and kids' love has always been essential to my ability to do my job and come through dark periods. I also wrote this book to share with my eight grandchildren some of the most important things that the "bag man" they call Poppy is still learning: Our lives and work are a blend of opportunities and preparation, serendipity and intention, magic and logic, fear and drive. We do our best to control what we can, including how we respond to things we can't control, and remind ourselves to be grateful for it all.

If you're a Coach fan, I also want to thank you. You were at the center of all we did, so I hope you'll appreciate how far Coach has come with you in mind. If you're less familiar with Coach, I hope you'll enjoy this behind-the-scenes look at the improbable journey of the business and brand.

Lew

New York City
April 2025

PART ONE

Early Years

CHAPTER 1

Growing Up in the Bronx

It's hard to believe that something can happen in the future if you can't envision it in the present. This outlook has been true for most of my career, but I first learned about it from my mother.

In the fall of 1959, the two of us were summoned to the office of my junior high school's guidance counselor, the formidable Mr. Schmutter. He was dressed in a suit and tie, and I can still feel the man peering at us under his bushy eyebrows, my file on his desk. I was in ninth grade, and not a very engaged student, which is why we were there. Mr. Schmutter settled his gaze on my mother and suggested that instead of attending a regular high school, perhaps the New York School of Printing was a better fit for me.

"There's a lot of opportunity for people who can set type," he said to the woman who'd been taking me to the public library since I was six and once a week sent me off to school with a yellow envelope stuffed with crinkled dollar bills to deposit in New York City's college savings program. My mother, who didn't have a formal education past high school and never worked outside our home, wasn't having Mr. Schmutter's future.

"My son is going to college," she said, then shot up from her chair. "Lewis, we're leaving." Anne Hershkowitz Frankfort clutched her handbag and exited without even saying goodbye. I stayed seated for a grueling few seconds, paralyzed with embarrassment. I was less bothered by Mr. Schmutter's opinion that I wasn't college material—*and did he even say those exact words?*—than I was worried by my mother's abrupt disregard for whatever authority I assumed this man had.

At 13, I was witnessing my mother standing up for her beliefs by advocating for her son, who didn't yet have the chutzpah to stand up for himself. My mother believed that I would go to college. For me, college was an abstract concept. No one in my family had ever gone, aside from my sister, Claire, who was eight years older and took night classes at a community college. Before I could believe college was my future, I had to envision it, too. See it in my mind's eye. That is vision, and once we have it, we can begin to take the steps on the path to achieve it.

The experience in my guidance counselor's office may have been the first time I finally saw myself in college one day, because eventually I got up and followed my mother out of the room. I loved her. I wanted to please her. But more important, I believed her more than I believed Mr. Schmutter.

• • •

A lot of us come from humble roots that shape our drive and our values. When I look back on my years before joining Coach, I see origins of other beliefs, not just about my future, but about the way the world could be. The way I might be. Those experiences would one day help shape a company.

My father, Abraham, who went by Max, was a New York City policeman who worked eight-hour shifts, sometimes 8 a.m. to 4 p.m., sometimes midnight until morning. He'd walk or drive the streets of his Harlem beat, earning paychecks that just covered our family's basic living expenses, including the $65-a-month rent of our first-floor, two-bedroom apartment in a four-story tenement in the Bronx. My father retired from the police force in his late forties when cataract surgery compromised his eyesight. He then worked at the post office before becoming a security guard at the Fifth Avenue flagship store of luxury jeweler Harry Winston, where he worked for many years.

We lived in a working-class section of the Bronx that was filled with families of mixed ethnicities. Jewish, like my family, as well as Italians and Irish. Stores near us were mostly family owned. The photography shop across the avenue. The candy store down the block. The pizzeria, and the bagel place where I worked behind the counter in high school. There were no indoor malls back then, and my mother's occasional trips to an outdoor shopping center in Yonkers required two buses and a train. I once went with her to buy school clothes and saw a Macy's department store that opened up next to a Gimbels. I remember wondering why one department store wanted to open so close to one of its competitors.

At home I listened to the Lone Ranger fight for justice and watched sitcoms like *Leave It to Beaver* on our black-and-white TV. An upper-middle-class family living in a two-story house in a green-grassed suburb was as foreign to me as a masked cowboy riding the range. I was an urban kid. A backyard and my own bedroom were luxuries my parents couldn't afford but that they wanted for me one day. I assumed these things were attainable because my parents raised me to believe that we lived in a country where the son of a cop could one day access a better life. Not by some divine right, however. I'd have to earn it through education and hard work.

I was a lousy athlete, better at playing marbles than stickball. I was the only kid on my block who never hit the ball over the stone wall for a home run. I also had a speech impediment. A late talker, I didn't say much until I was three or four. When I finally started speaking, my lips and tongue couldn't sync to express what I was thinking. *R*'s and *L*'s came out like *W*'s, and I couldn't pronounce certain combinations of letters.

In first grade I repeatedly tried to tell my parents that I needed a costume for my public school's annual neighborhood Halloween parade, but they couldn't understand what I was saying. On the day of the costume parade I showed up as the only child at P.S. 91 not dressed like a cowboy, or an animal, or anything other than an elementary school kid. I was told I couldn't be part of the parade and had to walk at the tail end of the procession. A lone, plain-clothed caboose behind the towering teacher Mr. Salant and a lively line of costumed characters. I was really embarrassed, certain that the parents and neighbors watching saw the boy who showed up unprepared. It felt awful.

In third grade, I was in a hallway when I overheard one teacher tell my teacher that she couldn't understand me. "Why'd you send Lewis to my classroom to deliver that message? We can't understand him when he talks. You shouldn't send him on errands," she complained, clueless that I was within earshot. And I'd been so proud to be chosen for the task! I could stand up to bullies on the playground, or when a group of mean kids came to our street to beat us up, but the teacher's words sunk into me like a stain.

When it was suggested I go to a school for the speaking-impaired, my mother refused. Taking me out of regular public school would have derailed her future plans for me, so once a week I'd leave class to see a speech therapist who held up a small mirror in front of my face to teach me how to move my tongue to different places in my mouth. I was aware that people couldn't understand me, so I was careful to choose words I could pronounce.

Claire was the one person who usually understood me. Some days our mother had to wait until my sister got home from school so she could tell my mom what I was trying to say, and stop my tears of frustration. Claire was my interpreter and caretaker. She stayed home with me when our mother ran errands, and she took me everywhere, alone and with her friends. The beach. The movies. The Museum of Natural History. The day I found $10 on the street, Claire was the person I wanted to spend it with. We got seats behind home plate at Yankee Stadium, then went to a Chinese restaurant. Claire had a big, playful heart back then, and still does. She was nice and easygoing, and despite sharing a room, the two of us never argued, even when I took all her clothes out of the dresser drawers and scattered them on the floor. She just laughed at her younger brother's practical joke. To this day, my sister and I have never had a fight.

• • •

After middle school, I attended the all-boys DeWitt Clinton High School—not the vocational option, and not the public school for the smartest kids, but the one in the middle. I excelled at math, not so much in English, and I found a crew of fun, equally mischievous friends to run with. My grades and my confidence improved. My voice also deepened into what would eventually become a distinctive and later gritty baritone that lent a weight to my words, even when they came out slightly mispronounced. I also was growing into my eventual 6-foot frame, and by age 17 I stood a few inches taller than most of my peers.

My world was expanding, too, amid the social consciousness of the 1960s. Not from anything my parents said. I didn't come from a politically charged home. But whatever I heard Walter Cronkite say on the nightly news or read in a headline when I passed a newsstand piqued an interest in politics and government. I was 14 when I pushed through crowds to shake John F. Kennedy's hand as he drove through the Bronx, campaigning for president. I liked the young senator's optimism that things could change, even though at that age I was hard-pressed to know what, exactly, had to change.

I did, however, have a profound sense that we lived in a dangerous world, a fear linked to the era in which I grew up, when the threat of atomic war was terrifyingly real. In elementary school we were taught to duck and cover during mock air-raid drills that were part of the Federal Civil Defense Administration program to teach Americans how to protect themselves from an atomic bomb—as if hiding under a wooden desk was going to save us from radiation. At one junior high school assembly, a representative from the Office of Civil Defense showed a dystopian slideshow about what would happen if a bomb hit the Empire State Building. He told an auditorium full of 11-, 12-, and 13-year-olds that everyone who lived below 161st Street in the Bronx was doomed to die. I lived on 180th, but the 19-block difference didn't make me feel especially safe. Neither did the potential of nuclear war from the Cuban Missile Crisis in 1962, when I was a junior in high school and started to seriously wonder if I'd make it to adulthood because there was a real chance the world would blow up. I think these years seeded in me a lifelong existential anxiety about a potential apocalypse, which in my later years triggered emotional reactions to wars and even a fascination with weather as the earth's climate warmed and posed a global threat. Luckily, as a young person, even though I sometimes had nightmares, my fears about the end of the world weren't all-consuming or debilitating.

In 1963, my mother's plan for me unfolded when I became the first in my family to go to a four-year college. By 17 I was no longer that caboose of a kid struggling to express himself, but an outgoing young man with a quick smile who was interested in the world beyond the Bronx and increasingly had something to say about it.

• • •

Hunter College was a gateway school for students like me who were the first in their families to get a traditional higher education. It was a commuter school, so most of us lived with our parents, who to a large extent were immigrants or, like mine, second-generation Americans. To me, Hunter's Bronx campus felt like a community. Maybe it was the stately Gothic architecture, but I sensed it was a place with possibilities.

I enjoyed classes if I found the topic intriguing, especially psychology and my major, political science. I liked learning what made people tick, but I was easily bored so I sought out teachers who could hold my attention. I loved the freedom college afforded. I could create my own structure, control my time and what I studied, even though I wasn't a big studier, which my B average reflected. I preferred hanging around interesting people to doing homework. I'd have dreams that I showed up to a final exam but failed to learn the material. The fear of flunking out was a constant hum in the back of my mind, and I was traumatized when I got a D in zoology. And yet, I still focused less energy on studying and more on what went on outside the classrooms.

• • •

The 1960s were among the more provocative decades to be a college student. The mood on campus for my first year and a half felt optimistic, but Hunter's student body became more vocally divided as students tried to figure out what role our generation would play in the country's future. We were conflicted between accepting what people in authority said and challenging what they did.

My own relationship with authority was influenced by my parents. When your father is a policeman, you pretty much grow up respecting authority. It was my outspoken mother who showed me that respect for authority didn't have to be absolute. Just because someone has a title doesn't mean they're right. I embraced liberal social views, considered myself part of the civil rights movement, and marched against the war in Vietnam. Mostly I tried to spark change closer to home. I got involved in student politics during my sophomore year and by the end of my junior year had been elected student body president for my senior year. "Performance, Not Promises" was my campaign motto.

I had much to learn about wielding my own authority, and my strengths and weaknesses in that regard were noticed by a faculty liaison between students and the administration named Dr. Mary Rita Donleavy. She was an irreverent, feisty professor unlike any adult I knew. Not condescending or dictatorial, she spoke to us with honesty and was a sincere, optimistic voice on campus. She was also attuned to the counterculture that the 1960s had given rise to, as well as the Human Potential Movement, which believed that through disciplines like self-examination, honest interpersonal communication, experimentation, and openness to new experiences, people could become the best versions of themselves. To help me tap my potential and prepare for my role as president, Mary Rita got Hunter to fund my attendance at a two-week summer workshop in group dynamics at a remote town in Maine. As soon as junior year ended I drove my four-door 1957 green Plymouth Belvedere—my first car, which I bought because it only cost $425—from the Bronx to a leafy compound in Bethel, Maine. A nonprofit organization called National Training Laboratories (NTL) had become a popular place for companies and universities to send people to so they could learn how to be more empathic communicators. I had no idea what to expect but went in with an open mind, feeling grateful for the opportunity.

I spent most days sitting in circles with other student leaders as well as teachers, social workers, and deans from other schools talking about how to improve education. The point of the group sessions was less what we discussed than how we discussed them. The NTL facilitators encouraged us to give each other feedback on our respective communication styles. I became aware of how I could impact others if I understood them as individuals—Jim avoids conflict, Julie is aggressive, Mike likes positive reinforcement—and better understood myself—Lew can get impatient. I also became aware of how my voice and personality could command and even repel attention, and that I could adjust my behavior to suit someone else's style, if I chose to.

My time in Bethel widened my aperture on leadership. Instead of telling people what to do, I could get people's buy-in. Most important, I better understood the power of a group versus the power of one person. A leader could urge people to come together toward a common goal, rather than telling everyone what to do. I also realized I had to be a better listener. Hearing opinions from so many smart people showed me that instead of assuming I was right, it was possible, even preferable, to hold different views in my mind at the same time and try to see the merits of each before making a decision or finding compromise. Easier said than done, of course, but the seed was planted.

When the workshop ended, I exceeded the speed limit driving from Bethel to Parksville, New York, to start my summer job as head waiter at a small resort in the Catskills called the Grand Hotel. I was eager to try out my newly acquired skills on the eleven waiters and busboys I managed. Before the hotel opened for the season, I arranged some dining room chairs in a circle and asked the waitstaff to sit, then encouraged them to discuss ways we could work better together to serve the hotel's guests. The guys thought that I was out of my mind. They just wanted to serve people their meals and then go party. But I persisted. Most days before the dining room opened I had us gather in a circle for a five-minute meeting to talk about the day ahead: the menu, which entrees we should push if the kitchen was running low on the most popular dishes, or how to ramp up if the hotel was booked to capacity. Some of the waiters shared grievances from the day before, or complained about the kitchen, or each other, or me. I was woefully ill-equipped to be a group moderator, but I tried to keep peace and focus on how we could make good tips, while balancing the needs of the hotel guests, our bosses, and each other.

My experiences that summer left me with a positive feeling that I could actually move a group of people to act differently. I was grateful to Mary Rita for exposing me to these ideas, and for believing in me.

During my time in student government I pushed for changes students said they wanted. From the mundane, like keeping lounges open on weekends, to the ambitious, like free tuition. I fought for lower cafeteria prices, and I fought to get closed-door faculty meetings open to student observers so there would be more transparency and communication among teachers and students when it came to setting policies.

Overall, my college causes were pretty tame compared to what was going on in the world. I wasn't an angry rebel or particularly courageous. More of a by-the-book, outspoken activist who didn't want to break rules, just challenge them. If I annoyed or angered the administration, so be it. But I wasn't out to be disrespectful or violent—just an idealistic young person experimenting with how far I could go to improve the world with all the earnest conviction I could muster, and without getting into trouble. I was mostly successful.

The most trouble I got into was during my senior year, when I was on the steering committee of an organization that opposed the Vietnam War, and for a few weeks our group's demonstrations got out of control. Not violent, just disruptive. One incident unfolded in the office of the dean of students, who claimed the demonstrators impeded the freedoms of faculty, staff, and students in the building. I wasn't there when protesters reportedly stormed in and staged a sit-in, but as an officer of the group I was held accountable for its actions, so the dean put me on disciplinary probation. I accepted responsibility but not blame, defending myself in a letter to the dean denying the accusation that the group's actions were premeditated.

My mother would have been furious that I'd put my education in jeopardy, which for her was more important than protesting the war. The first time she heard I'd been suspended was decades later, when a friend recounted the story at my 60th birthday party.

Back then, she and my dad just wanted their son to get a college degree, live a better life, and not become a socialist. I wanted to please my parents, but I did not fear letting them down or choosing a path they might disagree with. For the most part, I believed that their acceptance and love for me was unconditional. My own desires toggled between politics and business. I was conflicted about which I wanted more—to make the world a better place or to make it into the middle class.

I graduated from Hunter in 1967 with a degree in political science. But more than any one subject, the most meaningful thing I learned in college was the power of curiosity and investigative skills. It was possible to have no knowledge about a subject but through a didactic process become conversant, maybe even smart about it.

There was a lot I didn't know, but almost nothing I couldn't try to learn.

But what was I curious about? I was still debating between a career in politics or business. Activism or capitalism? Each satisfied a different hunger. I wanted the world to be a more just, equitable place, but I also wanted to join the middle class and make enough money to support myself outside the neighborhood I grew up in. The idea that I could do both in the same job—earn a good salary while working for some bigger purpose—didn't occur to me. At the very least, I had no idea what that might look like. I certainly didn't predict that a botched stint on Wall Street followed by 10 years in city government would help prepare me to one day run a handbag business, of all things.

CHAPTER 2

Troubleshooting in Government

After college, I was intent on working and living in Manhattan, so I put all my eggs in one basket and applied to one graduate program, Columbia Business School. My college grades were a bit of a mixed bag, but my test scores were strong so, thankfully, I was admitted.

Student aid covered 25% of tuition, and I took out student loans for the rest. I focused on marketing and took classes outside the MBA curriculum in psychology and sociology, which catered to my curiosity about the human condition. Much of marketing, I realized, was an exercise in interpreting human behavior.

It's hard to overstate how much attending Columbia impacted my perspective on business and on myself. Just as Hunter opened me to possibilities, Columbia broadened my views on what they could be and how to succeed. The school's case-study teaching method focused on problem-solving to deliver an education that went beyond theories. Graduate school also expanded the opportunities open to someone like me, who had no connections in the business world. It also further boosted my self-confidence. Not many people in my life had told me, directly or indirectly, that I was capable, aside from my parents and Mary Rita. I was naturally outgoing and social, which translated into a presence that projected confidence. But Mr. Schmutter's unintentionally demeaning assessment of my intelligence back in middle school lingered at the back of my mind.

So did insecurities that my speech impediment triggered. Traces of that childhood disability still affected how I pronounced certain letters. Combined with my Bronx accent, I developed a distinctive "voice." Some words ending in *a* sounded like they ended in a soft *er*. Nostalgia was *nostalger*. And my *R*s still sounded like *W*s.

When I graduated, I joined the army reserves and spent four months at a military base in Fort Knox, Kentucky, the first two in basic training and the second two as a cook's helper in a company kitchen, mainly peeling potatoes and making pancake batter for 200 soldiers. Afterward, I returned to New York City, and because I had those student loans to pay off I looked to Wall Street for higher-paying jobs.

My first job was as a junior analyst for the large securities firm F. I. duPont, Glore Forgan & Co. My job was to find new public companies for our clients to invest in. I was given little training and had barely any oversight. Early on, anxious to impress, I eagerly pushed shares of an artificial Christmas tree business I'd discovered, but without doing enough due diligence. When the workers went on strike, the company couldn't produce enough trees for the holiday season, so after an initial pop from my recommendation, the stock tanked along with my nascent reputation.

A pissed-off broker sent me a Telex, the email of its day: "Next time you recommend a stock, let me know and I'll take the day off." His rebuke sank my stomach. It was a sobering wake-up call that I had no idea what I was doing when it came to investments. I'd failed to do my homework and was superficial in my assessment. I hadn't researched the company enough. I should have flown to their headquarters in the South and walked the factory floor. I didn't ask enough questions, or the right questions, and I didn't push back on the answers they gave me. If I had, I would have known that they had a union, and that the union contract was almost up—and I probably wouldn't have recommended the company. The lesson I learned? I needed to be a rigorous investigator.

I was hardly the first young person to make a mistake in their first job, and one day it would make for a humorous story to tell my kids about how dad screwed up. But at that formative age, the incident felt all-consuming as it shook my sense of self-worth. I equated a mistake with being a failure. My lack of due diligence, and how terrible the outcome made me feel, were two experiences I never wanted to repeat.

I wasn't immediately fired, but I was included in a slew of the firm's layoffs during a Wall Street slowdown. I hit the job market with few prospects, questioning my business prowess, and thinking that maybe I'd made a mistake not pursuing work in the public sector.

Luckily, the City of New York was hiring.

• • •

In 1970, New York City was a fiscal, political, and social mess. Mayor John Lindsay had inherited rising crime, racial tensions, and rampant poverty, and his administration was recruiting young idealists from the private sector to bring management skills to the city's byzantine bureaucracy. I saw an opportunity to do some good, so I took a salary cut to become an entry-level analyst in the Municipal Services Administration, where I spent an underwhelming year surrounded by many people more interested in getting to Friday than improving the quality of life for people in the city. My boss was a nice guy, but he was no change agent, nor was he someone who'd teach me all the things I didn't even know I needed to learn.

When a mentor doesn't find you, you have to find them, so I looked for people in the administration with smarts and commitment. Someone I could work for and learn from.

Herb Rosenzweig had been one of the so-called whiz kids who'd gone to work for the US Defense Department under Robert S. McNamara. He served as Assistant Secretary of Defense in the mid-1960s, and he resigned because of his opposition to the Vietnam War. He was subsequently recruited to bring rigor to New York City's Human Resources Administration. Herb ran a small policy group to advise the department on human and social service strategies. He was well respected, and I wrote him a note asking to meet. When his assistant Edna called me she said Herb liked to go to a nearby bar called Galloway's.

"Go meet him for lunch sometime."

I arrived to find him gobbling down a roast beef sandwich on a Kaiser roll with gravy dripping down his chin and tie. I told the waitress to bring me the same thing. I was 25. Herb was 41. I wasn't intimidated, since most of my friends were older, but I was nervous because of his reputation. People had warned me that while brilliant, he was difficult to work for. We talked and ate for about 45 minutes. I remember thinking this man was a global citizen sincerely concerned with justice and equality. I told Herb I wanted to work for him. He told me to come to his office and meet his staff.

"He's impossible," they told me. One person called him a madman. Others said he was irascible and irreverent. I was undeterred, more compelled by his intentions than repelled by his style. When I was offered the opportunity to join his team, I took it.

My first 90 days were like boot camp. I went through a rigorous onboarding process that included learning about the city's poorest, most vulnerable citizens and the services they needed just to survive: childcare, homeless shelters, elder care, welfare. I wanted to be challenged, and Herb delivered, so much so that I wasn't sure I would pass whatever tests he put me through.

"Are you kidding me?" he'd say after looking over my work those first weeks. He was unapologetically direct, but I saw through his rough edges to his genius and framed his criticisms as education rather than insults. I was just grateful I'd found a mentor.

Herb had two traits I'd yet to encounter. One of them was his incisiveness. I watched as people bombarded him with information, and I marveled at his ability to hear it all and then cut through it to find its essence. He synthesized data, connected dots, simplified complex subjects, and could rank competing issues in order of importance. If I came to Herb with three ideas to solve a particular problem, I'd leave with one, or a hybrid, and understand why the other two wouldn't work nearly as well.

Herb was also capable of taking in ideas different than his own and holding antithetical views in his mind at the same time, evaluating them on their merits based on the thoroughness of his understanding, and pivoting as circumstances warranted. This willingness to deviate from an original plan and approach problems in new ways was a form of what I would one day refer to as lateral thinking. It's what helped him be so incisive and confident in the views he did hold. Under Herb, who also happened to be a grand master at chess, my own thinking got more sophisticated and my method of review and inquiry more rigorous.

Herb's skills were widely known, and he was often summoned to the mayor's office to provide his take on the intractable issue of the day. For all his brilliance and sense of greater purpose, Herb had terrible interpersonal skills. He was acerbic, impatient, and hot-tempered. He cared more about getting to the outcome he wanted and less about how he got there. Demanding, with high standards, he didn't suffer fools. I had no reason to believe I wasn't one, so I worked my butt off to keep up, eager to learn and simultaneously afraid that he'd terminate me. The fear wasn't paralyzing: I just funneled it into being laser-focused on learning so I could meet his expectations.

Six months into the job Herb began asking me to come with him to City Hall, and sometimes to present on his behalf so he wouldn't lose his cool. I wasn't a yeller, but I think my deeper voice gave me gravitas beyond my years, and Herb knew I could read a room and modulate my tone or approach, which I learned from my NTL training.

When Herb took on a new assignment, he brought me along as his first deputy, making me his de facto number two. Eventually I had a staff of almost 500 in charge of personnel policies, budgets, and staffing for 25,000 city employees. I participated in labor relations disputes, and I was learning to make hard choices. I also became more incisive and confident. At 30, I began to feel like a competent adult.

My four years working with Herb were also noteworthy for what I observed. He insisted people take accountability, and he didn't care if people disliked him because of it. He took responsibility for unpopular decisions when he believed they achieved a larger goal. Herb wasn't beloved, but he was respected.

Besides being my mentor, Herb became my closest friend, and our relationship became the catalyst for the most consequential event of my life. During a weekend in the spring of 1973, we drove upstate to Woodstock, New York, where we stayed at a counterculture hotel that attracted a lot of young people. At breakfast one morning we struck up a conversation with two young women living in Queens. Later, we all went for a walk and I got to talking with Roberta Rosenberg, an assistant professor at Brooklyn College, who went by Bobbie. She was extremely bright, with a broad smile and genuine warmth. She also seemed to be a woman who marched to her own beat. I was intrigued, and I asked if she would come for dinner at my apartment when we were back in Manhattan, despite the fact that I didn't cook, which I didn't mention.

Bobbie arrived at my studio apartment a week later where my table was set for a dinner that a friend had to help me prepare—a fact that Bobbie only found out about years later. She was born in Manhattan and raised in Long Island and New Jersey. She was close with her parents, whom I would come to love and admire, and her father, who went by Robe, ran a second-generation family business that made men's neckwear. She was earning her PhD in the history of education at New York University, and working on her thesis, which became the book *Collegiate Women: Domesticity and Career in Turn-of-the-Century America*, a provocative study of how higher education shaped young women's lives. I was impressed by her dedication to education, particularly the power of education to shape people's lives, a value we shared. She was also interested in making the world a better place, with more equality and more opportunity for the disenfranchised, so we had a lot to talk about. As first dates go, it was pretty great, and it was clear that I'd met a very special woman who, eventually and thankfully, was as interested in me as I was in her.

Two years later, in August 1975, Bobbie and I were married, surrounded by close friends and family at her parents' home in Englewood, New Jersey.

• • •

Shortly after we met, Bobbie and I moved into a one-bedroom apartment at 66th Street and West End Avenue. We felt safe in our neighborhood, but we knew we'd be crazy to walk through Central Park when it was dark. Crime in New York City had reached a tipping point, indicative of other problems. The city was on the edge of bankruptcy, and the state had forced the new mayor, Abraham Beame, to put together a fiscal committee that became part of the state's Emergency Financial Control Board to oversee management and solve its biggest problems.

One of the most severe was the city's day care system and federally funded Head Start program, which together were responsible for the safety, health, and early education of some 50,000 children from lower-income families. The nation's largest day care program was overseen by the Agency for Child Development (ACD), which had about 500 employees and funded just over 400 day care centers, most operated by nonprofit agencies. A majority of programs were well run, but a significant number were not. Some were led by self-interested community leaders with no experience. Others operated out of shoddy facilities that didn't meet health codes, including storefronts and church basements. Some centers were overcrowded, others underutilized. There were also many thousands of families using the day care system who weren't legally eligible. The agency itself was filled with good-intentioned people, but it was also a thicket of backlogged paperwork and outdated policies.

In March 1976, a task force report concluded that the agency was "a management and fiscal crisis of staggering proportion." It advised putting the ACD under the supervision of an interim Deputy Commissioner. When First Deputy Mayor John E. Zuccotti asked me to take the role, I said yes only when he promised that City Hall wouldn't interfere with the tough choices I would need to make, which I wanted to make based on merit and data, not the political pressure or favoritism I knew from my previous years was all too common. The mayor's office was more than happy to keep its distance. Let Lew be the face of the troubled day care system, for better or worse.

The only instructions came from Zuccotti, when he summoned me to his office.

"Be decisive," he said.

• • •

My mandate was to reinvent the city's childcare operation so it could do more with less—essentially, provide healthy care for children from the city's poorest households on a much lower budget. My vision went beyond cutting costs, to include giving kids safe places to go and an enriched experience with activities like reading and art where possible. Not just babysitting. I knew education was vital to giving kids of poor families a head start in life.

I was also keenly aware that I was a young white man with no social services experience in charge of an organization where more than half the staff was Black or Hispanic, and where most were women. And the decisions I had to make would mostly affect Black and Hispanic families, including many led by single mothers. I also didn't look like a typical conservative civil servant with my untamed curls and scruffy beard.

My title gave me a degree of power. Credibility I had to earn.

I knew I couldn't do the job unless I had a team with different backgrounds and expertise to make up for my own deficits. A mix of right- and left-brained thinkers willing to put in long hours. I surrounded myself with people like Shirley Lewis, a former case worker who also had a master's degree in social services administration from the University of Chicago. "To whom much is given, much is required," Shirley said to me when I first interviewed her. I also brought in people from the private sector who'd never worked in government but had skills we needed.

A small article that the *New York Post* did about my appointment called me "the young troubleshooter charged with the task of shaking up the ACD." The headline, "Municipal Mr. Fix It," was the most optimistic take on the job I'd heard yet. The reporter must have asked me why I chose to work in government, because she quoted me as saying that as a child I "wanted to be a cop on the side of justice and good" and that as a teenager I wanted to "change the face of the earth." A bit grandiose but I was an unapologetic product of the 1960s. I did, however, have a self-imposed goal to ensure that every eligible child from a center we closed had an alternative center nearby.

Any idealism I still clung to clashed with reality when just weeks into the new role a memo from New York City's Bureau of the Budget landed on my desk, ordering me to slash the ACD's already-reduced $150 million budget another 23% to $115 million. The cut was so massive I thought it was a typo. The bulk of the funds paid for day care centers, which meant many more than I anticipated would have to close. It was a breathtaking directive with no leeway.

The next few months were a high-stakes marathon. I visited dozens of day care facilities, where I talked with teachers and kneeled on rugs with kids playing blocks. I met with parents to explain budget challenges and heard their panicked pleas not to close their center. At public hearings, I sometimes faced protests.

The painful truth was that for most day care programs to survive, the number of facilities and staff had to be cut. For the most part the mayor's office stuck to its agreement not to interfere, but a few politicians didn't accept the math. At one point an outspoken congressman named Ed Koch showed up at my office to convince me to keep open a facility in a neighborhood he did not represent, but where 80% of the families using day care were ineligible. I told the congressman there was nothing I could do; the numbers spoke for themselves. He wasn't interested in facts.

"I hope you make the right decision," he said. We disagreed on the definition of "right," and I stuck with my team's decision to defund those centers.

So many people and issues vied for attention each day that I had to figure out how to organize my time and thoughts. It could feel overwhelming. Time management wasn't my forte, so I came up with tools to give me a sense of control over the chaos. I began each week with six lists—projects, tasks, problems, meetings, pending activities, and daily activities—which I updated daily. I also came up with a framework for my team: issues we had no control over I labeled "gravity," which deserved no more than 5% of our time. If something was important but not easily addressable in a given moment, we would "park it" and give the item a specific date to be revisited. Just knowing it was temporarily parked, but not forgotten, allowed me to stop fretting about it so I could focus on what mattered in the moment.

Ultimately, the ACD achieved substantial cost savings from closing mismanaged day care facilities, consolidating others, and finding creative ways to shave expenses, like renegotiating bad leases the previous administration had signed. Inside the ACD, we instituted performance metrics and developed new processes to determine eligibility. We strengthened site licensing procedures and added more training to improve the quality of care.

We didn't right all the wrongs, but we did what many people thought impossible—reduce the budget by $35 million while restoring a sense of accountability and integrity. And every eligible child who was displaced was offered access to alternative care. A *New York Times* piece in March 1979 headlined "The City's Day-Care System: Resilient in Difficult Times" described our progress. I was proud of what the ACD had done to preserve government-funded day care, which, as I told the *Times*, was "the best legacy we have of the 1960s New Society." I was still the practical activist I'd been at Hunter, looking to make the world a better place within the guardrails of what was possible.

• • •

Looking back on my government years, I recognize skills and lessons that followed me into my next chapter, even elements of magic and logic. At the

ACD, data analysis and accountability allowed us to meet budget targets, while courage and imagination allowed us to break from broken and entrenched government traditions and improve how the agency operated. I also saw just how much a results-oriented, passionate, collaborative team was capable of achieving, especially when given a purpose beyond themselves—a greater good. Unfortunately, all that rarely came together in New York City's government at the time, which was one reason I was thinking of leaving.

Another factor that would hasten the end of my government career was not getting the job I wanted next, which involved being responsible for negotiating city workers' union contracts. It was a meaty role with huge potential to improve worker performance and reduce cronyism. Unfortunately, the former congressman who once marched into my office and had since been elected New York City's mayor, Ed Koch, passed me over for the job because, as he confided to me, "I was too principled." Years later when I recounted that story publicly, the former mayor denied it.

My decade working for the City of New York added to my early ideas about leadership. I saw how people could abuse authority, and I encountered people who were granted power because of *who* they knew, not *what* they knew, which drove me crazy because I believed in a meritocracy. It's no wonder I found my government years as frustrating as they were fulfilling and educational. This didn't extinguish my desire to advocate for the less advantaged, but I was doubting whether government was my destined path. I just had no idea what that path was until a serendipitous cab ride opened a door to a future that was completely unexpected.

CHAPTER 3

The Product Is the Hero

In the spring of 1979 I spoke to an evening class of graduate students at Columbia University for a course on social services administration. The instructor, Dr. Mel Herman, also worked for the Department of Health, Education and Welfare (HEW). Mel was an esteemed voice in government affairs, and he and I were in touch from time to time. He'd given his students a case study that Boston University put together about ACD's challenges and turnaround efforts, and he invited me to speak to his students about the work. After the class Mel and I hailed a taxi on Broadway at 116th Street to share the ride downtown.

"So Lew," he asked, "what do you do for an encore?"

I said I wasn't sure. There was so much more work to do at ACD, and for the city in general. But I was also growing weary of government's general lack of accountability, and I contemplated leaving for a job in the private sector. Bobbie and I had two kids now. Tamara was 2, and our son, Sam, was almost 1. We needed a bigger apartment—or a house in Brooklyn or one outside the city, which I wanted. I'd grown up playing stickball on concrete playgrounds, but for our kids, and for myself, I wanted lawns and more space than the cramped two-bedroom we could afford at West End and 66th Street. I wanted a different life than my parents, with the freedom that having discretionary resources afforded. Again, dual motivations that I was trying to reconcile. What did it look like to have both? I wasn't committed to leaving government, but I also wasn't interested in doing just any job simply to make money.

Other than having a vague inkling that I wanted to build something, I knew more about what I didn't want than what I did want. Joining a consulting firm, a common next step for people worn out from government, was out. I could have made much more than my current $42,000 salary, but the consultants I'd met were thinkers at 10,000 feet, not doers on the ground. I wanted to roll up my sleeves and do the work of the work. I also had no interest in joining a large company. At a place like Procter & Gamble I worried I'd feel like a cog in a wheel, trapped in an endless hierarchy. Besides, I was probably too brash to make it in a keep-your-head-down corporate culture. I was making assumptions, of course, because aside from my failed stint on Wall Street I'd never worked in a real business.

Our cab jolted over potholes in midtown traffic as Mel told me about a childhood friend of his who ran a small pocketbook company. "He's 60 and doesn't think any of his three kids will succeed him. He's looking for a protégé, someone that has nothing to do with the garment business but has good values. You could be right up his alley."

This wasn't a suggestion I expected from Mel, but I had too much respect for him to rebuff what seemed like an unlikely match.

Coincidentally, something else kept me from rejecting the idea outright. I already knew a bit about the business of bags. Nearly two years earlier, not long after Tamara was born, Bobbie and a friend started a business called Sandbox Industries to design and sell diaper bags, which she began to run in addition to teaching.

As a new mom, she was frustrated when the only diaper bags she could find were ugly and impractical, and heavy to carry once filled with all the infant paraphernalia. Bobbie and her friend designed the cleverly named Shoulder Stroller Bag, which had the novel feature of a strap that latched onto a stroller. It was helpful that Bobbie came from a textile and apparel family. Her grandfather and father had a successful business making men's neck ties. Her Aunt Frankie had a bag and basket business with a factory in Jacksonville, Texas, where Bobbie manufactured Sandbox's different bag styles as the business grew. Sandbox's bags were practical, attractive, and well made. And they sold well enough that eventually Bobbie left her teaching career to run Sandbox full-time.

Bobbie's work gave me an appreciation for the bag business that I wouldn't have had otherwise. And because I put my MBA to use helping with some financial aspects of the business, I knew it could be profitable. If Mel Herman's friend made dresses or hats, I might have been less inclined to investigate.

I thanked Mel for the referral and told him to give my information to his friend.

"What's the name of his company?" I asked.

"Coach Products," he said. I'd never heard of it.

• • •

I diligently prepped for my interview with Coach's founder, Miles Cahn. I was intent on doing my homework to know exactly what I might be getting myself into, learning as much as I could about something I didn't know was a habit ingrained from Herb and from the Christmas tree company debacle, when a lack of due diligence probably cost me my job. Never again would I not be prepared. I started my inquiry by calling buyers at a few department stores, pretending to be a freelance reporter for *BusinessWeek* magazine who was writing an article about Coach. The buyer at Bloomingdale's told me the store ran out of Coach handbags around Thanksgiving and couldn't get enough inventory to replenish by the holidays.

"They don't make enough fast enough," she said.

A buyer for Bonwit Teller named Avril described Coach bags as phenomenal and very durable, with heavy-duty stitching and leather that wore very well.

"It acquires a patina," she told me. "Other bag makers try to recreate it but they can't get the same look of the leather. Knockoffs can't come close. They're extremely good value for the money." She said some customers collect them. But it was a small northeastern brand that didn't make enough to sell around the country. I found her testimonial almost overpowering; at least that's what I wrote in my notes. I asked what the profit was on a typical Coach bag, but she politely declined to say.

Betty, a buyer at the higher-end department store Bergdorf Goodman, told me the store had stopped carrying Coach because it didn't sell well. Their customers wanted something "less basic," she said, then discreetly added, "but it's a wonderful, quality product."

One of Coach's most popular and unique bags, the slouchy but sturdy Duffle Sac, retailed at about $90, I learned, which was about 20% of the retail price of the designer handbags Bergdorf typically carried, but more than most bags on the market, which weren't made as well.

One weekend I visited a handbag store on the Upper West Side, on 72nd Street. I walked up to a display of Coach bags in black and shades of brown. The bags struck me as plain but distinctive. Not fancy, more practical. I picked up various styles. The leather was soft but sturdy. I peeked inside. The Coach name was pressed into the interior of each bag, and the inside material felt rough but also soft. Suede. The bags had a raw, authentic aesthetic, not overdesigned. Some of the flaps closed with a simple little brass turnlock, and a leather tag the same color as the bag dangled from each strap on a short, beaded brass chain, embossed with the Coach name on one side.

Frankly, I thought the bags were more handsome than pretty, and I asked the salesperson if they sold well.

"Very well," she said, and she added that women old and young bought them. "They have a cult following." I was curious. *Why did so many women love these bags?*

The company was private, so there was little public information, but I went to the library and made a copy of Coach's Dun & Bradstreet report, which revealed some basic facts that I'd eventually fill in with more detail. In 1941, a man named William Lipp founded Gail Leather Products with four investors who each put up $1,000. One of the investors was Jacob Cahn, Miles's father. Miles was in his mid-twenties when he went to work at the company for $50 a week in 1946. The company branched out from wallets to desk accessories and other small leather goods in the 1950s, and in 1957, Gail Leather Products changed its name to Coach Leatherware. Miles and his wife, Lillian, bought the business in 1961 from Will Lipp with the help of a bank loan.

The Coach name was first used on products in 1962.

Coach employed about 100 people and had annual sales of $6 million, 60% of which came from men's and women's bags, and the rest from other leather products like wallets, toiletries kits, and men's belts. The company had no debt, and its peak seasons were September through Christmas, and January through March. I deduced that leather products sold better in colder months, and Coach products were often given as holiday gifts.

The day of my first interview on April 26, 1979, I arrived at Coach's offices at 516 West 34th Street. This was New York City's buzzing garment district, and according to Dun & Bradstreet the company's fourth location. A previous one was almost destroyed by a fire from another tenant. I entered the 12-story brick building, stepped into a narrow, manually operated elevator, and asked the older gentleman seated on a stool to please take me to the 10th floor. He rattled shut the iron gates, and ever so slowly we ascended before jolting to a stop. The gate trundled open and I stepped out to face two white doors. I opened one and was inundated with the rhythmic whir of sewing machines, what sounded like pounding or hammering, and a rugged, leathery scent. Light streamed in from wide windows that stretched to a ceiling with exposed wood beams. To my left were rows of long tables cluttered with pieces of fabrics and small machines and tools and dozens of people in stained smocks with their heads down, working diligently with their hands. To my right there was an enclosed glass section with eight desks, and three private offices. The large one belonged to Miles.

He came out to greet me. Miles was dressed in jeans and a worn sweater over a woven shirt, and his eyes sparkled under a mane of white hair. He had a strong presence.

We walked around Coach's factory, showroom, and shipping area. Like its bags, Coach's facility was clean and unpretentious. A place of hard work.

Miles went to City College of New York, the other school I'd been accepted to after high school, and had a degree in business administration with a major in advertising. He'd gone to work for Coach because William Lipp was looking for an assistant to run the business one day. That's what Miles told me he was looking for, a potential successor who could learn the business and take over once he and Lillian decided what to do with their company. But he hadn't made a decision yet about when they were leaving, not wanting to put "the cart before the horse," he said.

"I've learned many nice things about you," he told me. I assumed they came from Mel.

Our meeting was pleasant, and I left the interview intrigued. Miles and his wife had clearly built a small, successful business by making quality products at a fair price that a lot of people liked. If they made more of these products, they could undoubtedly generate more sales, at least from what I'd gleaned from the department store buyers I'd interviewed. But Miles didn't strike me as all that eager to fill more orders to keep stores stocked, which I found curious and of possible concern that he might limit the company's growth.

Forty-five minutes before our second interview I was running late, and still feeling uncomfortable with leaving the ACD behind. I called Bobbie at about 3:15 p.m. from my office and told her I was thinking of canceling the meeting with Miles.

"The work here isn't done," I said, half indifferent to the new job, half not wanting to hustle 40 blocks uptown by 4 p.m. Bobbie wasn't having my indecision before a decision even had to be made. She'd also done some reconnaissance and asked friends if they knew Coach. They really liked the bags.

"Stop it," she said. "You aren't backing out now. Go to the second interview and we can deal with your leaving if you even get the offer." She was right and I went.

One of the first questions Miles asked me was if I'd be satisfied working at a small company after such a big city government job.

"You'll start with a desk outside my office, maybe shortly get your own office. But you won't have a team to lead. Can you adjust to that?" It was a fair question.

Everyone has their own definition of success, and mine was evolving as I contemplated leaving civic work for the private sector. I was still searching for some balance between "being on the side of justice and good," as I'd told the *New York Post*, and having a job that gave me the financial means to live with more opportunities than I grew up with. I wanted to make money but also achieve things that had meaning beyond my own benefit. That's what propelled me to do more than just cut spending at the ACD but do it in a way that genuinely served kids and families. The *why* of my work had to achieve some greater good. Such an ideal outcome requires more than intent, but also thoughtful, rigorous execution. Great things don't just happen. We have to do everything in our power to bring them to fruition.

Success, as I would come to define it, was to achieve excellence in execution and outcome, and for a purpose I believed in.

Where my drive for excellence came from is hard to pinpoint. My mother certainly had aspirations for me beyond the status quo. But I didn't harbor some deep-seated, unmet need to get my parents' approval for me to be happy. If anything, I'd already exceeded their expectations. I'd also read 19th-century philosopher John Stuart Mill, probably back in college, whose theory of utilitarianism promotes decisions that produce "the greatest amount of good for the greatest amount of people." No doubt that concept stuck with me and became part of how I defined excellence. And I am sure Herb's sense of purpose and uncompromising standards were also imprinted upon me.

I couldn't articulate all of this even to myself when Miles asked me if I would be satisfied with a job at Coach. At some level, though, I knew that if I believed in an endeavor I would work hard to make it successful, and I would find satisfaction in both the effort and the outcome.

"I believe so," I said, and I assured him that no task would be too small. I also suggested introducing Miles to Bobbie and our kids. Coach was a family-owned business, after all, and I thought Miles might appreciate meeting my family, and seeing how important they were to me. He didn't take me up on the offer, although when I told him about Bobbie's diaper bag business, he made it clear that he would not want me taking time away from Coach to spend on Sandbox. Fair enough.

I went back to my office and made a list of pros and cons—which I've kept all these years. On the down side, a job at Coach would be a sacrifice in any status I'd earned in government. I'd also sacrifice a salary boost, at least for the next few years. I could easily make $55,000 to $60,000 a year at a big company, versus the $800 a week Miles would pay me to start, which was what I currently made. He said my compensation would go up if I contributed to the business, but he was unclear about how and when I might get a piece of the profits. I wondered, could I become an owner? Get shares? The idea of one day potentially being in charge was a definite pro. The uncertainty of it happening a definite con. Or at least a risk.

Another con: I'd be swapping the positional authority I enjoyed at my government job to answer to one person who held all the power.

Under "Misgivings" I wrote, "Can MC share decision-making?"

Then there was the office. I wouldn't have one. The benefit of being close to coworkers was that I'd overhear conversations, could ask lots of questions, and get to know the team and industry more quickly. But I was a planner who liked space to think things through in private and hold some conversations behind a closed door. Would the less-than-desirable office situation make me feel too vulnerable? Exposed? Self-conscious? "Might inhibit performance," I scribbled in pencil. I was contemplating all this when Miles asked for a third meeting.

The next time, at his request, he and Lillian came to my office on Church Street in lower Manhattan to see how I went about my day. I showed them my yellow legal pads and explained how I organized my time each morning, with handwritten to-do lists sorting projects and tasks, problems, meetings, and pending activities.

Was he impressed? Hard to say, but he asked for a fourth interview and gave me an assignment to write a newspaper ad for Coach. Unlike Miles, who'd majored in advertising, I'd never written a word of ad copy. Coach didn't do much advertising, but I reviewed its small, rectangular black-and-white ads in the *New York Times* and *Playbill,* the ad-filled programs handed to New York City theatergoers. These so-called tombstone ads were simple, just a drawing of a single Coach bag with a blunt headline, such as "It's not a Coach bag without a Coach tag."

I spent a taxing weekend attempting to emulate the pithy style with an original flair that might impress Miles, and I got help from my mother-in-law, Elaine, who was an excellent writer. When I handed Miles my amateur ad copy, he barely glanced at it before setting the pages aside without comment. It wouldn't be the last time he rebuffed my ideas. But he offered me a job, and we came up with a title, Vice President of Marketing and Special Projects.

Coach was a very different environment than the one I currently occupied. There would be a major adjustment. But Bobbie and I had talked. Not many job opportunities came along with the potential to help build a business, and maybe even run it one day. I was willing to make the short-term sacrifices in salary and status for the potential upside.

A more existential concern was whether the role would fit me. My daily focus would shift from trying to be in service of people in need, to selling products that people didn't really need. I was ready to funnel energy into building something, but I worried whether working for Miles would give me a big enough sense of purpose, and enough control. Coach seemed like a great product with an ethos. My biggest reservation was whether I'd be able to work effectively with Miles.

In early June 1979, I signed the short letter of employment Miles had typed and mailed to my apartment. It confirmed my title, as well as my salary, and an October 1 start date. The letter also stated that either of us could terminate my employment with 30 days' notice. Years later, when someone asked Lillian why Miles hired me, she replied, "Lew was the only candidate." I knew that she wasn't joking, and that Miles had hired me despite his own misgivings.

I copied the employment letter to keep with notes I'd made during the interview process. Before filing them away, I glanced at my pro and con lists. Under "sacrifices" I'd written "frightening," because it was.

• • •

Joining Coach was humbling. No one there cared that I'd been in meetings with the mayor, or featured in the *New York Post*, or testified in front of congressional committees. I was on their terrain now and had to prove myself all over again. I also had to honor my promise to Miles that there was no task too small that I wouldn't willingly take on. I shifted my mind and attitude into learning mode and spent the first few months losing sleep at night, worried Miles might fire me.

My first project was the unglamorous task of installing air conditioning on the factory floor before next summer's heat poured through our glass windows. I couldn't have known less about HVAC systems, but by the time I was done researching vendors, negotiating contracts, and supervising the install, I was an expert on cooling a 20,000-square-foot space, and I became friendly with some of the factory workers.

At the same time Miles asked me to answer the customer mail that was piling up in his office. The handwritten notes offered a trove of insight into our customers, and reading them extinguished any lingering doubts I had that a Coach bag was just a bag to carry stuff. Women wrote about buying their first Coach bag for interviews or for a first job, and about buying their second Coach bag after being promoted. Our bags in black and British tan were gifted as coming-of-age gifts, for graduations and milestone birthdays. A Coach bag was a treat as well as a practical investment. Women carried their Coach to work, but also on weekends, for nights out, and to travel. They used their bag for almost any occasion.

Miles and Lillian pinned their favorite letters to a bulletin board. One of my most memorable letters was from a woman who was going through a difficult time in her life after a divorce, and decided to travel to Europe for three weeks, alone, with just a Eurail Pass, no specific destination, one piece of luggage, and her Coach bag. She was on the first leg of her train journey when she spotted another American woman also carrying a Coach bag, and traveling alone. According to the letter the customer wrote us, she introduced herself, sure the two had more in common than just good taste in bags. The women wound up traveling together for weeks and became lasting friends.

Another memorable story was from a woman whose Coach bag fell into a lake when she was on a boat. Years later, the lake was dredged and her handbag was found and returned to her. She shipped it to us to restore and when it arrived the leather was damaged from water and mud. I was amazed when our craftsmen restored it to wearable condition. In fact, many customers also sent their worn bags and briefcases to our factory to be refurbished as part of our lifetime guarantee of free repairs and restorations, no matter what the bag had been through—a rare level of customer service for an accessory.

Coach bags were meant to be used for years, and our customers valued the authenticity and durability of our leather. Most other handbags were coated to ensure they looked shiny and new for as long as possible. Instead, our thick, naked leather was free to absorb oil, dirt, and other particles that naturally changed its appearance as it rubbed up against clothing and was exposed to natural elements. The idea that you'd have your Coach bag for years was innate to its appeal, and customers went on and on about how long "my Coach" lasted.

"Our products wear in, they don't wear out," was a marketing refrain we used to highlight the natural markings from the cowhide and human use that also made each bag personal to its owner. Two women could place their black zippered pouch bags side by side and easily identify which was theirs.

There was a real pride of ownership associated with Coach, and a kindred spirit shared among many of the people who carried our bags.

I was also beginning to appreciate how intensely personal a handbag could be. The outside projected your sense of self to the world. *I am serious. I am practical. I am professional. I have style.* The inside of each bag was your private inner world, holding valuables like keys, a wallet, an appointment book, photos of family, and, one day in the future, your phone. A bag was a home-away-from-home that you held in your hand, that hung from your shoulder, or that you wore across your body. Women had undeniable emotional ties with their bags. Like constant companions, a bag could be beloved, which if you think about it makes logical sense. Here is this thing you carry all day long. Touching. Opening and closing. Reaching into for your essentials. And because Coach leather developed that patina, it felt uniquely yours. The experiences people had with their Coach, and how they grew to cherish it, was a kind of magic.

I was coming to see why Coach was worth paying a bit more for than most bags on the market—you really got a great value for the price. I also appreciated why our products engendered such loyalty, and our customers' love enhanced Coach's appeal to me. I was proud to work for a business that sold products so many people felt so good about. I wasn't in civil service anymore, but our customers' unusual devotion gave my work added purpose.

• • •

Until the early 1960s, Coach had mostly produced practical products that prioritized function over fashion: small leather goods like wallets, billfolds, belts, keyholders, luggage tags, and desk sets made from a type of leather Coach called No. 66 Water Buffalo produced exclusively for Coach by an English tannery. The products, mostly for men, were primarily sold through executive gift catalogs.

It was Lillian who got Coach into the women's handbag business. As Miles told it, he'd scoffed when she first suggested that in addition to men's accessories they should also make pocketbooks. Lillian persisted and encouraged Miles to hire a talented young sportswear designer named Bonnie Cashin.

For about 15 years, Bonnie's eponymous Cashin Carry Collection of bags and even some clothing introduced the Coach name to a new consumer: women. Her creations were playful with a New-York-in-the-'60s attitude. Bonnie's modern, quirky stylings sometimes mixed fabrics with leather, and they had punchy names like the Feedbag, Big Mouth, Cylinder, Bucket Tote, and Swinger to reflect their unconventional shapes. The Duffle Sac was one of Bonnie's most iconic shapes. Introduced in 1971, it became a hit that we introduced in different sizes, materials, and iterations through the decades, making it a consistent customer favorite.

Her bags also had novel features like outside pockets and trigger-snap locks that attached straps to the bag itself. Bonnie's most lasting innovation was probably the turnlock fastener. Coach lore has it that Bonnie fashioned hers after the devices that secured the fabric rooftops of vintage convertibles to the car's body. In fact, such closures had been used on bags for decades, although not as a style statement.

Blending a spirit of cool and timelessness was Bonnie's magic, and she got the attention of fashion editors and industry publications that featured Bonnie and her bags on the pages of their magazines. *Women's Wear Daily,* the fashion industry's bible, dubbed Bonnie's Shopping Bag tote "the snob tote" because it was modeled after the paper shopping bags that Bonnie saw women carrying in the city. The first shopping tote made out of leather became a hit.

Bonnie's bags were popular but not as profitable as Miles wanted, so he'd come up with a more basic style: unlined bags in simple shapes that replaced the inside-seam construction used on most handbags with an unusual external binding. The bags were also made out of a kind of leather that Miles had created years prior to replicate the suppleness and durability of a baseball glove. Like a well-worn catcher's mitt, the bags developed that rich, darkened patina over time. Miles called it glovetanned cowhide, and its properties, paired with the external bound stitching, gave the Coach bag a distinctively recognizable "look."

I was surprised by how labor intensive it was to perfect our leather and make our products.

Creating the look and feel Miles wanted to achieve was difficult, partly because it was a contradiction of traits. The leather had to be soft yet virtually indestructible. It had to be natural, but could not fade when exposed to light, or stain when it got wet. It couldn't look like plastic, or like it was coated, because it wasn't. The leather also had to feel supple, yet it had to be taut enough to hold structured shapes. If you bent a piece of Coach leather backward, it didn't wrinkle. But over time it did show markings from use, which was part of its allure. A Coach bag became *your* Coach bag.

Getting all these qualities right was like making fine wine. You couldn't just know what to do, you also had to feel it. It took a lot of experimentation to develop a replicable process.

All the cowhides we used were from cattle raised for their meat. Without food production, there would be no Coach leather. Turning a hide into leather is called tanning, and making Coach's glovetanned cowhide began on location at our tanning partners, which were often businesses passed down from generations that had long relationships to Coach. First, the tanners selected the cleanest cowhides before putting them through a process that changed a hide's chemistry so it didn't deteriorate over time. Once tanned, each piece was inspected for imperfections. We didn't use finishes or pigments to cover up natural blemishes or discolorations, so they had to choose hides that were close to perfect. One by one the acceptable pieces were inserted into a splitting machine to separate the top grain of the hide, which was then fed through a shaving machine to give it uniform thickness. Next, all the pieces were put into a giant rotating drum to soak in oils and organic compounds, to make the hide more supple.

During the next phase tanning science became tanning art. The soaked pieces were put into other huge vats where color was added, and for as many as eight hours the leather tumbled to ensure the dyes permeated. Then a vacuum dryer shrunk the leather to give it the necessary Coach tightness. The leather then stayed outside for 24 hours, giving up moisture until it reached an ideal state of equilibrium for the buttery feel Coach leather was known for.

Every leather hide was scrutinized for thickness, color, and texture before arriving at our 34th Street factory. There, our expert pattern cutters would lay a single skin across their workbench and determine the most effective way to cut the various pieces needed for a single bag. The cutter's job was to ensure the best parts of the leather were the most visible. Even more importantly, the cutter assured that the integrity of each product was maintained so it kept its shape, delivered on its functionality, and retained its beauty—all while using as much of the leather as possible to avoid waste. It was like a puzzle. It could take more than 100 steps and up to two weeks to produce a single Coach bag.

Most of our workers had been with Coach for years before I arrived. They came from the many ethnic communities that made up New York's five boroughs. Someone once compared their graceful movements to a well-choreographed ballet. The most skilled among them was Myron Delman, who was very knowledgeable and a bit of a curmudgeon. Everyone called him Myer. He had had been with Coach for 20 years by the time I joined, overseeing the factory. During lunch breaks he'd hold court with three or four other workers, orchestrating a daily card game.

Our workers' collective skills and passion for the work went into the details that made Coach products attractive, functional, and durable—and so distinctive.

• • •

The product is the hero.

This was Miles's philosophy, and by the time I came to Coach he had brilliant clarity on Coach's core values, benefits, and design. There was no one original Coach bag, but there was an original Coach look and ethos, and all our bags derived from a singular design concept. The straightforward shapes with no gimmicky ornamentations. The authentic durability of our full-grain leather and solid brass hardware. The quality of our well-crafted construction. The functionality of features like adjustable straps; spacious interiors with no fabric linings that might rip; inside compartments and outside pockets; easy closures; or tuck-in flaps to adjust a bag's size to its contents. The trust of standing behind our products with free repairs and replacements. Miles relentlessly focused on those attributes, ensuring our marketing materials as well as our products conveyed them, and our customer service reinforced them.

After Bonnie Cashin left Coach in the early 1970s, the company was left without a true designer. Miles stopped producing her more whimsical styles and focused on about two dozen more simple silhouettes that had what Miles called classic shapes that were not beholden to the whims of fashion. The Basic Bag, a slim zippered clutch with detachable shoulder straps, and the roomier north-to-south rectangular Compact Pouch, with a full flap and turnlock closure, easily transitioned from day to night, season to season, year to year.

The burnished brass turnlocks were so distinctive on our simply styled bags that they became one of Coach's product codes, an image that people would come to associate with the Coach name. If you saw a turnlock on a leather bag or briefcase, you knew it was probably a Coach.

With the Cashin Carry name no longer part of the business, Miles rebranded all the handbags "Coach," and embossed the moniker on the interior of each bag. On the outside, he hung a small, rectangular, Coach-embossed leather tag—always the same color as the bag—from a short brass beaded chain. Miles called it the Coach lozenge. Even though the chain was detachable, most customers chose to keep it, a sort of status symbol for some. The company actually got a remarkable number of requests from customers to replace their lost tags.

From that point on, almost all Coach bags were produced in our glovetanned cowhide of varying neutral hues, which we gave eclectic names like tabac, mocha, and saddle. Every style also incorporated discernable, signature features, or brand codes, that told you it was a Coach bag. The adjustable, double-loop buckles that resembled hardware on a bridle. Bonnie's turnlocks. The hanging lozenge. Together, they contributed to the wide recognition Coach bags enjoyed.

On marketing materials, Miles continued to use one of the brand codes that Coach came up with during the 1950s: the horse and carriage. The stately drawing of a coachman seated atop a carriage drawn by two prancing horses. The horse-and-buggy was a symbol of luxury in the days when cobblestones lined New York City streets, making them bumpy and difficult to walk on. The image also was a loose reference to the durable, smooth harness leather of saddles, and elements of the horse's tack that influenced some of our bags' unique features, like the adjustable straps.

Coincidentally, or maybe not, the luxury brand Hermès, which began in 1837 when horse harness-maker Thierry Hermès opened a workshop in Paris, also had a horse-drawn carriage logo. Our two logos may have been similar, but by the 1970s, a Coach bag was about 4% of the price of an Hermès.

Miles was a savvy, intuitive marketer who educated people about the specialness of Coach leather. Prior to the famous lozenge, a baseball-shaped leather tag hung from the straps, with an embossed phrase that urged customers to "Feel It." Inside every bag, embossed onto a leather patch, was an explanation of Coach's leather: "This is a Coach bag. It is made of completely natural glovetanned cowhide."

He also wrote a tiny, four-page booklet that told you why Coach was special.

This bag is different.

The scars, scratches, veins and wrinkles that are characteristics of full-grain leather have deliberately not been covered over with paint.

Instead, far more interesting gradations of color have been achieved with a clean aniline dye that enhances rather than conceals these beautiful natural markings.

It is just this absence of heavy, artificial finish that gives our leather its marvelous feel, or "hand."

What should you do to break in and care for your bag?

Absolutely nothing!

This extraordinary leather will virtually take care of itself.

Hug it. Drape it. Squash it. Hold it in your hands. Wear it every day. Like a well-worn English Saddle, your bag will gradually take on the rich patina and warm glow of real leather.

Do not try to remove occasional spots or stains. Left alone, they will fade away and blend into the leather as it begins to grow darker with normal use.

The leather should be allowed to darken naturally. It will ultimately take on a most pleasing over-all burnished appearance that will identify your Coach bag as the much-loved, frequently worn, favorite accessory that it is sure to become.

This post-purchase reinforcement encouraged you to feel good about what you bought. We needed you to understand that a perceived imperfection in the leather wasn't a defect but part of the bag's hallmark beauty. And we needed you to know how to extend the life of that beauty.

The authenticity of natural imperfection was part of Coach's unique value.

The equities baked into Coach products formed their identity, and began to permeate American pop culture. In 1980, *The Official Preppy Handbook* became a satirical guide that nonetheless mirrored and influenced upscale American lifestyles. It singled out Coach as a purse of choice: "Good materials, good workmanship, classic design, lasts for years." That same year, *Fortune* magazine ran a photo spread titled "Things Made Well" featuring Coach bags alongside nine other US and international consumer goods perceived as high quality, like Baccarat crystal, Cross pens, Toshiba calculators, and Olympus cameras. Media coverage like this reflected and reinforced Coach's evolving place in the American zeitgeist. Priceless acknowledgments.

With credit to Miles, the product said it all. That was part of his magic.

Asking me when and why I came to love Coach is like asking me when I fell in love with my wife, Bobbie. I knew how I was feeling before I could even articulate why. And then, one day, it was part of me. In retrospect, I can say that Coach's prestige-without-pretention vibe first endeared me. I was a working-class kid who grew up with a distaste for elitism. But there was something deeper. The bags themselves, the artisans that made them, and our customers' loyalty represented values that I believed in, too.

I understood that the values and emotions associated with our products formed the foundations of Coach's identity and needed to be preserved to ensure the integrity of the evolving Coach brand.

In my own mind, I began to form a romantic if idealistic notion of Coach the brand and Coach the business as a microcosm of traits I liked most about America: Authenticity. Aspiration. Originality. Individuality. Invention. Reinvention. Drive. And the idea that beautiful, well-made products could be accessible to more people. These were things I felt good about, and why working for Coach was becoming more than just a job, but a real passion.

Did I articulate all this immediately? No. But by the end of my first year I had deep respect for what Miles and Lillian had built, and I was passionate about the product, the budding brand, and the potential of the business.

In a way, I saw Coach as the story of the self-made individual.

CHAPTER 4

Becoming Multichannel

I didn't have a sense of style when I joined Coach, and one thing about not having a good sense of style is that you don't realize it until someone tells you.

About 10 months into my job I bought a new pair of casual leather shoes. I had no idea what company made them; I just knew they fit well and were natural leather, like Coach products. To my non-discerning eye my new shoes looked perfectly fine. I remember wearing them to work and telling Miles, "If Coach made shoes, this is what they would look like." He looked down at my feet and paused a moment before he spoke.

"Are you sure, Lew?" His question was rhetorical. Miles's unsubtle disdain for my fashion sense hearkened back to my year on Wall Street when my inexpensive suits made it clear to others that I came from a working-class family. I wasn't ashamed of that, but I did aspire to rise above it. My city government years were just the opposite. Being unfashionable, even disheveled and sloppy like Herb, was a badge of honor, as if caring too much about what you wore somehow diminished your civic duty or overshadowed your intelligence.

Both of those jobs showed me that how we move up in the world of work is intertwined with how we present ourselves; they inform and influence each other, and I admit that I was caught between caring and not caring about what I looked like. I wanted to be judged by the merit of my performance, but I also liked feeling good in what I wore.

In hindsight, I can see that not having a fashion background was an advantage. I came into the accessories business with no preconceived ideas about what a handbag should be or look like. I also had no opinion about what made one handbag better than another. Elite brand names didn't intimidate me, either. Rather, they intrigued me. *Why would someone pay so much money for a bag?* Miles and Coach were giving me an appreciation for the value of something that was well-made, aesthetically pleasing, and stood for something more than sheer utility.

Luxury items had long been associated with exclusivity and indulgence, something that goes beyond satisfying a need to catering to a desire. And for centuries that idea was the sole province of the very wealthy, who could afford to indulge in things they didn't need. Luxury was also a symbol of class.

As a market, luxury became a category of goods that cost more than "premium" products, which cost more than "mass-market" products. There are nuances in each category, but if you break it down to basics, a mass-market product does a necessary job and is affordable to a majority of consumers. A mass-market car, like a Toyota, gets you where you need to go. A premium or super-premium product does the job and then some for a bit more money, and because of how it's made delivers benefits beyond basic functionality. A luxury automobile like a BMW has unnecessary but desirable features, like a suspension that offers a smoother ride and a heated steering wheel. A luxury item's value is less about need and more about perceived need and the emotional and psychological benefits it delivers.

For a long time, luxury items were cost-prohibitive to most people. They conferred a certain identity about the owner to the world, and to the owner. You have money. You have taste. You have status. You have choices. Luxury brands were, for some, a shortcut to style; we trust a brand to tell us what looks good. Emotionally, maybe it makes you feel successful, in the know, special.

The connotations of luxury would expand over time, but in the early 1980s there were no American bag brands that were even remotely equivalent to bags produced by the highest-end European design houses like Louis Vuitton, Gucci, and Hermès, among others. These brands were revered for their superior craftmanship, exceptional materials, and their bags' signature looks and logos. The story of their heritage also was part of their allure. Luxury bags were, and still can be, a very lucrative business. Because of the emotional connection many women have to those bags, they are extremely loyal to their favorites and are willing to pay whatever is required to purchase one. In the 1980s that would have meant more than $2,000, the equivalent of about $7,000 today. Luxury brands understood all of this long ago.

Their distribution and availability in the United States, however, was quite limited, with only a handful of luxury brands in their own freestanding stores or high-end flagship department stores, like Bergdorf Goodman and Saks Fifth Avenue.

In contrast, mass-market bags from fashion brands like Nine West and Anne Klein dominated the US market, as did bags with no recognizable brand. There were probably 50 or 75 companies making pocketbooks, and it was a fragmented category with no industry leaders. Mostly manufacturers with private label programs or small brands. One of the rare higher-end American brands was Mark Cross, a tiny Boston-based company with a heritage of tailored bags and briefcases.

Coach was different. Most of our bags averaged less than $100, about twice as much as mass-market brands but only a fraction of the price of European luxury. Miles had created a product that was special enough to pay somewhat more for, yet still affordable to nearly half of US households. Our product also embodied the utility of mass-market and the quality of luxury.

Handbags, I was learning, were a unique business in the world of fashion and apparel. For consumers, the acts of buying and owning a bag were relatively easy propositions compared to buying and owning shoes or clothes. You didn't actually have to try on a bag in a store, or alter it, because the same bag could hang from almost any shoulder or be grasped by any hand regardless of your height or weight. You never had to worry about a bag losing its fit as your body changed over time. This meant that a bag manufacturer or seller didn't have to produce or stock multiple sizes of one style. For consumers, there was also low risk of feeling physically uncomfortable while using a bag, whereas with shoes or pants a heel could be too high or a waistband too tight. Bags were also more age-neutral than a lot of fashion apparel.

The bag category was also underdeveloped. Most women in the early 1980s weren't changing out their bags from day to day. They had two or three go-to bags at any given time and could be perfectly happy wearing a single, neutral-colored bag with a variety of outfits. They were not yet compelled to own a diverse array of bags. Clearly, there was untapped potential for handbags to play a much more significant role in women's lives, which posed a great opportunity for Coach

The more I understood the uniqueness of the handbag business and the accessories market in general, the more excited I became about our future. And, the more I tried to succinctly articulate how Coach fit into the market. My instinct was to contrast Coach to the European luxury brands. Where they were pricey, Coach was affordable. Where they were snooty and elitist, Coach was friendly and accepting. Where they were exclusive, we were inviting. If Louis Vuitton attracted the top 1% of household incomes, Coach skewed to the top 20%. If a luxury handbag told the world a woman had arrived, Coach was for women who wanted the world to know she was working her way up, and succeeding on the way. Did this make us a premium product? Maybe. At some point I started calling Coach democratized luxury, which felt right. Selling to the many versus just the few synced with my own sensibilities. I was proud of Coach.

Again, did I realize all this during my first year on the job? Of course not. But it was nonetheless the world I was being exposed to every day, and the accumulation of knowledge informed my thinking.

• • •

The company was getting letters from people who wanted to buy Coach products but couldn't find them. The only way to buy Coach was in select department stores or specialty shops. We didn't sell directly to consumers; we sold wholesale to retailers. By not being more accessible, we were missing out on sales, and people were missing out on Coach. That's why Miles wanted to start a direct-to-consumer business by creating our first catalog to send to people so they could order Coach products from us, from their home. We had to go to them.

It was a smart idea, but Coach didn't have a mailing list, just thousands of cards, kept in some disarray. For years, every Coach bag had a unique serial number hot-stamped inside the bag, on the leather. It also came with a card for new owners to fill out and mail to us. People could register their bag's number with us so if it ever needed repair we could identify its production date and lot. The serial number also gave the bag's owner a sense of purchasing a bespoke product, while registration established a relationship. The card's very existence was a testament to Miles's brilliance at creating that consumer connection. At the time about 20% of customers sent the cards back to us, a pretty decent return rate. Over the years, Coach had amassed about 20,000 handwritten cards, unceremoniously kept in dozens of dusty shoeboxes, their value diminishing over time. We knew where our customers lived and could bring Coach to them.

Miles assigned me the job of creating a mail-order business. I knew almost less about mail order than I did about commercial air conditioning, and I was shocked the first time I laid eyes on the shoeboxes. We set about alphabetizing the cards and one by one manually input each name, address, and serial number into a data-entry device called a keypunch machine.

I began educating myself on the mail-order business. I met with the heads of Brooks Brothers, Tiffany, L.L.Bean, and others that did mail order exceptionally well so we could understand their strategies. To help me, I hired a former colleague from city government who was analytical and had good investigative skills.

We began designing Coach's first true mail-order catalog, with all photography approved by Miles. At the same time, we wanted to get an early sense of how current customers would respond to buying from us directly. So, we took the existing wholesale catalog that showcased our products to store buyers, replaced the prices with marked-up retail prices, and mailed that version to all the names from the shoeboxes. The week after sending them was quiet. I knew the third-class mail would take a while to arrive at people's homes and every day we waited for phones to ring and envelopes to arrive with orders. I was in our shipping room one morning when Miles popped his head in.

"How many orders did you receive?" He wanted numbers.

"Two," I told him, which was not a number that either of us wanted.

It was a slow roll. Two became five, five became eight. Orders trickled in, but not as many as we expected. It was disappointing, but I was not deterred. I felt confident that we'd have more success once we had a real catalog and expanded our mailings. I'd already learned that most companies rented or exchanged mailing lists of consumers that fit targeted profiles. So that's what we did. In the months that followed, we sent Coach's first official consumer catalog to lists that we bought or exchanged with complementary brands, as well as brokers. For instance, we mailed our catalog to 100,000 names and addresses of people living in certain zip codes who recently spent more than $150 through Ann Taylor's catalog. Or women between 25 and 40 who earned above a certain income.

We also invested in software and began to segment customers into different categories. Decades before big data, there were countless ways to parse consumers based on past purchases, demographics, and psychographics. I found database analysis fascinating—human behavior sliced and diced.

Another thing I figured out was that we didn't have to create a whole new catalog for each mailing. Just changing the bag we featured on the cover and rearranging the layout of the first and last eight pages telegraphed newness. This was a significant learning about the power of merchandising: how products are showcased influences your likeliness to purchase. It meant that we didn't have to introduce a new bag to broaden Coach's appeal.

The mail-order business succeeded because it was an exercise in deliberate, strategic data management. The logic of it gave me a sense of control and potential in an industry I once thought I had little to offer. Style and creativity weren't the only things that could lead Coach to more success. Just as important was studying people's shopping patterns and respecting what they revealed. I didn't have to be a designer to sell bags as long as I was curious about people and proficient with numbers, which I was.

Year by year, Coach's mail-order business grew and spread awareness of Coach outside the Northeast. The catalog was Coach's first substantial sales channel beyond department and specialty stores, and it was a thrill for me and for Miles to see so many people who had never heard of Coach want our products. It was also a chance for me to prove to Miles, and to myself, that I could make a substantial contribution to the business and take on bigger assignments.

• • •

In the spring of 1981, I left our 34th Street offices and headed uptown to a meeting with the CEO of Bloomingdale's, an imposing man named Marvin Traub. At the time, he was considered one of the most powerful people in retail—the equivalent of royalty in New York City's heady fashion world. I considered myself an outsider to that world, so I was less intimidated by Marvin than respectful of what he'd achieved.

Bloomingdale's was one of America's oldest department stores, founded by a family who sold hoopskirts in Manhattan's Lower East Side in the 1860s. By the 1920s, its store took up a whole city block on Lexington Avenue between 59th and 60th Streets. Marvin had worked his way up from the store's bargain basement in the 1950s, and at Bloomingdale's he was reinventing what shopping looked and even felt like.

Not until I joined Coach did I have any idea what it meant to be a merchant, and Marvin was known as a master. Bloomingdale's didn't just display products in its New York City store; it tried to create theater, especially in its windows, showcasing wares from clothes to furniture with lavish staging that made you feel like you were visiting a home in Italy, or China, or the Museum of Modern Art. Walking Bloomie's was an event, and for a small leather handbag maker like Coach, being sold there was a big deal.

Going with me to Bloomingdale's that day was Coach's longtime head of wholesale, Dick Rose, who managed our relationship with retailers and was quite agitated at the moment. We were about to tell Marvin that Coach was going to open its own store a few blocks away. This was somewhat unheard of back then. Higher-end American brands didn't have their own stores, aside from a handful of exceptions like Ralph Lauren, which opened its first store in Beverly Hills in 1971, selling apparel, but did not yet have a store in Manhattan. Most American accessory and clothing brands were sold in department stores and boutiques. Dick feared that if Bloomingdale's viewed a Coach store as competition, they might drop us.

I'd gone to Miles with the idea of opening our own store because I knew from my research that luxury handbag maker Louis Vuitton had its own stores, which gave it more control of its destiny. As a retailer, not a wholesaler, LV had decision-making power over which of its products it sold, instead of another retailer choosing what they liked. LV could decide how their products were displayed and how salespeople talked with customers, as well as how its bags were priced. And, it didn't have to share revenue.

Opening a Coach store would also give us a third sales channel, although it wouldn't be our first store. Coach had a small one in Paris, which Miles and Lillian opened after taking regular trips to the city, thinking it might add intrigue to the brand for our US buyers. "Le Coach Bag" was on the Left Bank at 23 rue Jacob and did indeed confer on Coach a halo of prestige back in the states.

Now Miles wanted to open our first US store on 57th Street, across from Carnegie Hall, in a space for rent between a small BBQ chicken place and an umbrella shop. His rationale was that Coach advertised in the *Playbill* handed to theatergoers, who were our primary constituency. I disagreed. Someone was unlikely to buy a new bag or belt before or after the symphony. I felt that Coach's first store needed to be in a dedicated shopping area trafficked by locals and tourists, where it would build brand awareness and generate new customers. Lillian agreed with me, and I asked her to convince Miles that a store on Madison Avenue, just a few blocks east of Carnegie Hall, was a more lucrative option despite its pricier rent. Miles stuck to his guns, but Lillian's vote broke our tie.

When we told Dick our plan after signing the $50,000-a-year lease, he went crazy. He saw a Coach store as a threat to our wholesale business, and to him. Dick had long-standing relationships with our retailers.

"It's going to fail," he said. And then, "We have to tell Bloomingdale's. They'll throw us out."

Miles and I tried to tell Dick that a Coach store would enhance our prestige and be like a laboratory where we could pilot which products sold well so department stores could use that information to stock models that consumers were most interested in. Was I 100% certain Bloomingdale's would see it that way? Of course not, but I did believe that Coach had to start taking more control over our destiny. Why let someone else dictate how Coach bags were displayed? We could make shopping at Coach an experience that reflected our values and voice. The product would still be the hero, but a store designed the right way, with staff trained the right way, would elevate and reinforce what we stood for. Quality and service. Surely a smart man like Marvin would get that. But Dick was convinced he'd be furious. Either way, we'd already signed the lease.

At Bloomingdale's offices Dick and I walked into a large conference room. On the wall hung portraits of people who I assumed were generations of Bloomingdales. Coach was a minor player in a long history of American retail, here to assert itself. I introduced myself to Marvin, a tall, imposing man. He asked me to step outside, alone. Dick winced. *I told you so,* his wide eyes read. Marvin and I left the room. There I was, alone in the hallway with the king of retail.

"I know why you're here," he said, flatly. I steeled myself. "When we go back in there, I'm going to beat you up, and tell everyone that what you're doing is awful, not something partners do to each other. But," he paused,

"I want you to know that I think opening your own stores is the smartest thing that you can do. However, do not tell a soul I said that." I nodded, keeping my cool. Not only would he not throw us out, but his approval was a vote of confidence. The two of us walked back into the meeting room, our faces revealing nothing.

I sat down next to Dick, who leaned over and whispered, "I told you they'd drop us."

"We'll see," I said.

I never told Dick or Miles about that hallway conversation with Marvin—if you can even call it a conversation.

We went ahead with our plans and Dick remained skeptical. "When the store fails, can you go back to city government?" he asked me again and again. "Miles will terminate you because he doesn't like failure."

• • •

What did a Coach store look like?

We had to figure out how to design our first retail space in a way that felt like Coach, but on a slim budget, and on a sliver of real estate, located at 754 Madison Avenue, between 65th and 66th Streets, next to a women's casual clothing shop. Unlike Marvin Traub, I was no master merchant. But I did have an idea. One day I took a cab to 116th Street and went inside Butler Library on Columbia University's campus. It's a massive building with a facade of 14 ionic columns that convey the seriousness of the place. The interior has a high-ceilinged grandeur but also a quiet intimacy, especially among the stacks, where I swear you could hear people thinking. Being at Butler felt purposeful and special, and that's what came to my mind as I thought about what a Coach store might look and feel like. For inspiration, I walked around Butler and took pictures of rows of its leatherbound encyclopedias and other thick tomes lined up next to each other. All those shelves of stately book spines had a calming, reverent aesthetic.

We designed our store to look and feel like a library. On one wall, custom-built oak shelves—which we stained to look like the more expensive reddish-brown of mahogany—housed satchels, clutches, totes, or shoulder bags, most styles in six shades of brown, as well as in red, navy, or sage. Their gussets mimicked book spines when placed side by side. We even added a rolling wooden ladder so we could reach bags on higher shelves. On another wall hung belts. Glass cases displayed wallets and other leather goods, and oak and marble finishes reinforced the timelessness of our bags' natural materials. The palpable scent of naked leather permeated the space, creating a more immersive atmosphere, and because the 450-square-foot space was only 11 feet wide, the shop felt intimate. Above the wall of hanging belts were large photographs of our craftspeople working at our factory.

We guided the store's staff to treat customers like they were guests in their homes. Welcome them in. Ask questions. Listen. Care. Let them touch and hold every product. We didn't try to protect smaller items from theft by locking them away in cases, so the merchandise would be accessible, which was intended to confer trust and stimulate purchases.

On our first day, in October of 1981, we were surprised when people lined up outside the Coach Store well before it opened. And we weren't even displaying merchandise in the window! At Christmas, we had lines out the door and down the block as people waited to get in. By the end of our first year our little store had achieved $1 million in sales. We knew we had something special.

For the first six months I spent about two days a week there. Observing customers while they shopped. Or manning the cash register, chatting people up as I made change or ran credit cards. What prompted you to visit today? How did you hear about Coach? Are you here to buy something for yourself, or a gift for someone else? I was genuinely fascinated. Some people already received our catalogs. But many were tourists or people who'd come into the city for the day to shop. They'd never heard of Coach until they walked by the store. It didn't take long for our sales per square foot to exceed sales of Coach products in department stores, without cutting into our wholesale business. Sales at Bloomingdale's on 59th Street even went up.

I remember thinking, *It's working,* and that we were damn lucky we hadn't opened across from Carnegie Hall.

The product was the hero but in stores it didn't necessarily sell itself. Our salespeople became knowledgeable, passionate ambassadors of Coach, and had to be naturally good with people. Maybe you came in not planning to buy a thing, but you liked the supple feel of the change purse you held in your hand as you browsed, but not until the salesperson explained that the wallet was made of our unique glovetanned leather that developed a patina over time did you decide to buy it.

A few things became clear. One, what was true for a luxury brand like Louis Vuitton was true for a lower-priced brand like Coach. Wealthy people weren't the only consumers that wanted to shop in bespoke environments. Many people enjoyed being immersed in the essence of a brand and seeing an entire collection of products in one place. They responded when our salespeople explained why Coach was special, and how we stood behind our products with a lifetime guarantee. Send it back to us, we'll fix it. Look inside, each bag has its own serial number and there's a card so you can register your bag. We'll keep your name on file and can mail you catalogs with what's new. People appreciated the attention.

Our multiple sales channels fed rather than cannibalized each other, meeting people wherever they chose to shop. Today, most premier consumer brands have omnichannel strategies. But in 1981, when Coach opened its first store in addition to its wholesale and catalog businesses, we were among the few brands to reach customers in these different ways.

Over the next few years, Coach would operate thriving stores in Boston, Washington, DC, San Francisco, and Seattle, giving us a blueprint for future growth and expansion. When it came to the scale of that growth, Miles and I had very different aspirations.

CHAPTER 5

Selling to an Unlikely Buyer

My recurring nightmares began soon after my family moved out of New York City in 1982 and into an 80-year-old Colonial house in Tenafly, New Jersey, about an hour's drive from Coach's offices, depending on traffic. The house was on a quiet street and sat on nearly an acre of land with beautiful old oak trees. I now had a lawn, two floors, and five bedrooms. I was living what I'd grown up picturing as the American Dream, and learning that the dream came with a mortgage, as well as a personal loan. Bobbie and I used some of our savings to pay for the down payment, along with $70,000 we borrowed from our parents. I was grateful that they were able to help us financially, and I felt intense responsibility to repay them as quickly as possible.

I had more at stake now than when I started my job at Coach, and I was feeling increasing pressure to succeed. With my salary so dependent on the financial performance of the business, my ability to make money was intertwined with Coach's ability to make money. Maybe that's what spurred the nightmares, which always began the same way. I'd see a beautiful home that looked a lot like ours perched atop a very high hill. In one version, I run around the inside of the house feverishly closing windows and doors to protect my family—from what isn't clear. In another version, I open the back door to realize that the house is on the verge of sliding down the hill's steep slope and into a devastated version of the South Bronx neighborhood where I grew up. Looking down into the distance, I could see buildings toppled, as if after an earthquake or maybe a war. I'd awake drenched in sweat, the symbolism obvious: I was scared of losing everything.

Maybe that's why I tried so hard to control outcomes in my everyday life. And at Coach I saw the potential for amazing outcomes, but only if we became more strategic in our planning, invested in more stores, expanded production, and became more rigorous in our overall execution. But Miles wasn't keen on growing the business. He and Lillian were quite content with the current level of profits, and they were focused on a very different endeavor, building a goat farm and cheese production business on land that he and Lillian had recently bought in upstate New York. Coach's owner, my boss, had a new venture he was excited about, making goat cheese and yogurt. I didn't begrudge Miles his new passion, but I was at a different place in my life, with a long career ahead of me as well as a young family to support. I also wanted more than a paycheck, more than to just keep the company humming along. My drive for excellence translated to building Coach into the best business it could be.

So I was excited when Miles called me into his office at the end of 1983 to discuss the year ahead.

"We have to plan what we want sales to be for next year," he said.

I had ideas that I was eager to implement and told him I'd put something on paper. Within days I handed Miles my amateur but earnest attempt at an operating plan. How many new stores we could open. How to grow catalog circulation from 2.5 million to 4 million. Raw material purchases based on future demand, and how many people we'd need to hire. I proposed introducing more styles more often, maybe in sync with the seasons.

I heard nothing from Miles for about a week. Finally, I went into his office for a scheduled meeting, with my usual to-do list on my yellow legal pad.

"What's on your list?" I asked first, always curious to see if what was on Miles's was also on mine. I then asked what order he wanted to discuss things, to purposefully let Miles lead how we dove into the work of the work. We were destined to differ on some things, and I figured it would be easier to persuade him to see my points of view if he knew that I knew he was in charge. I'd learned that my proactive nature violated Miles's ingrained sense of hierarchy. For 40 years, nearly everyone who worked for him had stayed in their lane. Then I came along with my energy and ideas. But that day I was antsy, and I had to ask if he'd reviewed my proposed plan.

"I read it," he said, barely looking up at me. "I put it in there," he said, turning his head and pointing to the wastebasket next to his desk. He had filed my plan in the trash. I was more astonished than insulted, yet not completely surprised. "I don't want you directing me. I want to keep it informal," he said. "I know what we need to do." I didn't argue; I just nodded and told him I understood.

People can have complicated relationships with their bosses and mentors, benefiting from their gifts while navigating their shortcomings. This was true for me with Miles. I admired him. He paid his factory workers well above union scale. He also established a familial, collegial workplace where people genuinely liked working together. He was a philanthropist, and even an environmentalist in his time, conserving waste, committing to organic leather, and closing the business on Earth Day every year. He also taught me that the most important element of satisfying and delighting customers was to consistently create a great product. I had such admiration for how he thought about cementing a product's relationship to a person.

But for all his creative genius, aspects of his personality were maddening. In my experience, Miles rarely sought out input or entertained ideas if they were different than his. He also tried to keep a boundary between employees and his family; in addition to Lillian, one of his three children also worked for Coach. When one of Miles's daughters invited me and Bobbie to her wedding, Miles later disinvited me. "Under different circumstances I would love for you to come," he told me, "but I don't want to mix work and family. I hope that's okay with you." It wasn't, and I didn't try to placate what I could tell was his guilt. I assumed Miles didn't want me there because he didn't like to mix social classes. Or did he just not like me?

I had a lot of respect for Miles, but he made it hard for me to like him unconditionally.

I don't think he ever wanted me to be truly comfortable working for him, and his demeanor often put me on edge. As time went by, though, he needed me more. I'd built and managed teams that drove more than half of Coach's revenues, and I had close working relationships with many of them. Still, I never felt indispensable. I had seen Miles let people go, so to avoid getting myself fired I was extra careful with what I said or did not say to him, and how and when I said it. Out of necessity I was learning to manage up.

Having opposing ideas with people you work with is inevitable, but I don't think Miles saw disagreements as a path to improvement. Stubborn, he'd dismiss me from his office with a hand wave rather than have a respectful argument. Was he risk averse or just content with Coach's achievement? Maybe a bit of both. Whatever his motivation, his behavior occasionally drove me crazy. I was grateful he'd hired me into his family business, but I was also frustrated at his lack of interest in growing that business.

If Miles was intuitive about the product, I was intuitive about how to grow the business, which was no doubt informed by things I'd learned at business school, but also by common sense, my own values, even my fear of failure and drive for excellence. During those years working for Miles my strategy was to attend to what I could control, and heavily influence, and to learn as much as I could. I poured myself into our mail-order business and our stores, as well as my ongoing fascination with consumer research. When I told Miles I wanted to conduct focus groups, he fired back, "We don't need them." As far as he was concerned, the business was performing so well. Why bother?

"Indulge me," I said, and did them anyway. I wanted to know: What else did our customers like about Coach? What kind of bags did they wish we made?

I was especially intrigued by the increasing number of Japanese tourists visiting our stores. From studying Louis Vuitton, I knew that the Japanese had an affinity for luxury accessories, bags in particular, and a centuries-old history of coveting well-made items. Many were quite discerning and would examine several versions of the same Coach bag before selecting which one to buy. They also tended to buy multiple handbags, wallets, and other items to take back to Japan. I was curious to learn how they had heard of us and what they found so appealing about our products. We hired a salesperson at our Madison Avenue store who spoke Japanese, and she helped me converse with tourists. I asked what brought them in, and it turned out that many knew about Coach before they even arrived in the United States because someone recommended that they visit us. There were even some Japanese travel groups, so prevalent in the 1980s, that prescheduled stops at Coach stores. Japanese business culture also had a tradition of gifting to show respect and formally presenting business cards to new associates. These two rituals made Coach's smaller products, like card cases, popular to this consumer segment that one day would be critical to Coach's growth.

Inside Coach, I also saw logical ways to improve operations, and I developed a plan to strengthen our infrastructure and recruit experienced leaders to expand production. Just planning for the future gave me a sense of control. Miles never again threw my ideas in the trash because I never told him.

However, part of my employment agreement was that Miles would increase my pay as I demonstrated my value. He had denied my first raise request in 1980, asking me to be patient, but then he had given me a hefty bump that put me on par with his longer-term direct reports. I also got an office. But as we made more money, my compensation didn't reflect it. We'd grown into a multichannel business that was on our way to hitting $20 million in annual revenue, a 300% jump since I joined, with more than half generated by the standalone stores and mail-order businesses, which I'd started and oversaw. My efforts were making Coach, and Miles, more money.

In late 1984 I went to him with a request I knew he'd find difficult to embrace, but that I felt justified to make. I explained in a patient, logical way why I'd earned the right to participate in future growth more directly. "I think we need to structure something that would give me equity in the business," I said. Miles didn't disagree, but he replied that he'd also have to give equity to a few people who'd been around a lot longer than me, like Myer Delman and Dick Rose. I wholeheartedly agreed. We were a team.

After about two months of not hearing more from Miles, I got up the courage to ask him where we were.

"I decided," he said. "You're not getting any equity." There were two reasons. First, he told me that he didn't want anyone looking at his travel and entertainment vouchers, judging how he spent the company's money. That was his prerogative. After all, he was the owner. If that were the only reason, however, I would have been frustrated. His second reason for not giving me equity was that he was ready to sell the business, which was good news. And, he'd already retained a boutique investment banking firm, Rothschild & Co, to shop it. His intent was to leave immediately after selling. Literally the next day. After a lifetime of being in charge, Miles couldn't fathom even one day working for someone else. Apparently, Rothschild had told him that he had to identify a successor to potential buyers, so in a way that only Miles could, he said he needed me and in the same breath put me in my place.

"Lew, if you oversee the sale with the bankers, I'll recommend that you replace me, even though you aren't qualified." That last part was meant to stay between us, of course. Miles was convinced that I was ill-equipped to oversee parts of Coach where he excelled, mainly product design, marketing, and manufacturing. "You're not ready to be a CEO, Lew, understand that. However, I am going to say that you are." Even if Miles was right, and I didn't believe he was, it didn't dampen my excitement.

Five years after taking a leap of faith to join a handbag manufacturer, I had come to love Coach. Our offices and people were a home away from home. I came in early and left late and thought about the business incessantly. Not because I had to, but because I wanted to. I believed in our products, which were considered beloved companions for good reason, and I was certain that the business was capable of so much more. I had no intention of letting it go from my life. With the right buyer I would have the latitude I craved to unleash Coach so it could achieve a greater destiny. We would both be unshackled.

Together Miles and I worked with a bright, thoughtful young banker from Rothschild named Irene Miller to identify potential buyers. There were several very interested companies that came in and really kicked the tires. A close friend of mine, Eric Weber, was a senior exec at Dancer Fitzgerald Sample, the ad agency that handled the account for Sara Lee (SL), a $20 billion food and apparel conglomerate that owned dozens of companies. Eric put us in touch, and before Irene, Miles, and I met with Sara Lee, I did some research. The Kitchens of Sara Lee had been a small chain of neighborhood bakeries founded in 1935 before being bought by Consolidated Foods Corporation, which itself descended from a single grocery store that started during the Civil War. Consolidated was changing its name to Sara Lee the year we approached them about adding Coach to their portfolio of well-known if unrelated brands, like Jimmy Dean sausage, which was founded by a meat-loving country-singer-turned-entrepreneur in 1969. And Hanes, a brand known for socks and underwear that went back to 1901. Sara Lee had corporate offices in Chicago and Winston-Salem, North Carolina, worlds away from Manhattan's scruffy garment district and Coach's peeling wallpaper and tattered rugs. Culturally our two companies could not have been more different.

I remember flying to Chicago and to Sara Lee's offices in Winston-Salem to meet with the company's senior executives, including CEO John Bryan, trying to sell them on my vision for Coach. By now I was very familiar with the French bag brand Louis Vuitton, and I told the execs that I wanted Coach to become a democratized version of European luxury in America. That probably sounded very grandiose if not pompous to business professionals who were 15 years my senior and sold pantyhose and frozen pastries for a living.

When Sara Lee Corporation paid $30 million in 1985 to buy a small pocketbook company, some people scratched their heads and even laughed. But I knew why Sara Lee wanted Coach, and it wasn't because the executives believed in my vision or were particularly impressed with our products. More compelling were Coach's trifecta of businesses—wholesale, mail order, and freestanding retail stores—which were the rare model of a multichannel consumer business. We now had five stores, mailed out more than 2 million Coach catalogs a year, and were in about 900 department store locations. Sara Lee wanted to learn from the channels' "synergy," and from my expertise. I was hardly a multichannel expert; I just knew what we'd done. Still, Sara Lee's leaders seemed to think I was some sort of pioneer in this area. It also helped close a deal that both Miles and I wanted.

Why did I want to sell to Sara Lee when not that long ago I'd shunned the idea of working for a big corporation? Frankly, after six years of navigating the limitations and politics of a family-owned business, I craved an environment that valued and rewarded performance. I wanted to be surrounded by professionals I could learn from in an environment that measured progress. If Miles was right, that I wasn't ready to be a CEO, Sara Lee might help me become one.

Sara Lee also had the means to help us prosper. Running Coach inside a decentralized conglomerate with financial resources, marketing know-how, and consumer research expertise was a chance to turn our homespun approaches into strategically sound operations. We'd have access to capital to expand manufacturing, build new stores, hire regional sales reps, and grow the mail-order business. I could tap into their expertise in finance and marketing to build a real leadership team at Coach. I was also a numbers guy, and packaged goods companies breathed data, so I could adopt more sophisticated processes and analytics.

Miles gave $1 million of the sale's proceeds to Coach's union workers, divvying up the funds by seniority, writing some checks for as much as $200,000 in today's dollars. On this Miles and I agreed: everyone should share in a company's financial success. On top of that, he gave me and two others $250,000 each. The large influx of funds allowed Bobbie and me to pay back our parents, plus expand the house to make room for our growing family. Our third child, Alana, had been born a year earlier.

True to his word, Miles departed immediately after the sale in August 1985. He packed a few cartons, got into our creaky elevator, closed its iron gates, and left, leaving me with his legacy to uphold and build upon. I wouldn't see him again for several years, but it took a while before I stopped hearing his voice in my head.

Overnight, I was in charge of Coach. I also had a new employer—a public company with quarterly expectations and, I'd later find out, a snake-pit culture that would infuse my mind and body with heightened stress and anxieties I'd have to learn how to manage. If Miles had been content to steer a horse and buggy, Sara Lee wanted me to drive a race car. I was excited. Did I fear crashing, or that my house would slide down that steep slope? You bet I did.

PART TWO

Expansion Years

CHAPTER 6

Scrappy to Strategic

I held my first meeting as Coach's new CEO with our small business staff in the ninth-floor showroom. I wanted my eight colleagues to understand the magnitude of what it meant for a company with only $25 million in annual sales to become part of a multibillion-dollar global corporation. We had unlimited opportunities and significant changes ahead. I also told them that Sara Lee had no real understanding of our beloved product, brand, or our loyal customers. We had to safeguard what made Coach Coach. The product had to stay the hero but within the parameters of our new owner's regimented operations and high standards.

Sara Lee was a classic conglomerate. Its financially driven business model was to buy successful consumer goods companies, give them autonomy, and provide them with resources to grow. How each company grew wasn't really a concern, as long as it was ethical and legal. That said, Sara Lee monitored each company's financial performance with an iron fist to ensure it met specific objectives quarter after quarter. These targets were determined by operating plans that each company put together for approval by Sara Lee corporate. Once approved, the plan had to be achieved. This business model delivered returns to shareholders consistently over the years. However, it did not particularly inspire people inside Sara Lee to be bold in imagination or in their goals. "Make your plan" was the mantra.

All this accountability was normal for the packaged goods company, but it was a major mental and executional shift for Coach, and for me. I welcomed it, though, because the increased scrutiny and analytic rigor gave me more control over the business, and it represented an opportunity to maximize Coach's growth potential—which for me was much more than just "making plan."

My aspiration was for Coach to build a truly great brand. And I was eager to implement many of the ideas I'd come up with but that Miles hadn't been interested in pursuing. One strategy was to broaden our assortment and widen our appeal by creating differentiated collections. Every product in a collection would be labeled Coach, but like retail boutiques or department stores that carried different bag brands, our collections would have subtle style and thematic differences but an aesthetic that still read Coach. I envisioned that each collection would be displayed in its own dedicated zone in a store and have its own section in a catalog.

Our first official stab at this strategy was the Lightweight Collection. By skiving the thickness of our cowhide in half, we could offer a collection of bags that were half the weight of our existing bags. The softer, drapier leather also lent itself to different shapes. And because the glovetanned cowhide was half as thick, it could accommodate new features like drawstring closures and less structured shapes. The bags also felt more appropriate for warmer climates and seasons.

Our traditional bags became part of what we called the Classic Collection, and in 1989, we launched the Sheridan Collection, our first handbags with fabric linings, followed by the Travel Collection, and so on.

The product assortment format that we would adhere to for decades was born, and eventually we'd get more creative with their names. The Soho and Manhattan Collections of the early 1990s ushered in a nomenclature that emphasized our New York City sensibility through neighborhood and street names. But those collections were years down the road. For now, we played it safe.

• • •

After the Sara Lee sale, my biggest concern wasn't introducing new products or even branding. More urgent was transforming a business run on instinct and tradition into a more professional, accountable company. I was revved up and optimistic but also aware that I'd inherited a heritage that needed to be preserved for the business to grow. I felt pressure to make sure that what Miles had started didn't fail but was also as successful as I wanted it to be. My boss was gone, but I could still hear his voice of judgment. *You're not ready to be a CEO, Lew.* Talking to people helped ground me in reality. One day I went to see my friend Eric Weber's father for advice. I told him about the changes I was making at Coach, and I wondered aloud what Miles would think. He looked at me with the wisdom of experience.

"Lew, you've got to get rid of the bird on your shoulder," he said. "Miles is out of your life. You can't look for his validation. It doesn't serve you well. Let it go. Whenever you think about him, brush it away. Otherwise, you'll never be free."

Even if I could let go of Miles, how did I let go of all the negative voices in my head? Also, I was hardly free at Sara Lee. In selling Coach I'd swapped one controlling force for another. Sara Lee's culture was unapologetically demanding. Business divisions were given a lot of autonomy, but its top executives were maniacal about financial performance, to the point of vindictiveness. In some years, when the company held an annual meeting for its 100 or so senior leaders, headshots of all the division executives were projected on a huge screen with a black box around the photo of anyone who failed to achieve their plan and make their numbers.

Sara Lee also had a quarterly ritual to keep us on track. Officially, these were called business review meetings. Unofficially, Sara Lee employees called them barrel meetings, an allusion to the interior of a submarine—that claustrophobic, contained, pressurized environment where there's no room for human error, and success depends on everyone doing their jobs perfectly. A much less generous interpretation equated the meetings with its attendees "being over a barrel," and at someone else's mercy. Both connotations adequately described the tone of the reviews, which could be serious, and for many people, nerve-racking affairs. The rapid-fire inquiry was a wildly different tempo than my meandering conversations with Miles, when we compared to-do lists. My approach to these corporate rituals was to be overprepared, and to have everyone on my team armed with such deep knowledge about Coach's business that there was no issue we couldn't address. It also helped that Coach consistently met or exceeded plan.

With Miles, my attempts at rigor had been rebuffed. At Sara Lee, rigor was something we had in common, and I embraced it. Still, I had to adjust to the new situation and to personalities very different from my own.

• • •

My boss was no longer a self-assured, scrappy entrepreneur, but a posse of career executives whose goals were less about building great brands than looking good to their superiors and getting their full bonus at the end of the year. I did not think people at Sara Lee had the same passion for pantyhose or cheesecake that my coworkers and I had for Coach's products.

When I showed up at Sara Lee's offices in Winston-Salem I was viewed as someone of a different ilk. Granted, I adapted by wearing jackets and ties, because when in Rome, but I was also the bearded New Yorker in a sea of clean-shaven southern professionals. I could be outspoken in meetings, and some considered me difficult to deal with, or, in their words, a pain in the ass. It was an environment where positional authority dictated who had power, not necessarily who had the best ideas, and that drove me crazy. I had zero interest in getting caught up in their politics of hierarchy and frankly wanted to deal with it as little as possible. To keep perspective I broke my job down to basics: The fundamental strategy that guided Sara Lee was sales growth with profit improvement, quarter after quarter. All Coach had to do was make Sara Lee more money each quarter and they'd leave us alone to build the brand I believed that Coach could become.

My intent going into those first few years was to learn how to operate a rapidly growing business by acquiring the know-how, processes, technology, and other resources that Coach needed from our new owner to achieve our goals. The arrangement had echoes of my time in New York City government, when turning around the Agency for Child Development (ACD) required me to slash the budget while caring for the kids in day care. The tough choices I had to make back then were driven by data, not to appease politicians. I'm not sure I even saw these parallels at the time, or recalled the deputy mayor's directive to "be decisive." But I did know that as CEO of Coach I would make decisions that wouldn't please everyone. I didn't fear upsetting people. What I feared was failing to meet Sara Lee's expectations, as well as my own.

Our vulnerabilities often drive us and, in my case, fear served as a forcing function to perform at my very best, which I couldn't do unless I had a strong team that performed at its very best. Again, not so different from how I ran

ACD. I needed to surround myself with a level of talent and thought partners the likes of which did not yet exist at Coach.

• • •

The people a business hires when it's young set the foundation of the company it becomes. Their values imprint on the culture. I was out to build a high-performance team with a gung-ho spirit, fueled by passion for the brand and a belief in the potential of the business. One where character and knowledge were more important than titles. Anyone I drafted had to play well with others and had to complement rather than compete with Coach's long-timers, who had institutional knowledge and relationships we valued.

Most importantly, we needed a chief financial officer who could become my business partner. I flew to Winston-Salem, where Sara Lee's non-food businesses were based, to interview three candidates they selected, current CFOs at other businesses Sara Lee owned. I wasn't yet a strategic interviewer, but I was instinctive enough to sense who'd be a cultural fit and to sniff out the vacationer mindset I'd often encountered in city government. I rejected Sara Lee's three candidates—not for lack of experience, but for lack of drive and curiosity. I asked a senior Sara Lee exec who else they had, like someone on the road to being a CFO, because I figured that person would be hungry. I was given the name of a person in his early thirties, who was raised in India, had an MBA from Wake Forest University, and had worked at Sara Lee long enough to garner respect. A "good guy" who was "moving up quickly," but some thought he wasn't "ready to be a CFO." I'd heard that tune before. "But if you want someone who'll work 24-7, give you heart and head, consider him," they said.

In some functions attitude and intelligence are more valuable than experience, so I asked to meet him.

Arun Rao was smart, respectful, and at the same time feisty. We liked each other immediately, and I convinced Sara Lee to let me appoint him Coach's first CFO. Arun relocated his young family from North Carolina to New Jersey, and when he arrived, Bobbie, the kids, and I met Arun and his family at the airport to give them a warm welcome and drive them to their new home, not far from Tenafly.

Arun proved himself invaluable. A gem of a human and a leader who helped me more fully understand Sara Lee's culture and expectations and develop financial and inventory planning systems that enabled Coach to measure our performance against those expectations. Arun was one of those people who knew what to do and how to do it well. During the next several years he would play significant roles evolving Coach's supply chain, opening factories, and negotiating vendor contracts.

He was also the perfect intermediary with Sara Lee because of his credibility. He helped me navigate SL's hierarchy, and he became my de facto number two. People went to him with questions or for permission to do things, and because Arun knew I'd want a strong rationale behind any decision, and because he wanted the same thing, he held people to high standards, too. He also had what others described as a beautiful soul, and he was beloved for his integrity and his energy. We all came to know Arun as hard charging but also caring.

Every CEO dreams of an operating partner of infinite capacity, with shared values and shared vision. That's what I had in Arun, someone I trusted to do what was best for the greater good of business. I'd leave him in charge if I was traveling or unreachable. With him, it was like I was able to multiply myself. And not since Herb had I made a true friend at work.

• • •

At the same time that we were beginning to get our operational house in order, we needed to transform our department store business, mainly by convincing the stores to display Coach products in image-enhancing ways. Until that point, Coach had willingly sold our products to anyone that paid their bills, regardless of how they showcased our products. No more. Meeting Sara Lee's revenue and profit requirements was as much about volume as it was about how people perceived Coach, and that required a more discerning distribution and merchandising strategy.

There was someone from the Hanes division of Sara Lee that I wanted to meet, a nine-year veteran named Gary Dembart, to find out if he could oversee our wholesale distribution.

Hanes was widely respected for how it had disrupted a mass-market category, hosiery. Back in 1968, a Hanes executive set up a secret project to figure out how to increase the frequency and volume of hosiery sales by selling pantyhose at grocery stores, because women shopped there more often than they went to department stores and boutiques, where most pantyhose was sold in flat, clear envelopes wrapped around a piece of cardboard. But typical hosiery displays took up a lot of space, too much space for a supermarket, where every inch of floor was valuable. Two designers came up with bold new packaging and merchandising: vertical, end-of-aisle shelves custom-built to fit egg-shaped plastic containers about the size of your fist that each held a scrunched-up pair of pantyhose. Cleverly named L'eggs, the pantyhose helped Hanes dominate the hosiery market for almost two decades, changing how women perceived and bought the product. It's a terrific story of what can happen when insights into people's behaviors and creativity come together. Gary was schooled in that tradition.

When I first called Gary, he was in his 24th-floor office at 30 Rockefeller Plaza, overlooking the famed ice rink. I introduced myself and asked him to come to our 34th Street offices to interview to be Coach's new director of sales. He never got back to me. Not many Sara Lee executives were clamoring to work for a small leather goods manufacturer, Arun being an exception. I'd have to sell Gary so he'd believe that Coach could be a $500 million business one day, a joke to most people at the time. First, of course, I had to get Gary to show up, so I played some Sara Lee politics and called his boss's boss.

A few days later Gary's office phone rang at 8 a.m. "Do you know who this is?" The gruff voice belonged to Gary's hard-nosed vice president who often screamed at executives from the stage at the annual conference.

"Yes, I do," said Gary.

"Do you also know that it's inappropriate to turn down a division president for an interview?" He was referring, of course, to me. Again, Gary said yes. The telephone line clicked quiet. Gary walked to his boss's office and asked if he still had a job. His boss laughed and said, "I think you need to pick up the phone and call Lew Frankfort. Tell him you'd be happy to come by." This was vintage Sara Lee.

A few days later Gary arrived at Coach's offices for our interview.

"Sara Lee has no clue what they bought," I told him. "We're a jewel in the rough."

This was hard for him to accept, sitting in our scrappy showroom with its fraying rug. It can be hard to believe that something can happen in the future if you can't envision it in the present, so I painted a picture of the growth rate I envisioned. It certainly was not what he expected. Neither was my enthusiasm as I walked him through our showroom, picking up sample bags perched on bakers' shelves, describing why our leather was unique, and why so many women loved their Coach bags. About halfway through our meeting, Gary was selling me on why I should hire him. Two weeks later he showed up at Coach in jeans, Timberland boots, and a sweater. I remember Gary saying it was the first time he hadn't worn a suit to the office in more than a decade.

I had him report to Dick Rose, our longtime head of wholesale. I don't think Dick ever liked me much. Everything I oversaw—mail order, Coach's stores—risked compromising his relationships with retailers. He also wasn't impressed by Gary. "We're not just making little eggs you can easily replace on a rack," he told his new direct report. "It takes weeks to make a Coach handbag."

Gary and I agreed we had to curtail sales to most specialty retailers because they lacked the sales volume or the merchandising wherewithal to adequately represent our brand. The mom-and-pop shops weren't a viable sales channel. This logical decision put Dick in the unpleasant position of cutting ties with business owners he'd known for many years, some for decades. He took out his frustration with me on Gary, who to his credit was able to hold empathy for his older colleague while doing the very task that caused the man grief. Juggling our two personalities and priorities wasn't easy on Gary. Nonetheless, he did a great job at it while rapidly growing our wholesale distribution in department stores and improving how Coach showed up to consumers.

Not long after Coach was acquired, I'd walked into the Sixth Avenue entrance of Macy's flagship store in New York City's Herald Square. I looked around at all the handbags for sale along the perimeter of the vast floor, then I looked at the cases of jewelry and perfume situated just inside the entrance, where customers inevitably walked as they came in and out. That coveted floor space was where I wanted Coach to open a small shop. Now that I had decision-making power, I was keen to elevate our department store strategy to ensure we had better positioning. I did some retail math in my head to figure out what Macy's was netting from the jewelry and perfume displays, then went straight to the top, arranging a meeting with the CEO of Macy's East, Art Reiner. I told Art that if Coach took over the space, we'd guarantee the $250,000 annual margin Macy's was already getting from us—and pay the difference even if our sales alone didn't meet that goal. He shook his head, insisting we'd never make it back because moving Coach away from other handbags would hurt our sales. I told him I was in a different place. Moving our location was an opportunity to create a shop, not just a display, which would boost sales. I was promising that Macy's wouldn't lose money even if he was right and our sales lapsed. Art agreed, which was how Coach relocated to the center of Macy's main floor, a strategy Gary would successfully implement in department stores across the country.

One reason I was so confident we'd make the sales number was because Coach already was consistently oversold during the holiday season. Miles purposefully kept supply less than demand so that we would always be in that oversold condition, in part to retain Coach's allure, and in part because he didn't want to increase production if it meant having everyone work longer hours. By mid-December, we usually ran out of our bestselling styles. To better meet demand all we had to do was ramp up and expand supply, another change I'd already begun. We couldn't sell more bags unless we made more bags.

• • •

When it came to Coach's leather, Miles had kept me at arm's length from the leathermaking process, only letting me meet with tanners when they came to Coach. I'd never even visited a tannery to witness the tanning process until the 30-day period before the Sara Lee deal closed, when we both figured I'd better get up to speed. When Miles left, his raw materials expertise also walked out the door. Now I needed to replace it.

Ken Purdy was the owner of one of the nation's largest tanneries, Prime Tanning, and he pointed me to an industry veteran with a promising nickname: Mr. Leather. When I met Fred Friesenhahn, he told me his remarkable story. He was born in Romania and was a shoemaker by trade who opened his own factory before joining the Hungarian army during World War II. After the war, he came to the United States with his wife, Trudy, and just one suitcase, which carried his shoe-making tools. Mr. Leather was now 60, and I was so appreciative that he'd agreed to work for Coach. He was a rare talent who for many years would make us much better than we would have been otherwise. America's retail and garment industries were rife with immigrants like Fred, or the children of immigrants, who had arrived with so little and built lives for themselves and their families. I never ceased being touched by their stories when I came across them, which was like listening to the American Dream on repeat.

Constructing most Coach bags required obsessive attention to detail by skilled craftspeople. Our challenge was to keep making quality products priced to be easily accessible to the top 20% of bag consumers, and aspirational but not out of reach for the next 20%, while giving the company the opportunity to make a fair return. We first began to scale manufacturing by renting space in an existing Florida factory. Around this time I also brought in an Atlanta consulting firm to help us implement a more modern production process. One of the firm's two partners, Bill Page, worked with Coach full-time, commuting from his home in Atlanta every week.

Bill implemented just-in-time manufacturing, or JIT, the Japanese methodology that uses formulas and layouts to maximize efficiency, costs, quality, and productivity. In the United States, JIT hadn't gained much traction among smaller manufacturers like us, but that didn't deter us from recognizing its benefit, and so in the late 1980s we began applying the same approach to constructing handbags that Toyota used to build cars. JIT did not require our craftspeople to work faster, just differently. Bill, with Myer's support, reorganized our process from one continuous production stream into teams of 15 to 25 people, which each produced products from start to finish. Most workers were cross-trained so they could swap jobs or fill in for each other. Everyone also learned quality inspection so we could spot problems as they occurred. Without compromising our products' quality, or lowering morale, or upsetting the union, we reduced what took two weeks on average to only a few days. To his credit, Myer saw these changes not as a threat to him but as a benefit to Coach. He and Bill worked beautifully together in a respectful collaboration of new knowledge and old know-how.

Bill also worked with Arun to help expand manufacturing, warehousing, and logistics, and make our entire operation more efficient. Eventually, a tragedy would compel me to hire Bill full-time, when Coach would need his expertise to keep us moving forward.

• • •

There was also the fundamental issue of Coach's culture to consider. I had no intention of adopting Sara Lee's stiff corporate workplace. I wanted to maintain our more entrepreneurial, familial atmosphere, where smart, nice, hardworking people were aligned on a common purpose, the success of the business, and the preservation of the brand. A place where they did their absolute best to perform at a high level, and where people were promoted and judged on their value to the company, not by where they came from, or where they went to school, or by their gender, or race, or sexual preference. I'd believed for years that ideas mattered most. In principle, I wanted Coach to be an inclusive meritocracy.

I also wanted Coach to be a workplace where people believed in the products we brought into the world and believed in each other. Creating a sense of loyalty and even love for a business that sells a discretionary product is not easy to do, and yet Coach had never felt like a place that just sold bags—at least not since I'd been there. My team and I had a sense of shared purpose that the products we made mattered. I intended to build on that shared sense of purpose as we grew and hired more people. Our employees had to believe, as I had come to believe, that growing a company that democratized luxury was a worthy pursuit, and they had to take pride in how we achieved it. Our policies had to treat employees as we would want to be treated, with respect and dignity. The culture had to embody our values just as our bags embodied equities like durability. But crafting our culture would be a more complex endeavor than crafting a handbag. I intended to work closely with the right person to figure it out.

I didn't use this language at the time, but what I was attempting to do was blend magic and logic by cultivating a workforce that had a genuine passion for the undertaking as well as a commitment to rigorous execution and accountability. Finding this balance could make Coach a very special place to work.

When I went looking for our first official head of human resources, I wanted someone who had the courage to establish Coach's own culture by embracing my values and their own, as well as Coach's ethos, but also someone who had the patience and gravitas to deal with Sara Lee's HR department.

Maxine Fechter came recommended by a mutual acquaintance. She'd spent eight years in personnel at the British retailer Conran's, known for curating exceptional shopping experiences. She currently worked for a small gourmet retailer out of Boston, commuting from her home in the New York suburbs. Maxine had never heard of Coach, and when she went to look at our bags in a store she found them heavy and not particularly attractive. Of course, she didn't tell me this when we first met.

During our interview I sensed that she was a person of high integrity. I also realized that her background was more administrative than strategic. When I described the role, Maxine told me straight up that she thought it might be more than she could handle. She'd never worked for a big corporation. Honesty was a trait I valued, and it overshadowed her lack of experience. Maxine was feisty and smart. She would learn whatever she didn't yet know. Moreover, she had a mature, even maternal quality that could help shape the familial culture I wanted Coach to maintain. Coach needed Maxine, I just knew it.

"I promise that you'll fly here, you'll soar." She hesitated. She had to be home for dinner at least three nights a week because her younger daughter was still in high school. This, she said, was nonnegotiable. "Absolutely," I assured her. I didn't want her leaving my office without saying yes. "You need to take this job," I pleaded with her. When she finally accepted I was so happy I hugged her. I looked her in the eyes. "Maxine, we'll take this journey together."

Maxine intuitively understood that people, policies, and one-off choices shape workplace culture. She imbued ours with her own integrity, and shared my belief that as a company we should treat people the way we would want to be treated, which sometimes meant disregarding Sara Lee's policies.

For example, the year our factory in Florida produced excess inventory, Sara Lee insisted we shut it temporarily to catch up. The idea of not paying employees for any amount of time was unthinkable to Maxine and me; hourly workers especially counted on every paycheck. We agreed to close the factory for a week but we kept paying everyone who worked there without telling Sara Lee. And when the head of that facility contracted AIDS and had to stop working to receive treatment, we kept him on our payroll for years, unbeknownst to Sara Lee, so he could retain his health insurance. Coach had a significant LGBTQ population, and under Maxine we also began offering domestic-partner health care benefits, as well as maternity leave, well before the 1998 New York State Domestic Partnership Registration Law gave same-sex and different-sex couples the opportunity to receive the same medical benefits afforded married couples. Sara Lee had no such policy, so to prevent it from stopping us Maxine didn't inform Sara Lee until after we announced the benefit to employees. Maxine also created protocols to help us hire and promote people with a mix of traits we came to call "Coach smart." To be Coach smart was to be knowledgeable in your area of expertise, curious, and a constant learner. If you were Coach smart, you were rigorous by nature and held yourself to high standards. You were also self-motivated and collaborative, empathic and analytical, and a hard worker. If you were Coach smart, you were optimistic, honest, and most importantly nice. Nice was a big word at Coach. After you came to our offices to interview for a job, Maxine and her staff always asked the receptionist how you treated them on your way in and your way out. If you weren't respectful you probably wouldn't be invited back.

I came to describe our culture as a "performance family," a term I coined to articulate an ethos of hard work and high standards coexisting with a spirit of cooperation and collaboration. Using the word *family* in an office setting didn't have the insincere or even manipulative connotations that it does today. Back then, it was rare to think about coworkers as family, and it set a compelling tone that we cared about and supported each other. Unlike a family, however, Coach was a business, and you would be asked to leave if you didn't perform. Ensuring we stayed true to that ethos was HR's role, and so I considered Maxine and her team as strategic to Coach's growth.

• • •

In 1988, I was looking for a new executive assistant, and an employment agency was sending candidates for me to interview. Pat Cherry walked into my office carrying a new Coach handbag she'd coincidentally bought for the interview before the agency told her that Coach was the company that was looking to hire. Pat was a quiet force with a genuine smile who knew a thing or two about corporate culture and working with demanding personalities. When I told her I spent long hours at the office, she said the job wasn't for her because she'd have too long a commute to come in very early and stay past 5 p.m. We parted amicably so she could pursue other opportunities. I interviewed others, but no one came close to Pat. I asked her to please return for a second interview. She did, and we agreed she'd only stay late a few days a week.

Not long after she started, the assistant Pat was replacing told her that I always worked through lunch so Pat should bring me my meal every day. Pat fired back that she wasn't hired to be a waitress. Fair enough, I said, when my outgoing assistant told me, and I agreed to get lunch another way. Months passed, and Pat and I established a relationship of mutual respect and familiarity. Eventually she realized that she worked for a person who was perpetually "on" and spent his days in back-to-back meetings. If a sandwich didn't appear on my desk I might not eat at all. Bringing me lunch wasn't about serving me, Pat decided, but keeping me fed so I could keep working. She began asking me what I'd like for lunch, which I greatly appreciated.

An executive assistant for a CEO is a demanding role that requires a commitment to excellence, the ability to read people and situations, juggle personalities, get through endless to-do lists, keep secrets, and know when to follow the leader, and when to lead the leader. A trusted assistant who understands their boss's proclivities and tolerates their quirks is irreplaceable. That's Pat. She had my back, but she could also confront me with what I needed to hear. Like when she warned me to stop so aggressively rebelling against Sara Lee's corporate culture. "You'll never win," she said. She was right, and I even pulled back a little. She also did her best to get me to stick to a schedule, an almost impossible task given my penchant for running over and asking for last-minute meetings. I often came into the office with something on my mind that I felt the need to address right away, so I'd delay my first meeting, which would disrupt the day's calendar and other people's schedules, too. At one point Pat threatened to quit if I didn't at least try to be more disciplined and organized—"like a professional CEO," as she put it—instead of letting my whims dictate the day. Again, I did my best, but in truth this part of my personality was hard to corral.

For all our skirmishes and a battle or two, Pat and I always found our way through. She got me, tolerated me, taught me, and we came to feel like real family.

Pat truly loved Coach's people and considered herself an ambassador for the brand, which may be why she put up with some of my behavior when I got stressed or frustrated, which would frequently happen as my own job became more intense. I realized that great executive assistants were hard to find. I would tell people that if they had one, they should do everything within reason to keep them. I'm grateful that Pat is still with me.

• • •

Being owned by Sara Lee gave Coach resources to grow, and grow we did under the strict, watchful eye of SL executives who had no tolerance for failure, which was stressful. In fact, shortly after Coach was acquired, I began suffering from lower back pain and stiff shoulders. Sitting or walking, my carriage just felt off. It was uncomfortable and distracting.

Stress takes physical manifestations, and my body was showing signs that the mental weight of Sara Lee's constant measured scrutiny and my own drive to achieve outstanding performance were taking a toll. Sometimes, when I felt particularly tense, I would walk our factory floor, where the hum of sewing machines and the quiet concentration of our craftspeople soothed me. When I got home after work, I frequently went on a run to decompress. I needed to let my body express itself, and after a jog or a workout my muscles seemed to relax. I also found a trainer who understood human anatomy and physiology, and who helped me reduce stress in addition to building strength and endurance.

I wasn't sure what else I could do until I told a close friend about my chronic pains and aches, and he recommended a massage therapist who he thought was uniquely talented. I'd had massages from time to time, usually on vacation, and considered them a bit of a luxury. But the worse I felt the more I needed to loosen my muscles and reduce physical tension on a regular basis. I called the practitioner my friend recommended, Edgar Pena, and he came to my house, set up a massage table in one of the kids' rooms, and went to work on my back while Alana, who was a toddler at the time, played under the table.

"The problem with your neck is not your neck," said Edgar. "It's because your whole body is bent out of shape." One of my hips, he observed, was almost two inches higher than the other. I had no idea, and asked him all sorts of questions. Edgar had been curious about the non-physical aspects of the human body ever since he was just 14 years old, growing up in Colombia. He'd emigrated to the United States, and at 17 he began taking classes in metaphysics, eventually studying the connection between the mental and physical aspects of the human body, and how our psychology affects our physiology. After an hour with Edgar I felt more than just relaxed. The pain in my neck subsided, and my mind had quieted.

Edgar's rates were reasonable so I asked him to come back, and his visits became a weekly ritual to break up a relentless cycle of tension and pain.

"You have a lot on your shoulders," Edgar would say with his soft chuckle. "It's what happens when your mind shows up in your body."

The connection between our minds and bodies became less mystery and more science to me as Edgar shared teachings from various healers and scholars. I'm a logical person who likes proof of truth, but I'm also open-minded enough to entertain concepts that evade tangible evidence. Most of us can't see the energy centers, or chakras, that exist throughout our bodies and correspond to organs, glands, and our nervous system, as well as to our mental and emotional states. Scientifically, I know that the human body is made up of energy. I was learning that energy can be moved by trained healers like Edgar, and by our own minds based on what and how we think. Thoughts, after all, are also a form of energy.

When our energy gets stuck, or blocked, our physical body can get out of whack, a regular occurrence for me. It often took at least 60 minutes of massage and stretching for Edgar to reset my anatomical balance.

Over the years I benefited from Edgar's ongoing education as he learned and encouraged me to explore different kinds of body work, from the reflexology that he also practiced, to acupuncture and, years later, meditation. I became ever more attuned to my body, and emphatic that nurturing our "magnificent electric bioenergetic machine," as Edgar put it, was crucial to my mental and physical health.

Edgar's body work was better than going on a daily run. Never a one-time cure, but routine maintenance to ease physical manifestations of my anxiety and my racing mind. It allowed me to function better, at least for a few days. But by the middle or end of another long week, I was grateful when Edgar showed up at the house. I also was eager to share his gifts, and after many years of prodding he would eventually take me up on my offer to come to Coach's office once a week to treat any employee that was interested, for a modest rate per session. I eventually had a room at Coach set up just for him, so he could continue to see Coach employees at a discounted rate.

To this day, I still see Edgar almost every week.

• • •

The pressure I felt from Sara Lee and from myself also manifested in my psyche. As Coach grew, so did my responsibilities, and so did my fears of failing. A strong quarter didn't eradicate the nightmares of my house falling down that steep hill. In fact, I had those dreams more often. The more Coach gained, the more we, and I, stood to lose. I couldn't let the company crumble under my watch. Losing money was also part of it; so was my reputation, and keeping my job. But the fear I felt was deeper, as if something untenable, unfixable, unforgivable, even unfathomable might happen.

It's important to understand that "not failing" wasn't my definition of success. If I was only motivated to avoid failure I'd play it safe. Because I had that equally strong drive for excellence, I set ambitious goals, and to achieve them I dug deeper into every aspect of Coach's business. I challenged assumptions, and I looked for weak spots as well as opportunities to help ensure that the company so many people loved grew. A lot.

By the end of 1987, Coach had doubled our annual revenue to $50 million.

Just one year later, in 1988, we grew 60%, to $80 million. To celebrate we bought every factory worker a turkey for Thanksgiving.

By June 1989, we'd surpassed $100 million, quintupling sales in just four years.

Our rapid growth during these years was primarily due to how thoughtfully we expanded our distribution. In addition to our retail stores, up from five when we joined Sara Lee, our catalog business was buttressed by now more than 1 million names in our database. It was more than a numbers game, however, and I was fiercely protective of how Coach showed up in the marketplace. At one point, a Sara Lee colleague several notches above me insisted we start selling Coach products at JCPenney, which distributed Hanes and other Sara Lee–owned products. The retailer was holding back big purchases of underwear until Sara Lee brought in Coach.

"With all due respect, no way," I told him. JCPenney was a discount department store, which wasn't where our target consumers shopped. Penney's couldn't possibly maintain our price points. I fought his insistence even as he lost his temper. Coach never went into Penney's, and I never found out what happened to those stalled underwear orders.

In the department stores that did sell Coach, our sales more than tripled by 1989 thanks to better merchandising and more locations. Outside the United States, there was another department store where we were also thriving, in a country where customers were coming to covet Coach as much as Americans.

• • •

By the late 1980s, the Japanese tourists who had discovered Coach at the start of the decade were now shopping at Coach stores in droves. I'd learned more about them: The Japanese were intensely brand conscious and brand loyal, but Japan had no domestic accessory brands of consequence. Quality handbags there were imported from European luxury companies, and because they were so costly most people couldn't afford them. Those that could treated them as investment pieces, akin to works of art. (During a future trip to a remote Japanese village, I'd visit the home of a woman who knew I was from a handbag company. I still remember how she opened a cupboard and gingerly removed a Louis Vuitton handbag wrapped in cloth, which she'd acquired 25 years earlier and considered a family heirloom.)

It had become clear to me that Coach couldn't aspire to be a higher-end global brand without capturing the Japanese consumer, a population that, at that time, accounted for as much as 35% of the $24 billion global spend on luxury accessories. Coach needed to be in their home country.

The least-risky way for us to enter Japan was to partner with one of the country's high-end department stores, which would give us instant visibility in prime locations and credibility by association. The department store we approached was Mitsukoshi, a retailer whose origins stretched back to a kimono fabrics merchandising company founded in 1673. In addition to being one of the largest and most exclusive department stores in Japan, Mitsukoshi was known for superior customer service, which was so essential to our own brand.

In 1988, a few colleagues and I flew to Tokyo to meet Mitsukoshi's president and chief operating officer, Yoshiaki Sakakura, and convince him that Mitsukoshi should be our exclusive seller and distributor in the country. I still remember walking into a Tokyo conference room with my team and a Japanese translator and taking our assigned seats in upholstered chairs on one side of the room. We were offered tea and water while we waited for the esteemed Sakakura-San, who finally entered with his entourage. He sat directly across from me, while his top executives took their seats across from Coach's senior leaders. The rest sat in chairs along the wall. The formality of it all was a bit intimidating.

My team and I had prepared a presentation to introduce them to Coach. First, I told Sakakura-San about Miles's vision for a quality product that sold at a fair price. I told him about the cult following of our beloved bags, which had lured me to join the company. I described our unique glovetanned leather. Then I shared sales data we'd collected to prove how popular Coach was with Japanese travelers.

What really got Sakakura-San intrigued was the title of our presentation: Magic Plus Logic.

I'm pretty sure this was the first time I'd ever used that term. I'd come up with it when I was trying to divine how to communicate to someone from another culture what made Coach so special. For me, magic-plus-logic represented the unique look of Coach bags as well as the unconventional ways we were going about building the brand and the business.

Sakakura-San looked transfixed as I explained that our company was growing by blending magic and logic, and the concept was all he wanted to talk about. Not long after the meeting Mitsukoshi became the exclusive seller of Coach products in Japan, and for years Sakakura-San would affectionately refer to me as "magic-logic" during our animated discussions about Coach's Japanese business, which would eventually become a huge part of our global growth.

Coach eventually grew our brand in Japan and in other regions abroad. But it was that first meeting in Japan where magic-plus-logic originated as the umbrella term for our ethos.

After the Tokyo meeting, I started using the words back at our US offices in various incarnations. At a store managers' gathering in September 1989, I spoke about what the company was doing to attract more new customers and stimulate repurchases. In addition to sending 200,000 catalogs to American Express cardholders, "we're also exploring new ways to turn logic into magic," I said. The words weren't jargon or hyperbole because the concept described a way of working that already existed. There was no formal definition, but at the highest level most people intuited that magic-plus-logic meant a blend of creativity and business. To some people it was a mix of art and science; to others it was art and commerce. Maybe you saw it as heart and head. Or the syncing of the right and left brain. One person said it was inspiration plus intelligence.

One of my favorite interpretations came from a talented young designer, Ivy Ross, who would work with us for a few years in the mid-1990s. Ivy was the rare artist with a business sensibility. She went to school for jewelry design and had just finished an executive management program at Harvard when I interviewed her for a VP role.

"What do you enjoy doing most?" I asked her.

"Making magic," she replied.

In a memorable talk Ivy gave to Coach employees, she explained how Coach thought about product development. "The job of a designer," she said, "was to first understand the needs of the customer"—this was Coach's logic engine—"then use shape, form, and composition to guide the design to beauty. Various elements come together until the right combination strikes a spot and catches fire, a kind of spontaneous combustion to create a product whose spirit matches the user's personal values and actual lifestyle." That was the magic. "With this definition in mind, we look to the Coach product."

Ivy's description was as poetic as it was accurate.

Magic-plus-logic went beyond how we designed and marketed products, of course. There was also a blend of creativity and business elements in how we were building and running the company. We were a familial culture that also held each other accountable for results—a place where the acquisition of new knowledge could change minds. We used imagination and information to expand our sales channels—first to catalogs, then to our own stores, then in how we showed up in department stores, and eventually to how we expanded abroad.

Magic-plus-logic was becoming embedded in how we approached our work. Our constant challenge was to get the blend right—and not to lean too heavily into one at the expense of the other.

CHAPTER 7

Centering on Consumers

Coach's products and identity weren't tied to a single, well-known designer, unlike some of the world's most famous luxury bag brands. Louis Vuitton meticulously crafted trunks for Parisian royalty before he founded his eponymous company in 1854. Guccio Gucci was a porter at London's luxurious Savoy Hotel before establishing his artisanal luggage workshop in Florence in 1921. Gabrielle "Coco" Chanel was a seamstress who opened a Paris boutique and designed elegantly simple women's apparel before creating Chanel No. 5, the fragrance that launched her fashion empire. These founding designers were the heart of European luxury houses, and their personalities and discerning, lavish lifestyles shaped the associations and emotions people had with their products.

In contrast, Coach's uniquely American handbags—more sturdy and functional than pretty and stereotypically luxurious—may have been designed initially by Miles Cahn, with Bonnie Cashin's influences, and the work of many others over the decades, but people didn't know their names or connect their stories with the Coach brand or our bags. Not being dependent on one person's creative vision was a mixed blessing, because we weren't at a loss if our creative visionary left us, but we also didn't have a creative visionary to lead us.

Rather than a designer-led brand, Coach was consumer-led, which meant one of the most important tools we had at our disposal was our curiosity to learn about consumers—mainly women's habits, values, and the roles bags played in their lives.

I had been curious about our customers since my first introduction to Coach. *Why did so many women love these bags?*

In 1987, a research firm did a study to help us understand the key components of our customers' satisfaction. Direct quotes from women interviewed reinforced five things we already believed were true. First, the quality of our craftsmanship: "It's made with love," said one woman. "For a lifetime of wear." Said another, "they are very conscious of what they are doing. I read it in the catalog, the other bags don't explain that to you." Second, customers said that the unique "soft" and "buttery" texture of our leather made Coach "a purse worth paying more for." Third, our customer service: "The salesgirl came over and told me a little bit about the history of Coach and that kind of got me all the more interested." They also liked that we offered free repairs and replacement. Fourth, the enduring simplicity of our bags' styles. According to one woman, "It's beautiful, not complicated, it will serve well and look good regardless of what I do with it." And, "I don't think there's a duplicate. You know a Coach bag." Finally, the sense of community and belonging that owning a Coach conferred, which echoed the sentiments I'd first heard in 1979.

"It's like a mini-cult," said one woman. "I saw another woman walking across the parking lot with a Coach pocketbook on her and knew we had something in common, and would immediately have something to talk about." It reminded me of one of my favorite customer letters, from the woman who met her friend on the train in Europe.

The researchers concluded that for some women, there was an almost personal relationship between themselves and their Coach bag. As a brand, Coach's "mini-cult" was not defined by status seekers, but a "specialness" that didn't arise when brands like Gucci, Louis Vuitton, or Dooney & Bourke came up in focus groups.

We wanted Coach to maintain and build upon these qualities and to learn more about our customers, asking more questions of women in general: What motivates you to buy something? What mental steps do you go through before deciding to purchase one product over another for yourself, or as a gift? How do those steps vary by age, income, or where people live? What's the importance of a brand name versus price versus convenience versus function versus style versus color, and so on? The answers would change as culture and the market changed, so we had to stay consistently curious.

Most people are curious, but some make up their minds and assume once a question has been asked the answer is final. They shut the door. Continuous learners, on the other hand, ask the same questions again and again, knowing the answers will change at some point. They always do.

Curiosity enabled me to acquire knowledge and insight. The way I saw it, knowledge is something derived from facts, raw data, education, and experience. Insight is a broader understanding of an issue, or an awareness of a situation, derived from connecting disparate pieces of information, including knowledge. Having knowledge and insight gave me a sense of control—which I needed to keep the potential of failure at bay. Knowledge and insight about our customers were also a hedge against risk. The more knowledge and insights Coach had, the better decisions we, and I, could make. This sounds obvious, but for me it was essential because I didn't come to Coach with a design background, some innate sense of style, or much business experience. Thankfully, I tried to be a continuous learner, and I was pretty good at connecting dots.

I also respected creative talent, and most of all I respected consumers.

By now I was, of course, cognizant of the intimacy that existed between a woman and her bag, a much more intimate connection than between a man and his wallet. If you think about it, a bag is an extension of the body. All day long you open and close it, put in valuables and take out essentials. Being consumer-led and product-centric was to be conscious about every aspect of this interaction and relationship. Like making sure the bag's zipper teeth didn't rake against your skin when you reached your hand in to search for keys, or that there was a pocket for easy access to credit cards or train tickets. Intangible things tie people to the items they choose to have in their lives, and managing a brand is in part an exercise in psychology, which requires getting close to people in all sorts of ways. You have to get inside their homes and their heads. Inside their closets.

One of my favorite things to do when I was visiting friends' homes was to peek inside their closets. I was fascinated by the number and kinds of bags that sat on a woman's shelves or hung from hooks. I wanted to know why she had so many black ones, and when was the last time she used the small one? And were there any kinds of bags she wished she had?

My whole approach to leading Coach was trying to understand the essence of the proposition between a brand, a product, consumers, and the marketplace. The intangible, emotional connection that makes you feel good when you see a favorite item in your closet, look forward to using it, and feel proud to wear it.

For someone who wasn't a designer and had a haunting fear of failure and an intense drive to succeed, being knowledge- and insight-driven was the only logical way to proceed in the mercurial world of bags.

• • •

In 1989, we knew that the core Coach customer was a classic rather than stylish woman who was driven to purchase products that were more functional than fashionable. She had the disposable income and the desire to buy a branded product, or a product that would deliver on a promise of lasting quality at a fair price.

By this time, I realized that one of our largest near-term opportunities was not just to expand distribution, but to broaden our appeal to people who knew of Coach but weren't compelled to buy from us. We called this target consumer group "aware non-buyers." If we could figure out how to entice these women to buy Coach, it would be a big unlock. Importantly, broadening our products' appeal would also entice existing customers to make more frequent purchases.

To realize these opportunities we had to get more serious about how we collected, analyzed, and interpreted information about women so we could, as Ivy put it, create products whose spirit matched a woman's values and lifestyle.

Being curious about people is one thing. Institutionalizing curiosity in a business to harness knowledge and insights is another, and it is something I tried to do at Coach since I'd first assembled focus groups and chatted up shoppers.

My appreciation for the powerful role market research could play at Coach intensified when I was introduced to Duty Free Shoppers (DFS), a global retailer that provided tax-free, lower-priced luxury products to international travelers. That now-ubiquitous concept you encounter at international airports originated in 1947, at a small airport in Shannon, Ireland, that was a popular refueling stop for overseas flights. Irishman Brendan O'Regan came up with the idea of selling local goods to airline passengers while they waited for their planes. He enticed them to buy local goods by taking advantage of a legal loophole so non-Irish citizens didn't have to pay tax. Thirteen years later, in 1960, the concept was adapted and scaled by two enterprising Americans, Charles Feeney and Robert W. Miller, who co-founded DFS, which targeted the luxury-minded Japanese traveler. By the late 1980s, DFS stores were situated in major cities and select airports.

I forget how I first came in contact with DFS, but I became friendly with its president, Fred Wilson, who was incredibly open with me about the company's brilliant strategy once Coach began to sell its products in DFS stores. Basically, DFS was an arbitrage-based business model that leveraged consumer data, trends, and regional pricing to sell premium fragrances, liquor, cosmetics, and handbags—most for significantly less than they cost in the country where you lived or where you were visiting.

I noticed how systematically DFS captured information about its customers, who by law had to share their passports to buy duty-free products. DFS captured this demographic data and shared it with vendors like Coach, so I was able to learn more about Coach's customers via DFS than I did by talking to people in our own stores.

DFS's rigorous analysis of the data was music to my ears and advanced my ideas about how similar analyses could benefit Coach.

Market research was normal for consumer packaged goods companies like Hanes, but it barely existed in discretionary categories like apparel and accessories. If a business as small as Coach did do it, the company probably outsourced it for the same reason a company retains advertising agencies: because it's not a core competency. But for a consumer- rather than a designer-led brand like Coach, run by a CEO who went to great lengths to make the best decision possible, it needed to become a core competency.

• • •

Data is just raw numbers. But analyzing data to glean insights that inform actions that result in products people love and smart business decisions is an art as well as a science. Logic as well as magic. At some point I changed the name of our market research capability to "consumer insights" to emphasize that the purpose of research was to extract knowledge. We also had to know the "why."

To develop this capability at Coach, we needed someone wise at the helm.

A recruiter found our first head of market research, Mary Grace Moore, who'd spent six years at the University of Michigan's Survey Research Center before working for Grey Advertising in New York City and then the financial firm Shearson Lehman. Mary Grace was a kindred spirit. She agreed that the goal of research was to help make informed business decisions by managing risk. She, too, was genuinely curious, and believed that when we understand people and why things happen, we can have more control over what we want to happen in the future.

Mary Grace joined us in 1989 as part of my expanding senior team. I put her office near mine so we could talk easily and often, but also as a symbol of how important insights were to Coach.

It was Mary Grace's analytical capabilities plus her people skills that elevated consumer insights to a respected role inside Coach during those formative years. She was a kind, humble, intelligent voice who loved statistics. She'd spend hours delving into stacks of computer printouts, listening to the human stories the data revealed, and then she would sit with our teams to help them understand the data. She never just spewed statistics; she communicated findings in a way that was meaningful, not mundane. A project management team would listen dutifully, then pull together a brief that described what a new product line should achieve to please current or potential customers, which the design team would then execute against.

The answers you get from research depend heavily on whom you ask and how you phrase questions. Mary Grace put together the right sample groups and crafted ever more nuanced queries about how women used bags in their everyday lives. She organized focus groups and sat with our senior leaders behind one-way glass, taking notes as women on the other side of the glass offered opinions about the ideal length of a bag strap or the depth of a pocket, and talked about where they shopped, how many bags they owned, how many they actually used regularly, and for what purposes.

Focus groups were revealing, but they didn't provide definitive direction because they were too small and risked bias if, say, one chatty person dominated a discussion. Mainly, they were a qualitative tool that guided us to what we should study quantitatively.

We'd also conduct phone surveys every three or six months with statistically projectable sample sizes as part of attitude and usage studies, or a brand equity study that told us how Coach stacked up to competitors. Over time we began to compare our research results from prior periods to track changes in, say, the level of brand recognition, product satisfaction, or a customer's willingness to recommend Coach to a friend. We also measured intent to purchase Coach in the future, a telling metric that reflected the brand's saliency.

Once we began to design new bags and collections, we made samples at a small workshop we maintained at our 34th Street offices. We invited employees to carry the model for a week or two. Walk around with it. Take it home. Bring it shopping and on vacation. Then write a report and keep the bag. We might even fill some bags with bricks, then have machines pull the straps to check their durability. Did Louis Vuitton do that? I don't think so.

For styles that went into development, we placed samples in stores and used professional interviewers to intercept shoppers and get their opinions. Do you like the bag? Would you buy it? If the bulk of feedback skewed extremely positive, we were confident we had a real winner. Consistent thumbs-down was an obvious strikeout. It got challenging when the majority of opinions fell in the middle, and we had to figure out how to improve the product. Delicately conveying negative feedback to designers was part of Mary Grace's value. She once compared the process of telling a designer what customers thought of her bag to telling a mother what strangers thought of her baby. Mary Grace didn't want the customers' critiques to extinguish a designer's creative fire, so she treaded lightly. Instead of, "People think your daughter isn't very pretty," she'd say, "They'd love your baby even more if it had dimples." Mary Grace's empathy was part of her magic.

Once we decided to bring a style or collection to market, we sometimes piloted it in select Coach stores, displaying 100 units of, say, a 10,000-unit run to gauge the level of interest. If the Murphy bag flew off shelves, we might ramp up production, highlight the bag in our catalogs, and encourage wholesale accounts to buy more. If the pilot didn't go well, we'd lower sales expectations and future production levels.

Knowing if a bag sold well also was not enough. We also wanted to know who was buying it, and why. Did it appeal to a long-time customer because it had a zip closure instead of a turnlock, or did it attract a first-time Coach buyer because it was a new color for us? We tried never to assume, so we always asked.

Mary Grace also kept me in check. Early on, when I wanted to raise prices, our department store group pushed back, insisting it would hurt sales volumes. I disagreed, so we put the question to Mary Grace. She polled consumers for insight into price elasticity of demand, which is the ratio of the percentage change in demand to the percentage change in price. I was ready to be right when I poked my head into a meeting as Mary Grace was presenting the findings to a few people.

"Well, what does the research say?" I asked.

"Lew, if we increase prices, sales will slow." I smiled, nodded, and left the room, no more explanation necessary. The numbers and Mary Grace had spoken. In fact, making sure we "did a Mary Grace" became internal code for collecting, parsing, and understanding data, then extracting insights to inform product decisions.

My own grounding in math helped me assess data, too, and I kept a statistics textbook in my office that I occasionally consulted. If, say, I wanted to make a decision with 95% confidence, the book told me how large the sample size had to be.

When research didn't reinforce our creative instincts, we'd pause. Take a breather. Maybe go back and talk to more women, or take a different turn. We couldn't forget the magic.

We called this practice of measuring, and then modifying, "working the business" and much of what I described evolved over the course of many years after Mary Grace arrived.

We also worked the market, collecting demographic information about people's ages, income levels, and where they lived, plus psychographics like their values and shopping habits. We'd triangulate data to identify trends by region, preferred channel, or age group. The collective knowledge was one factor we used to make business decisions, such as where to open new stores.

By 1991, we knew that the average Coach customer owned four Coach bags and that awareness of the Coach brand was rising, second only to Gucci in the United States. Around that time we began to segment consumers into three personas that we labeled classic, functional, and aspirational. Classic consumers wanted well-made products that didn't go out of style, and they tended to be brand loyal. A functional consumer wanted the most comfortable, durable bag at the lowest price, something she could rely on to do the job. Aspirational consumers desired the status that carrying a certain brand conferred.

Eventually we identified and created different "usage occasions," activities that might benefit from a specific bag size, color, or shape. Earlier attempts to associate a specific bag with a specific use could be seen in Coach's late 1980s advertisements. The spacious, slouchy Duffle Sac was pictured under the tag line, "The Coach for Weekends." Our pouch-shaped Riding Bag was dubbed "The Coach for Outdoors," and the single-flap Pocket Purse was "The Coach for Everyday." To identify less obvious occasions that could call for unique "carrying vessels," as we sometimes called them, we'd deconstruct the year—12 months, 52 weeks, seasons, weekends, weekdays, nights, days, lunch, dinner—and cross-reference holidays and events with different personas. What bag might a classic consumer carry at a Christmas party? Or for a weekend getaway? What kind of vessel would a functional consumer want to take on an overnight work trip?

Insights into women's preferences also helped us further succeed beyond the Northeast and Midwest. For instance, sales of Coach in warmer climates never did quite as well as in other parts of the country. Once we started probing to find out why, local focus groups told us that women in those regions didn't gravitate to our predominantly muted color palettes, which consisted primarily of our six different shades of brown, and of course black. Even our navy blue and forest green skewed dark.

In 1992, we recruited Alan Krantzler to head merchandising, and among the creative things he did was insist that we infuse vivid colors into our monotone mix to position Coach as more akin to the sunbelt lifestyle. There was some internal opposition, but Alan pushed and then worked closely with our manufacturing partners to incorporate purple, teal, and orange into the leathermaking process. Placing the brighter colors in window displays lured more local women into stores, even though most ultimately purchased a neutral-colored bag. Alan developed this merchandising approach to reflect human nature. He called it the "icing strategy": let shoppers see an array of cupcakes with different-colored frosting on display, even if they ultimately buy chocolate or vanilla. The strategy lifted our sales everywhere.

Inside our stores, Alan encouraged us to rethink the library look we'd pioneered, which lined up bags on the shelf like books, a look that had worked well for years when most of our bags were similar shapes, and when our stores had more limited shelf space. But lining up bags side by side didn't showcase enough of our increased variety. Alan knew from his experience consulting in the publishing industry that books with covers facing out on bookstore shelves tended to sell well, so he applied that maneuver to our bags so you could see the different silhouettes. It worked extremely well in the stores that adopted it.

In sum, Coach's qualitative and quantitative research into where consumers had been, where they were today, and where they were traveling became a competitive advantage. Department stores loved us because the sales data we collected from our own stores revealed bestsellers that Macy's or Bloomingdale's should heavily stock. Inside Coach, people expected data-driven thinking. Our customers, of course, had no idea the lengths we went to understand and delight them. They just liked what they saw.

If Coach could meet a larger portion of women's style preferences and needs for various purposes, we'd grow our brand's "share of closet," a term I coined to reference the percentage that bags made up of a woman's entire wardrobe spend, as well as the total number of bags she owned, and the percentage of those bags that were Coach. Increasing Coach's share of closet was going to be key to our success. Just as important would be broadening the way women in general thought about the role bags played in their lives, and the growth of the handbag category overall.

Coach's approach to consumer insights was part of our logic engine, of course, but it required an emotional element. Beneath all the data gathering and insights was also a deep love for our customer. All of us at Coach had to be genuinely curious about her. Care about her. Respect her. Her lifestyle and opinions influenced all we did. At the same time, we had to be imaginative and instinctive in how we interpreted, communicated, and applied her preferences.

For me, a non-designer running a creative brand, having so much insight into the mind of a consumer provided a much-needed sense of security because it increased the likelihood of Coach's success and reduced the chance we'd fail. That said, I'm also human, and there were times my own emotions overrode insight and logic. I could put blinders on if I sensed competitors encroaching.

By the late 1980s, the handbag brand Dooney & Bourke had become popular. The bags had a preppy, equestrian sensibility, and I saw them as Coach's most formidable US competitor. In response, I had us design a collection we called Dakota that reflected elements of Dooney & Bourke bags, mainly through contrasting colors and mixed materials, like navy box-grain-textured leather with brown bridle-leather trim. Our 1990 catalog even featured models in riding gear leaning against the white fence of a horse paddock with a $286 Coach Harvest Tote hanging from her shoulder. I wrongly assumed that Coach's brand codes like our lozenge hangtags would differentiate us by signaling to you that the bag was a Coach. There was little if any magic or logic to my decision, and sure enough testing revealed that the Dakota bags came off as Dooney & Bourke knockoffs. We pivoted back to our classic, monochromatic looks and more creative ways to refresh our assortments.

The temptation to veer out of our lane, and into the wrong one, would haunt me as we grew, in part because I didn't always recognize what was happening. Maybe it was a form of cognitive dissonance as I tried to deal with the discomfort that came from watching another brand's voice resonate.

Emulating a competitor might quell my fears that Coach could lose ground in the short-term, but it was a longer-term mistake. The opposite is refusing to innovate, or ignoring competitors altogether, which was a mistake I'd make, too, but not for many years.

• • •

In addition to studying people, we were mindful of society as a whole, diligent students of the American landscape, always aware that our longevity was linked to reflecting cultural changes.

Several macro trends fueled Coach's popularity throughout the 1980s and 1990s.

For one, the rise of women into professional fields gave them more reasons to buy more bags, and more disposable income to do so. Coach's ethos and brand equities—durability, quality, function, value for the dollar—fit right in with women working their way up. In 1986, our barrel-shaped Madison Satchel, with its strong, clean lines and rolled handle became a favorite among the professional set.

There's no doubt that Coach was a beneficiary of women's ascent in the workplace, and not just because they were our primary customers. Women also played vital roles in our company, making up a significant majority of Coach employees. Over the years, women held key jobs in all parts of our business, from marketing and operations to HR and finance. Many women who started as salespeople rose to store managers, and into significant operating positions.

Another trend that served Coach was the beginning of casualization in the workplace, which we leaned into. More relaxed dress policies and social mores invited more expressive office attire, which extended to accessories like handbags, scarves, and jewelry—easy items that showed your individuality. The traditional heavy briefcase for women and men fell out of favor, and Coach filled the void with an array of case styles in our soft, supple leather—lighter-weight, less-boxy alternatives that were practical, professional, and stylish, and daily staples women and men were willing to invest in, for themselves and as gifts.

More broadly, Coach's expansion during these decades coincided with macro-shifts in US consumer spending. The rise in disposable income gave people more money to spend for discretionary or commodity products that delivered real and perceived value for a higher price. Built into these goods was discernable value, like quality, but also sensory value, like how it made you feel.

This is the period when Starbucks began to change how people thought about coffee. Compared to the $1 cup of brewed coffee from a deli or the Styrofoam cup of Dunkin' Donuts, Starbucks roasted higher-quality beans for coffee served in a smooth paper cup by a friendly barista in a café where you could sit in comfortable chairs surrounded by music and other people enjoying their beverages. Starbucks founder Howard Schultz improved a commodity by imbuing it with craftsmanship and theater, as well as community.

Nike was also changing the way people thought about a category, with its running shoes engineered to improve athletes' performance and designed to look cool. Founder Phil Knight merged performance and fashion to create a sneaker even non-athletes were willing to pay more for. In the accessories category, Coach's distinctive, quality leather bags, which conferred a discerning authenticity and practical style, were also a beneficiary of, and a catalyst for, this rise of branded discretionary items.

A related cultural development was the proliferation of upscale shopping malls, which ignited shopping as an American pastime, and gave higher earners a place to indulge their newfound shopping habits. The so-called malling of America was driven by the rise of the middle class and its migration from cities to suburbs, where malls were frequent destinations even if you had nothing specific to buy. Teenagers hung out at the malls with friends—browsing stores, buying snacks, seeing a movie, getting ears pierced. Entire families went together, ate lunch at the food court, then split up to meander. Shopping as hobby also gave women more occasions to use different kinds of bags—the item itself was an essential piece of the uniform.

From an operations perspective, malls provided Coach with more locations to open. Mall stores were also substantially more profitable given the higher concentration of shoppers compared to most suburban or urban shopping districts. A handful of real estate development companies controlled a majority of malls, and they sought out Coach as an ideal tenant, one that performed very well and attracted other retailers. Developers also offered us deals on rent and construction costs, especially if we opened in multiple locations.

There was a related retail trend, which was the increasing popularity of discount retail in various incarnations. Coach had been selling select products at reduced prices ever since the mid-1970s, when Miles opened summer stores in Amagansett, New York, and in Vermont, to liquidate imperfect merchandise or sell discontinued products. I remember filling my station wagon with bags to deliver to the Hamptons on Fridays, driving my packed car the three-plus hours from Manhattan. Many mornings we had a line of people outside the store. We later opened several year-round outlet stores selling products for up to 50% off in tourist areas like Freeport, Maine, and Orlando, Florida, where $100,000 worth of goods might sell in a week, which blew me away. Even though we were selling discontinued and irregular bags, I saw a desire, and thus a market, for quality products for people who value brands but wanted to pay less than full price.

Our research told us that the value-conscious consumer fit the demographic of our core Coach customer: women between the ages of 21 and 50 in middle-income households with college educations and who were gainfully employed. One psychographic that differentiated the value-consumer was that she was willing to drive at least an hour for a good deal, and at least once a month. These so-called smart shoppers were a lucrative segment, but Coach was discerning in how we reached them, choosing almost never to sell excess bags at discount retailers like T.J. Maxx, where wall-to-wall racks of clothes and cluttered shelves weren't brand-enhancing environments. But we did, however, embrace the no-frills, clean, sprawling outdoor spaces of factory outlet malls, which were located at least an hour from major cities. This discount shopping experience offered Coach a channel to reach more price-conscious people, especially aspirational consumers, which was in line with my ethos of providing quality products at prices more people could afford.

I still envisioned Coach as an egalitarian version of luxury bag brands that were too expensive for 95% of consumers. We didn't tell people that this discount shopping experience was an intentional strategy; we just did it, with a lot of discipline.

• • •

At one point an article about Coach and me in *Barron's* ran with the headline, "The Accidental Fashionista," referring to the fact that I had no background in retail, accessories, or design prior to joining Coach. It was a catchy headline, but the truth was that there was nothing accidental about the way I led Coach.

And yet, I was also relationship-oriented, and I valued my colleagues' opinions when it came to business decisions. Perhaps no one more so than Arun, who had become my thought partner, dear friend, and a beloved fixture inside Coach. The two of us talked multiple times daily, and we often called each other before big meetings to discuss what we wanted to achieve. In January 1991, I was waiting for him at our New Jersey distribution center before we met with two Sara Lee executives flying in from Winston-Salem. The meeting was scheduled for 8 a.m. I waited for Arun as my watch ticked past eight o'clock. He never arrived.

That morning, Arun had suffered cardiac arrest while getting ready for work. He was just 39, and he left behind his wife, Nadine, and their young daughters, Priti and Sarada. Arun's passing was a massive shock felt by everyone within Coach, as if a life force had been sucked out of our offices.

We all loved him in our own ways. People had story after story of how he'd touched their lives, and how he'd imbued our culture with a heightened sense of teamwork, raising the performance bar for all of us, often with an affectionate smile.

Only once had I experienced the shock of someone I loved and cared about departing so unexpectedly, when my father suddenly passed away of a heart attack in 1980. When he died, I felt like I had lost a limb. With Arun's passing, I felt like I'd lost a brother. The finality was almost impossible to grasp. How was it that I'd never see my dear friend again? Or have his ear, or his wisdom? His death was a club to my gut. I was so broken up that I could barely write his eulogy.

A small funeral was held in New Jersey. My son, Sam, recalls that it was the first time he ever saw me cry. At a larger memorial I announced that Coach and Sara Lee had created a scholarship fund in Arun's name at his alma mater, Wake Forest University, as an appropriate tribute to a man who touched so many lives during his short life. Bobbie and I helped Nadine and their girls relocate to North Carolina to be near Nadine's family. Our two families were already close. My kids had fond memories of going to Arun's home for dinners and holidays, and we'd continue to vacation together. More than 20 years later, I would walk both Priti and Sarada down the aisle at their weddings.

I grieved for a long time, feeling a massive hole in my heart, but also in my days. There was no one of similar caliber and temperament to take his place. He was Arun. I felt his absence in all parts of the business, and especially as Coach's growth began to slow, and we needed new strategies.

CHAPTER 8

Brand Building, Extensions, and Acquisitions

When Coach celebrated its 50th anniversary in 1991, there was a lot we could feel proud about, and yet we were also at a precarious crossroads.

We now had 1,500 employees and more than $155 million in revenue, 85% of which had come in the six years since we'd been acquired. In addition to expanding distribution, we'd achieved such rapid growth by adding new collections. Now lightweight bags, more briefcases, business-related accessories, gloves, ties, and scarves contributed $60 million, more than twice the size of the entire company in 1985. We'd also expanded our distribution to 55 Coach stores, added 150 shop-in-shops inside department stores, 2 million names on our catalog mailing list, and a fourth channel, international, including 23 stores in Japan. All four channels had achieved outsize growth, delivering on that synergy that Sara Lee had admired when we first met.

Internally, we'd professionalized operations. Our profits had a compounded annual growth rate of 44%. Each year we'd received an award from Sara Lee for record performance, and for the most part they left us alone. Our scrappy days were behind us, but anyone at Coach would tell you we still felt like a small company. Our internal newsletter, "The Coach Courier," might include photos of employees' babies or birthday announcements. You likely knew your coworkers' kids and spouse, sometimes even their pets' names. People's families all came to our annual holiday parties. People worked hard, and there was a real sense of camaraderie, which was in part why Arun's loss was so deeply felt, as if we'd lost a family member, because we had.

So far it had been a great run, but because we tracked performance metrics so rigorously, we were becoming alarmed by a disturbing trend. The rate of sales growth at our catalog channel and Coach stores was declining. Where once our same-store sales had increased by double digits year-over-year, they were now flattening—a dangerous trend if we couldn't reverse it. The problem was compounded by a goal I'd set for us the prior year, when I was feeling more bullish. I'd told Sara Lee's board that Coach had an internal goal of reaching $500 million by 1995, a milestone that was going to be difficult if not impossible to achieve if the current situation continued. It actually felt quite scary watching those trend lines decline, and I worried I'd set Coach, and myself, up for failure if we couldn't meet the high expectations I'd created.

• • •

There were a variety of new ways to spur growth, but some I was less certain about than others.

First and nonnegotiable, we had to stay focused on the product, the heart of Coach, by creating even more compelling, relevant handbags to attract new customers and give our current ones good reasons to purchase another Coach bag. We'd try to do this in two ways. One, by updating existing bag styles with new attitudes, from the casual to the more sophisticated. We'd also try to come up with new bag styles that served new purposes, or use occasions. Here, we'd have to double down on magic and logic by blending our designers' imaginations with consumer insights.

Future growth could also come from brand extensions by offering merchandise beyond our current product assortments. Our research was telling us that Coach had earned enough credibility with consumers to extend our brand into related categories. But permission is no guarantee of success, and into which categories should we expand?

In addition to organic growth, one idea was that we could acquire another business. This was not my first choice, and even if we did, it had to be small because I had no intention of betting the ranch on another brand with so much growth potential in Coach. But I was open to the right opportunity if it crossed my desk.

A more indirect growth strategy was to strengthen our marketing, mainly by building out Coach brand's personality to appeal to more people.

This was about more than changing the look of our products; it was about imbuing the idea of Coach with more meaning.

During the next five years, Coach would pursue all of these strategies with varying degrees of success, and a lot of learning.

• • •

A product in and of itself is not a brand. A brand, as I was coming to define it in the early 1990s, is a collection of images, associations, and emotions that you consistently hold in your mind about an entity. Together they confer a product's unique identity.

Associating ourselves with a brand's identity is a shortcut that relates to our own identity—how we view ourselves, and how we want to be viewed by others. That association is part of a brand's perceived value. But only if a product consistently lives up to its tangible values and benefits. Together, perceived and tangible values and benefits make up a brand's equities. If your bag starts to rip at the seams after a few months, it's not worthy of being a Coach.

An essential part of Coach's identity, and thus its brand, stemmed from the tangible images that had long distinguished a Coach bag. These "product codes" included our natural glovetanned leather, external binding, turnlocks, and stirrup buckles to adjust strap length. And the hangtag. These physical attributes were unique in design and functional in purpose, and they made a Coach bag recognizable as well as memorable.

The positive associations that people had with Coach were among its equities. Every brand has its own collection of equities, which I think of as a pyramid. The thick base of the pyramid consists of underlying equities, which are universal to every brand to maintain its integrity. These underlying equities are essential to a brand's ability to survive. They include authenticity, which means the brand's products are distinctive in design and construction; they provide perceived value for your money, whether the product costs $50 or $500; and they convey trust, because the product delivers on promised or inferred benefits, and the company stands behind it.

The next layer of the pyramid includes foundational equities, attributes that are consistently distinct to a brand. Coach's foundational equities emanate from our core product. The durability of our natural glovetanned leather that develops a patina over time and the quality of our solid construction.

The functionality of our bags' features, from its adjustable straps, spacious interiors, inside pockets, and easy closures, to the basic, transitional shapes and neutral colors that mean your Coach bag won't go out of style and can be used for different occasions.

The top layer of the pyramid consists of emotional equities, which are the feelings that a brand inspires. Emotional equities emanate from the underlying and foundational equities, as well as the personality expressed in the aesthetics and look of the product and the intangible ideas associated with it. During the 1980s and early 1990s, Coach evoked feelings of pride, loyalty, individuality, belonging, and even love. For the most part we were not playful, and we certainly didn't confer a sense of superiority. Coach was special without being elitist. It had the kind of status that says you are an individual—notice the unique markings on *my* Coach bag—yet part of a community of people with similar tastes and values.

If you were to open a door and see the values of Coach standing there, you would likely see someone who was style-minded but not status-conscious, independent, pragmatic, and professional. Our bags, and thus our personality and emotional equities, were also not especially feminine, or categorically pretty, and that was okay—for now.

Coach's brand identity emanated from the product. Storytelling contributed to cultivating that identity, and Miles had been an intuitive storyteller for whom the Coach product was the strong, beloved protagonist. He did an excellent job articulating our product's unique equities—even though he didn't use that word—in a way that created the emotions that connected a bag and its owner. His storytelling was not literal but subtly conveyed. Like in the unique serial number and message hot-stamped on the interior of every bag: "This is a Coach bag. It is made out of completely natural glovetanned cowhide. The scars, scratches, veins, and wrinkles are natural markings characteristic of full-grained leathers." This little "story" telegraphed more than information; it evoked pride in ownership and a sense of individuality and loyalty. Again, Miles's storytelling was almost exclusively product focused.

But of course there was more to Coach than just recognizable well-made bags.

Our product needed to stay the hero, but to expand our appeal we could do a better job shaping the broader idea of Coach through less tangible equities.

Who was Coach beyond our product? What else did we stand for?

We didn't have to invent the answers because they were already part of our DNA. Coach had its own authentic heritage of craftsmanship as well as a history rooted in the entrepreneurial spirit of our country of origin, much like the renowned French and Italian luxury houses Louis Vuitton and Gucci were tied to *their* countries of origin. We were an original house of American leather, now dating back half a century, to 1941, when we were founded by a few enterprising individuals. During World War II, Coach had made leather dopp kits for the US military. Our signature leather was inspired by the sport known as America's favorite pastime, baseball. Coach was a true American entrepreneurial success story headquartered in the quintessential American city, New York. Our employees were a melting pot of skilled craftspeople from all over the world, many immigrants or descendants of immigrants who came to America to pursue their own dreams. These truths made Coach much more than some run-of-the-mill bag maker. Our company and products were part of the fabric of America. But not enough people knew this story.

Coach had a genuine origin story to tell, and it was Catherine Sadler who helped us start to tell it well. As head of marketing in the early- to mid-1990s, Catherine recognized our heritage was an asset we'd yet to leverage. She used her publishing and retail experience to amplify that asset in a variety of complementary ways. First she interviewed Miles, then she wrote the story of our founding in a small booklet we inserted into each bag, sharing it with every customer. It also was a means to articulate the Coach aesthetic: natural-grain leather crafted into bags with graceful lines and a purity in concept that kept Coach understated, confident, and never trendy.

Catherine also brought our values to life by producing an elegant coffee table–style book that used portrait photography to showcase our artisans in their workshop clad in smocks and goggles and wielding the tools of the trade. Like a trimmer using a flame to trim threads closer than could be done by the sharpest scissors. Or sewing 12 stitches to an inch through several layers of leather with a special machine. Or using a natural sponge to perfectly stain cut edges. "Portrait of a Leathergoods Factory" elevated the hero's story by illustrating the craftsmanship that went into making each bag. We put copies of the coffee table book in stores for shoppers to peruse.

Catherine and I also worked closely on Coach's first breakthrough marketing program developed with famed advertiser Richard Kirshenbaum. The "American Legacy Campaign" was intended to weave Coach into the American zeitgeist. The campaign included more than a dozen photographs that each featured a historical American figure's modern-day descendant in a curated setting that was relevant to their famous ancestor—and with a Coach bag. George Washington's great great great great great great granddaughter, Joanne Washington-Blodgett, leaned against a marble monument with a Coach Court bag hanging from her shoulder. Mark Twain's great great great great grandnephew, Clint Clemens, posed in front of floor-to-ceiling bookshelves, a Coach Metropolitan Briefcase on a desk in front of him. The sepia-toned photography imbued each scene with nostalgia. We used the campaign across all our mediums, from prominent placements in store windows and on walls, to catalogs, and to print ads in magazines and newspapers. The elegant, subtle message spurred people to rip out pages and take them into stores.

"I want this bag" they'd say, and point to the one in the photo.

Calling upon the legacies of American heroes cast Coach as another product of America. Punctuating our authentic roots distinguished us as part of the American landscape, associating Coach with our shared values of originality, possibility, hard work, and longevity. No other bag brand in the United States could claim such a legacy, nor could any other brand have run this campaign.

Coach was not, however, a legacy brand. I define a legacy brand as one that has captured people's hearts and created indelible images and associations we hold in our minds, but that also can withstand periods of turmoil, and come back after a spate of poor management or down economies because it is so well established and trusted. Legacy brands are not indestructible; they must still be nurtured.

Coach still had a lot to prove to earn that distinction, which had become my vision ever since we sold to Sara Lee in 1985. I still remember trying to explain to the executives that Coach had real potential to become part of a lasting place in the American landscape. Of course, they thought the idea was far-fetched.

• • •

At the same time we were evolving the brand in the early and mid-1990s, we were also experimenting with extending it to new products.

Shoes seemed a logical first choice given that handbags and footwear had a lot in common. Leather material. Attention to detailing. And each had a practical as well as a style component. Many women also bought handbags with shoes in mind to coordinate their outfits. Miles and I had contemplated the idea of a Coach shoe since before the sale to Sara Lee. He even had versions of loafers made to his specifications. At the time I barely knew anything about the footwear business, and frankly I underestimated its complexity. Ken Purdy, who ran Prime Tanning and had introduced me to Mr. Leather, now connected me to a private-label shoe business, Jimlar, run by two amicable brothers, Jim and Larry Tarica.

In 1991, Ken and I drove out to Jimlar's Long Island offices where the smiling duo greeted us with hearty handshakes and a table of bagels followed by a lesson in shoemaking as we toured their showrooms. For most of its customers, Jimlar designed, sourced, produced, and distributed all types of men's and women's shoes. I left their offices impressed, but not yet convinced Coach should put its name on shoes.

Footwear seemed a tough sell. In general, women viewed them as less utilitarian but more emotional purchases than handbags, and they were less loyal to shoe brands than intimate apparel, handbags, and outerwear. Footwear's gross margins—the percentage of revenue a business retains after accounting for the costs of making a product, mainly labor and materials—were also lower than handbags' gross margins, and a fairly large percentage of shoes were sold at a discount. Selling shoes at Coach stores also would be a logistical challenge given the amount of inventory shoes required; stockrooms had to house multiple sizes of each style, and our stores' back rooms already had limited space.

The barriers to success in shoes were higher than in bags, but they weren't insurmountable. Besides, our research revealed that our most loyal customers were keen to see what Coach shoes might look like.

We took it slow, and about a year into our exploration I turned to Larry after yet another meeting.

"Should we do this?"

He said yes, but he also said that Jimlar couldn't work with us. Given Coach's quality standards, he said, we needed to manufacture our shoes in Italy, where materials and production were of the highest caliber. Jimlar didn't have an office in Italy, so Larry said he'd help us find a local partner.

I was disappointed. Over the course of the year, the brothers had become enjoyable, trusted thought partners at a time when I felt I had a deficit of them in the wake of Arun's death. I respected that they were willing to give up our business to do the right thing for the Coach brand. Such trust is invaluable and usually harder to find than talent. So I told Larry that I didn't want another partner and asked Jimlar to commit to taking the journey with us, but not as a licensee. I wasn't ready to hand over that much control. Licensing was too big of a risk to the brand we were nurturing, at least for now.

The deal we cut with Jimlar gave Coach control of design while Jimlar oversaw the back end, mainly supply chain and distribution. Jimlar also invested in us, opening an office next to the design studio Coach had maintained in Florence since the late 1980s. Jimlar operated like a division of Coach, not a contractor. They pushed back when they believed something we liked wouldn't work, but they also knew when to stop pushing. Because we shared the same goals, it was easy to prioritize desired outcomes, ask the right questions, disagree, and debate without worrying about each other's motives.

Some of my colleagues thought we were taking on too much and diverting resources into a category that Coach knew little about. But building products was part of Coach's foundational ethos. Also, I saw shoes as more than just another revenue source. I envisioned Coach becoming a lifestyle brand, anchored by bags and extending to other categories.

When it came to designing shoes, our main question was how to translate Coach's equities and product codes to footwear, while maintaining consistent quality and aesthetics. I had a better sense of what a Coach shoe should *not* be than what it should be. Not flimsy. Not uncomfortable. And certainly not sexy. But was Coach a loafer? How high or thick was the heel? Our leather was too heavy for footwear, so how could our shoes be recognizable yet distinctive?

Our first iterations were quite literal in their interpretation, and their shapes were safe, simple, well-constructed silhouettes. Initial sales were disappointing given our expectations, so in 1996 I recruited a rising star at Cole Haan, then a premium footwear brand, to lead our effort. Frank Zambrelli began his career at Chanel, so he had some luxury sensibilities, and at Cole Haan he'd earned the equivalent of an MBA in the shoe business as he traveled the world visiting factories and getting to know distributors. He brought expertise as well as definitive ideas. Frank thought our collection was beautifully made but, as he put it, *"nonnina,"* which in Italian means little grandmother.

We still had a lot to learn about designing footwear. For many women, fit was less important than how the shoe made her feel, emotionally. Your sore toes weren't a deal breaker if you felt fabulous in three-inch heels. According to Frank, Coach shoes needed to be comfortable but more scintillating.

Just as we had much to learn from Frank, he had much to learn about Coach and our methodical approach to product development. As Frank recalls, his very first presentation to our leadership team was a rather robust PowerPoint presentation, and I stopped him before he got too far in and suggested he take a seat and listen for a bit before enlightening us. People who joined Coach from the fashion world didn't expect our well-oiled process, and they often assumed they knew better. Sometimes they did, sometimes they didn't. What I learned over time was that no matter what someone's experience was elsewhere, they needed about 12 months at Coach to understand our calendar, seasonality, the cycle of ups and downs. If after just three months with us you were sure you knew all the answers, or knew our customers, I'd tell you to talk to me again on your one-year anniversary, and see if you still felt the same way. More often than not, your opinion changed once you had more context. I don't know if this is true for all companies, but it was the case for us.

To Frank's credit and Coach's benefit, he figured out how to execute his vision in the context of how Coach operated. His influence elevated our shoe collections with design elements that titillated, while maintaining quality construction. Although the leather was thinner, its finishes and stitching mimicked our cowhide's grainy appearance and bound edges. Shoe hardware was derivative of our bags' clasps and locks, but more refined. Our higher heels were blocked or tapered for stability, without looking like a pair your grandma would wear.

By 1997, Coach's footwear collection would be taking more creative risks than our bags, gaining traction with existing customers and attracting new ones.

Frank and I agreed that Coach's shoe business was worth scaling, but doing so required significantly more investment than we could make at the time, and by then, other issues were commanding our resources. So to help reduce costs and risk I decided the time had come to change Coach's relationship with Jimlar to a close-knit licensing model.

Footwear was and would continue to be a very important category for us, but it had been a long and winding road so far. Still, I had no regrets about not licensing sooner. The chances that Jimlar or another external licensee would have interpreted and adapted Coach's codes faster than we eventually did was possible, but unlikely. Jimlar would remain Coach's sole shoe licensee for 20 more years, quite unheard of and a testament to both companies' willingness to work with one another in partnership for a greater good instead of an individual good. I was learning that extending the Coach ethos and aesthetic to other products presented opportunities but also potential distractions.

• • •

For our first foray into clothing, we focused on menswear.

We created a separate business unit, Coach Apparel, and I recruited an expert in the category, Terry Pillow, from Armani Exchange, a diffusion brand from the high-end Italian designer Giorgio Armani, which produced lower-priced apparel. Terry hired a small team to put together a head-to-toe, Coach-branded collection, as well as open half a dozen Coach for Men stores. The two of us worked well together. He didn't mind when I probed his decisions, which I did in large part because I was fascinated with the creative process, not just as Coach's CEO but as a man who wasn't a particularly stylish dresser. At one meeting Terry told me Coach shirts would have seven front buttons.

"Why seven?" I asked. He said seven was industry standard for high-quality dress shirts. "But why seven? Why not six? Or eight?" Everyone around the table looked at each other. No one actually knew. I was genuinely curious. Plus, an extra button might give tall men like me more material to tuck in.

Like Frank did with shoes, Terry and his team had to apply to men's clothes the attributes that made Coach's leather goods successful. They chose quality fabrics and sourced manufacturing from some of the best apparel makers in the United States. The first collections were what we called tailored sportswear, and everyone was proud of the handsome pieces produced—including dress shirts (with eight buttons)—which also received industry accolades.

Unfortunately, men were less enthusiastic. We'd set out to make a quality product for the discerning male, which we did, but it turned out that the American male wasn't all that discerning in the mid-1990s. Men were also slower than women to figure out how to dress for the trend of casual Fridays, when suits were no longer mandatory at offices the last day of the week. Most men leaned their attire toward the safe and bland: khakis and collared golf shirts that were more Gap, Brooks Brothers, or Ralph Lauren than Coach.

It didn't help that our materials and detailing required higher prices than our targeted customer was willing to spend on casual clothes for one day a week or weekends. The Coach brand for menswear was not a market fit—at least not yet.

Unlike the decision we made about shoes, we decided not to keep trying to grow the men's category. Part of the reason was timing. In the late 1990s, the women's bag market was also growing, and the opportunity was so large for Coach that we needed to pour more resources into it and exploit it. I decided menswear had become a distraction without a clear path to profitable growth. Could it have been a distraction we avoided if I'd done more market research up front? Hard to say. Another thing I was learning was that consumer research into product extensions can only go so far because it's difficult for people to imagine something that doesn't exist. You might say you love the idea of a Coach shoe or men's pants, but until you actually try them on you can only offer an opinion about the expression of the idea. But in this instance, and uncharacteristically, I chose to do virtually no research before launching our men's line and, instead, trust my team, who delivered a great product but for a market that wasn't big enough.

Closing the Coach for Men stores was a difficult decision, but we didn't completely abandon men. A corner of Coach stores would still sell an edited assortment of bags and accessories. We just reined it in until the time was right to revisit it.

• • •

Coach explored many brand extensions and collaborations over the years I was CEO, each executed depending on the category's ease of entry, the size of the opportunity, and the likelihood of success. Some went better than others. In 1998, Movado launched the first Coach watches for a partnership that benefited both companies. Estée Lauder would eventually produce Coach fragrances. We tried women's silk scarves, but the fabric demanded a higher price point too far from Coach's main products. For men's neckwear, we contracted with famed designer Joseph Abboud, who was a friend, and the results were beautiful, but Coach ties didn't gain traction. We also licensed a line of furniture that was exhibited in showrooms.

At one point, in the early 1990s, an executive at Ralph Lauren asked me if Coach would consider designing their handbags. I figured that putting Ralph Lauren in the bag business as a competitor was only worth it if they put us in the ready-to-wear business by designing Coach clothing, which I knew Ralph would never agree to.

We entered into some fun product collaborations that were less about making money than novel ways to reinforce Coach's premier status, giving the brand a so-called halo effect. Early in my tenure, I negotiated an agreement with United Airlines to create custom belts and bags for United's cabin crews, basically a slimmer version of our Stewardess bag, which we originally designed for flight attendants. The bag featured a special ID card holder on the inside front flap, which could be flipped up to show ID as an attendant passed through airport security. A few years later, we introduced a clutch purse that could be purchased by passengers in flight. The United bags were a way to build brand awareness and create purchase intent among flyers who were target customers.

We did something similar in the 1990s with Toyota USA's Lexus, its luxury automobile. In 1996, we cocreated the first of several Coach edition ES 300 Lexus vehicles with our glovetanned leather as its interior trim, and each car came with a set of Coach cabin bags. The 1997 Coach Edition Lexus LS 400 had seats upholstered in Coach leather, too, with the Coach logo subtly engraved on the back of each seat. Only 2,500 were made and a Coach cabin bag came with each car. In addition, a small champagne-toned, silver-plated medallion engraved with *Coach* was attached to the car's exterior, over the tire on the driver's side. I recall Lexus running out of medallions at one point, and many of the cars had to be delivered to buyers without it. I was shocked to learn later that about 70% of those buyers returned to the dealership to get the medallion once they were back in stock. Lexus did a superb marketing job, putting some $10 million into advertising. We also sold three Coach collaboration cars with Lexus in Japan. Such limited-edition, higher-end product collaborations felt novel 30 years ago. It was also a lucrative deal for Coach.

For the most part, we approached brand extensions with a level of discipline and performance benchmarks for what success looked like. We rigorously measured sales performance to calibrate our expectations, and we also targeted margins that were in line with our bags' high margins. If the brand extension's margins were too low, we made sure that incremental sales volume made up for it, which was the case with jewelry.

The wrong extensions can weaken a brand. Designer Pierre Cardin became revered in the 1960s for his avant-garde apparel and accessories, but then he cut hundreds of licensing deals that splashed his scripted signature on everything from soap to frying pans. The lack of focus and creative collaboration tarnished the brand and his name. We avoided certain categories, like bedding, because we knew sheets could be heavily discounted, and so it wouldn't give us the margins we needed, nor was it a category where our brand equity would resonate with people.

Over time we developed a philosophical playbook for whether and how to extend a brand. First, identify related products that loyal customers have expressed interest in by asking what they'd like to buy from you that you don't already offer. The question should be put to people whose hearts you've already captured, because they'll provide the most thoughtful, genuine responses. Second, understand the size and maturity of the category, and the share of your addressable market, which is the size of your potential opportunity. Third, examine the barriers to entry, assessing how difficult it will be to design, produce, and market the product yourself, instead of doing it with a partner or a licensee. Whomever you work with, make sure you stay active in the creative aspects like design and marketing. Both you and your partner or licensee should have skin in the game, standing to benefit from success, and trusting each other to make decisions in the best interest of the brand. Fourth, remember that equities are touchstones that people already associate with your brand, such as durability, so don't compromise by cutting corners or choosing vendors or partners that don't honor or understand your values and brand codes. Fifth, go in slowly, piloting products before major launches and with a willingness to adapt your plans to reflect consumer response. Finally, from the outset, define success in a measurable way that is consistent with how you judge the rest of your business.

• • •

I wasn't on the lookout for companies to buy, but in the early 1990s an offer to purchase the small, privately held Mark Cross company landed on my desk. Mark Cross was established in 1845, when Henry W. Cross founded a leather goods company in Boston, named after his son. The company was acquired by Patrick Murphy, who expanded the brand. When Patrick's son, Gerald, took over the company in 1934, he added new products, including evening bags. Some called Mark Cross the American Hermès, although its bags sold for a fraction of the price of the renowned French design house and had nothing close to the same name recognition. Mark Cross also had a few of its own stores for many years, including a flagship on Fifth Avenue.

I didn't see Mark Cross as a real competitor to Coach because its products were still priced higher than ours, and its brand had such low name recognition. With only $12 million in annual revenue, Mark Cross had thin profit margins and wasn't particularly well-run, so there was room for improvement on the front and back ends of its business. If we did it well, acquiring Mark Cross could help us grow sales by elevating our product offerings, something I'd already been toying with. With Mark Cross, we could enter the super-premium market, while delivering a more polished bag option for a different consumer profile, and for occasions that Coach bags didn't always serve. Turning Mark Cross into a powerhouse brand was not the goal. However, I did think we could build a profitable, complementary business.

Coach bought Mark Cross for about $5 million and I assigned some of our best talent to it, led by Alan Krantzler. Alan had been at Coach for 18 months, so he already possessed the requisite understanding of Coach's processes. He even had an emotional attachment to the brand—by coincidence, Alan's aunts had chipped in to buy him a Mark Cross briefcase for his first job after he graduated college many years earlier.

Alan closed unprofitable Mark Cross stores and redesigned others, and he gave the brand a facelift with an updated logo and designs that telegraphed an even more upscale feel. Operationally, Mark Cross leveraged Coach's infrastructure—distribution centers, IT systems, and tanneries. Our designers gravitated to Mark Cross because it was a chance to create products beyond Coach's design parameters. Mark Cross was free to build off its own codes or abandon them altogether.

Alan executed well in areas he could control, mainly product design and the store experience. Unfortunately, Mark Cross's small size relative to Coach-branded products had Alan vying for internal resources with footwear and menswear, mainly marketing support. So while store performance levels improved, store traffic remained low, in large part because Mark Cross didn't have the budget to raise awareness.

Also, something was happening that we did not anticipate. One in every two first-time Mark Cross buyers was an existing Coach customer. Rather than tapping into a non-Coach buyer, Mark Cross was cannibalizing Coach, not an outcome we expected, or welcomed.

It was Alan who suggested closing Mark Cross only a few years after we'd acquired it. He loved and was proud of what he and his team had built, with good reason. But he was also pragmatic and recognized that a dollar invested in Coach had a higher return than a dollar invested in Mark Cross. My decision to shutter stores and cease production was logical from a business standpoint, but it was an emotionally charged one for employees and customers that had a strong affinity to Mark Cross's heritage and the work that went into its revival. A few Mark Cross staff even picketed outside our offices.

Choosing to abandon a path is never easy. Once again, what I took away was the importance of keeping Coach in its brand lane, particularly when so much growth was still available. The experience also soured me on adding other brands during the rest of my tenure as CEO.

• • •

Despite closing Mark Cross and our slower evolution of brand extensions during the early 1990s, our other growth strategies—product development, enhanced marketing and branding, along with expansion of Coach retail and factory stores—got us back to growing same-store sales from one year to the next.

On the product side, we gave women more handbag options by further differentiating new collections from our classic look, while still updating and introducing new styles for different usage occasions. Our new collections were designed to reflect different lifestyles and attitudes by using a wider variety of high-quality materials in varying textures as well as familiar and fresh shapes. We continued the more modern Sheridan Collection, with its pebbly leather in colors like clover and red that contrasted with the tan bridle leather trim. The Soho Collection offered an easygoing elegance with lighter-weight, smooth leather that had just a hint of slouch, as well as hidden magnet closures and polished rather than burnished buckles. The Sonoma Collection's velvety, stain-resistant Nubuc in earth tones like sage and sand had unapologetically casual silhouettes, most with no unessential hardware, to emanate a laid-back, almost outdoorsy vibe. For women wanting a sophisticated aesthetic, the sleeker Madison Collection was our version of elegant glamour. Its tailored linings and sharper edges paired with brass turnlock closures had an air of refinement, like the petite Gracie Bag in white that we positioned as "perfect for evenings out."

Backpacks became one of our best new product offerings during the 1990s. We had the perfect leather for the shape, which offered a new, relevant use occasion for professionals whose workplaces were becoming more casual and self-expressive. I can still see the variety of backpacks filling the window display of our World Trade Center store, where thousands of commuters passed daily.

New collections were obvious departures from the classic Coach look yet they retained our quality craftsmanship as well as functionality, while attracting a wider continuum of personalities to the brand. In retrospect, however, I could see how the collections were more iterative rather than innovative or groundbreaking in their designs.

All of these efforts to build Coach unfolded while I was doing double duty. In addition to being Coach's CEO, I'd taken on a new job inside Sara Lee in what amounted to a monumental career shift that almost cost me my relationship with Coach and forced me to confront my limitations as a leader.

CHAPTER 9

Discovering My Best Destiny

In early 1990, I got word that Sara Lee was contemplating bringing in a McKinsey & Company consultant to oversee Coach as well as a business that it had recently acquired, the athletic apparel maker Champion Products USA. The consultant would be a group officer, and my boss. I couldn't even begin to envision reporting to someone who had no operational experience and had never built a brand.

I sat down to discuss it with one of my closest thought partners at the time, Maxine Fechter, our head of HR, as well as an executive coach that our senior leadership team was working with, Howard Guttman. Howard was driven, and he was helping us build on our culture of high performance. He also had zero tolerance for BS and always cut to the chase, even with me.

I shared with Maxine and Howard my idea of getting Sara Lee to consider me for the group officer role. The two agreed, and they helped me make the case. Soon the McKinsey consultant was out and I was appointed. Did I really want the job? Not as much as I wanted to avoid more direct oversight over Coach. Nonetheless, I studied the athletic apparel industry with genuine interest, and enjoyed my visits to Champion's headquarters in Rochester, New York. When I returned home with Champion gear for my kids, they were thrilled that dad finally had something besides handbags to share.

In June 1992, Sara Lee expanded my role to CEO of Sara Lee Accessories. Now I was overseeing a portfolio of businesses and brands including Coach, Champion USA, Champion Europe, Aris Isotoner, Bali, Playtex—which included WonderBra and Hanes women's underwear—as well as Sara Lee direct, its off-price channel distribution business. I was still Coach's CEO, but with my remit expanding I brought on a strong general manager, Laurence Franklin from Tumi Inc., to be Coach's president. Laurence was smart, and he understood brands and leather goods. To Sara Lee, I also brought two colleagues with me part-time, Maxine and Mary Grace, because I trusted their knowledge, and I knew they would operate in alignment with me as advisors to the other brands.

• • •

I had worked for 23 years for only three employers. I'd had two mentors, Miles and Herb, who, along with Sara Lee's executives, were my only real role models for how to work and how to lead. Mentors take different forms. Some, like Herb, actively instruct you. Herb had conviction and a sense of purpose, and he taught me to be rigorous, find clarity amid complexity, and take an analytical approach to problem-solving. Miles taught me more through his actions, mainly his single-minded, unswerving approach to brand building. From him I learned the commitment required to consistently reinforce brand attributes. Miles had a real clarity about what was required to get the job done, and he showed me the importance of being committed to do what was right for the business. What I learned from both Miles and Herb was to not compromise.

In retrospect, I see that I also adopted, consciously or not, some of their less admirable traits. Herb lacked the ability, and certainly the desire, to read a room and modulate his acerbic tone to win consensus. I was much more self-aware and socially adept than Herb considering that I could get along with diverse groups of people and adapt to a situation—if I chose to. But like Herb, and after seven years at Sara Lee, I was no longer motivated by wanting to be liked by people I worked with. Respect was different: I wanted to earn people's respect. But striving to be liked by everyone is a fool's errand that can distract from other goals and can lead to decisions that are intended to avoid conflict rather than achieve what's best for a business. Early on in my career I'd wanted to feel a sense of camaraderie with Miles, as well as get his approval, but his lack of both, combined with his need for control, frequently made me feel undermined and eroded. Sara Lee had scores of executives, which meant there were so many more people who could or could not like me. It's truly impossible to please everyone, so instead of trying, I was true to myself and tried to get comfortable being seen by some as a controversial person who was eclectic and eccentric. Definitely not one of the good ol' boys. Sara Lee's chairman and CEO, John Bryan, whom I deeply respected and with whom I had a close, informal relationship, advised me to modulate my personality and try to be more of a statesman to fit in, but I wasn't particularly successful changing my approach.

At age 47, not surprisingly, I continued to be motivated by a drive for excellence and my own fear of failure. I wanted to be as successful as possible at everything I did at work, which by extension meant making any business I oversaw as successful as possible. My measurements for success included growing revenue and profits, building strong brands, and developing staff. I saw my goals and the businesses' goals, and perhaps also our identities, as aligned and intertwined.

All these motivations had been manifesting in my life and work in ways good and bad, healthy and unhealthy, for years.

One of those ways was that I put more pressure on myself, intensifying my mental and physical stress. I was also a workaholic, at the office at least 50 hours most weeks and usually working five to 10 hours at home on weekends. I thought that's what it took, rather than doing a better job prioritizing or delegating.

On the upside, I leaned further into consumer research and analytics to better inform decision-making. I also paid attention to virtually every detail, because being grounded in the nitty-gritty gave me more certainty and that all-important sense of control. Nothing went unchecked. Every time I had to present to the higher-ups at Sara Lee, I used all the resources at my disposal to carefully prepare and be accurate in my supporting documentation. Was it overkill? Some people thought so, but we were doing so well that I didn't want to tamper with the process.

I expected the same rigor from people at the internal meetings I led at Coach. I used those gatherings as a tool to reinforce accountability and to move our business forward. Most meetings have four goals, in my view: to share information among the group, to advance everyone's individual thinking, to advance the group's collective thinking, and to align on next steps. Achieving those goals requires that everyone shows up with comprehensive knowledge of their part of the business.

A meeting to discuss a new bag, for example, would include everyone with a role in the product's creation, from design to distribution to marketing. Say we were trying to decide on the right price. I might ask production to provide a bill of materials so we could all understand the individual items that contributed to costs of production. If the total cost was, say, $40, I might ask market research if our customers were willing to pay $160, which was four times the cost of manufacturing, our general markup. If we decided, collectively, that $160 was indeed too high, then we'd ask designers and our merchants how we might alter the bag to reduce costs to price the bag for less while maintaining our high margins but without sacrificing quality and functionality. Should we eliminate a pocket, or alter the construction in some way? Production would weigh in as well. Would a change decrease labor costs, or add a step? Maybe I would notice that the bag's one-inch wide shoulder strap seemed too thin. Was anyone concerned it could cut into the customer's shoulder if the bag's contents were heavy? What would be the cost of making the leather strap an inch wider? Half an inch? Would it add $0.35? A dollar?

My questions were a way to get people to share information with each other so all of us could align, then agree on the best and next action, such as how to modify the product to meet our profit goals and quality standards. I expected everyone present to have the information we all needed to make informed decisions. I told people that the rigorous preparation they did before coming together would help them steer their part of the enterprise with more clarity and advance our collective thinking. So if you didn't have the information we needed to make those informed choices in the moment, the meeting and our progress stalled.

Once everyone understood that this level of rigor was the bar, they usually spent time prior to the meeting anticipating and answering potential problems and questions. And they probably brought more than just a notepad to the meeting, maybe even binders full of data—because this was before laptops gave us digital access to everything—so information was at their fingertips if an unexpected question or issue arose.

People knew I wanted them to get to the point quickly—start with the headline, not the narrative—but also that details mattered. If someone handed me a dense spreadsheet or a 20-page deck, I could quickly scan the critical numbers to see if they didn't compute, or were contradictory, or indicated a trend that could become a problem. Rather than take numbers at face value, I broke them apart, zeroing in on key metrics that begged explanation. Your same-store sales may have been up 10% in February, but I wanted to understand the trends underlying that increase: What were conversion rates? The dollar value of each purchase? The number of items sold in the transaction? Was traffic up or down? I also paid attention to more than numbers. If you spelled something wrong in your presentation, I probably noticed and found it hard to bite my tongue because it was indicative of being sloppy. If you couldn't get spelling right, what else were you getting wrong?

While I wanted to have empowered management teams that developed and implemented strategies based on our shared vision, I often had trouble entrusting enough people to care as much as I did and execute as well as I thought was required. Plus, I enjoyed impacting the blend of magic and logic to get to a better place, so it was hard for me to let go, which was ironic given my own frustration with Miles's controlling style. I was now a leader who had trouble relinquishing control in certain areas with most people. The ways I chose to lead were situational, based on the people involved and the circumstances, and I only felt comfortable fully empowering someone if I had complete confidence in their capacity, which meant they had mastery over their role, insatiable curiosity, took full ownership of their team's work, and, like Arun, shared my high standards. If you were one of those people I held you accountable for milestones and deliverables, but I didn't check in with every piece of work because I trusted you. In other situations, I felt the need to be more involved. But what I considered doing my job some saw as Lew swooping in unnecessarily to check progress and influence decision-making. In many cases it must have felt as frustrating to them as it felt to me under Miles.

At the same time, I highly valued the collective wisdom of interdisciplinary teams. Once I trusted you, as I trusted Maxine Fechter, Mary Grace Moore, Alan Krantzler, Howard Guttman, and others, I sought your counsel and actively supported your development and ascension. I'd stick my neck out on your behalf, and I'd grant you the benefit of the doubt. When people performed well, I provided enthusiastic appreciation. Public praise. Pats on the back. Kind words in a voicemail or note. I might invite you to lunch. I celebrated people and didn't take credit for others' accomplishments or ideas.

In fact, there were instances where I thought I received too much credit. For me, that kind of honesty was a matter of integrity.

The flip side is that I could be brutally honest when it came to expressing disappointment, especially with people I didn't highly regard, didn't trust, or whose performance I considered any less than excellent. I saw any weakness as a detriment to Coach, and I could push people to see if the team could depend on their knowledge, commitment, tenacity, and relentless curiosity to get the best outcome. I had no tolerance if I sensed you were winging it or faking it because you didn't prepare, lacked confidence, or weren't willing to admit what you didn't know, or were too concerned with looking good rather than being good. As much as I rewarded performance, I didn't gloss over mistakes. Especially the second or third time. Sometimes I asked questions to reinforce a point I believed needed reinforcing. If I asked you about something and you said, "I don't know but I'll find out for you, Lew," I usually replied, "Don't find out for me, find out for yourself and for your teams." I wanted people to leave no stone unturned in their analysis, all for the greater good of Coach. There was a reason behind my every query.

In my effort to instill a high-performance culture that protected and elevated our brand and grew the company, I did not suffer fools, and people knew it. If someone showed up unprepared, I called them out. My doggedness, however, could cause angst and have a chilling effect. I didn't yell, but my tone could be rough. When any authority figure doles out stern criticism—especially someone with a deep, gruff voice like mine—it carries emotional weight. Back in my city government days, people occasionally asked me how to deal with Herb. At Coach, some people sought advice from others about how to navigate me. No doubt, it helped if you had a thick skin. I didn't intend to cause people excess anxiety, but I also didn't try to avoid it.

By 1993, I knew I needed to figure out how to better modulate my behavior, especially in moments of frustration. I wanted to become more self-aware and perceptual, so I brought in the Center for Creative Leadership to conduct a deep-dive assessment of my strengths and weaknesses based on surveys and hours of interviews with me, my boss, and 14 Coach and Sara Lee colleagues. The results were collected in a bound report titled "Lew Frankfort's Managerial Approach" that included 86 pages of unvarnished, unedited qualitative feedback capped by a list of 98 skills for which my peers rated me either strong or in need of development. I took the thick report home to read. There, in black-and-white, were positive and negative aspects about myself that I already knew, didn't know, or didn't care to admit.

No one questioned my love for Coach, my integrity, or my commitment to do what was best for the business. They respected me as a "knowledgeable person" and "visionary" who could translate strategy into action, marshal resources to make big things happen, and motivate people toward a goal by creating a sense of purpose. I was seen as an optimist as well as an analytical person who was a "wizard with numbers" and a generator of new ideas. Not surprisingly, I also scored high on being logical and data-based. People also said I excelled at one-on-one communication. I appreciated the positivity but was more interested in problem areas where I needed to improve.

As I read through the list of skills, I circled the ones that everyone, or most people, rated me weak. People agreed that I paid too much attention to details, spread myself too thin, and needed to delegate more. None of that surprised me. I was more surprised that many thought I was stubborn, not willing to listen to or entertain ideas that contradicted my own, and made decisions in a vacuum. I considered myself someone who asked for opinions and could consider disparate ideas on their merits. Maybe it was impatience, but I clearly wasn't taking enough time to explain my decision-making process to win buy-in, or at least so that people understood my thinking. As a result, some perceived me as arrogant and my actions as arbitrary. I had to do better.

One person said that I didn't always consider people's feelings. Another commented that I could be callous and "not attuned to human frailty." One thing we all agreed on was that I was as hard on myself as I could be on colleagues, which was not necessarily a good thing.

An underlying truth was that my own drive for excellence and fear of failure could generate fear in others. Deep down I wasn't shocked, but I also wasn't proud.

Coach was an intense place to work, and I had no problem with that. We had high standards for a reason: Failure is so much easier than success, especially when you sell discretionary products. We had to take ourselves seriously to grow, starting with a shared belief that we would be unyielding in our pursuit of quality and never jeopardize the loyalty that customers had for Coach. So yes, I was tough. At the same time, I needed to be more conscious about my impact on others.

In the years to come I sought guidance from executive coaches and straight-shooting colleagues, who'd kick me under the table and pass me a note if I became too heated in a meeting, or they'd alert me if they felt I owed someone an apology, which I would usually deliver.

Not every culture is right for every person. People at Coach who didn't perform or appreciate our culture left. But there were scores of bright, talented, hardworking, and nice creatives and professionals who loved Coach as much as I did, rose to challenges, soared, stayed for many years, and would say they learned more and did more at Coach than at any other company they worked for. I know this to be true because many people still work at Coach, and former employees tell me and others that their Coach years were a highlight of their careers. I am grateful because neither Coach nor I could have succeeded without them.

Someone asked me if, given the historical success of Coach, I thought our business results would have been compromised if I had worked less, stressed less, demanded less, or was generally less fanatical. I'm not sure it's possible to know the answer, but I don't believe so. What I do believe is that it's possible, and preferable, to achieve results without being as difficult on people as I could be in certain situations and moments. So while I would never regret my high standards, I do regret how my style made some people feel.

• • •

It was with much of this in mind that I executed my role as group vice president of Sara Lee Accessories, overseeing a portfolio of companies starting in 1993.

The multiple businesses I inherited were at various stages of maturity. Some were doing well while others had stalled. My intent was to help ensure that every business would flourish by pursuing new opportunities, fulfilling unmet consumer needs, finding new channels of distribution, and diversifying products. What I did not appreciate was that managing this $3 billion collection of companies at Sara Lee was a completely different proposition from leading two much smaller businesses. Coach and Champion revenues combined were only about $600 million.

Basically, being a group officer was about managing people, not leading a business or a brand.

The nature of the Sara Lee culture enabled the CEOs I managed who were meeting their business expectations to rely on their positional authority and push back on, and even ignore, any of my ideas they didn't like, and in some cases they were right to push back. Most of the businesses had a different model than Coach, a fact that I failed either to recognize or accept, and instead I tried to force Coach's business model onto several of them.

My role was also more oversight than leadership, and I could be dogged with my inquiries about recent sales trends, earnings forecasts, major strategies, or initiatives underway. For instance, I've always believed the recent past is the best indicator of the near future, so if you showed me sales data over a three- or six-month period that was up 7%, I was more interested in sales over the last 30 days, which was usually a better indicator of what might happen in the next quarter.

"It's true your quarterly sales were up," I'd say, "but they were down 2% for the last month." A CEO who was perfectly happy that his overall performance beat plan might get annoyed that I wanted to talk about what the more recent data meant for the coming quarter, and what we should do about it.

I was misplaced in the role because, for one, I wasn't a packaged goods guy, and two, I had an entrepreneurial mindset, and I wanted to more rapidly grow brands and businesses to realize their full potential by taking big swings. I struggled with other CEOs' tamer, less ambitious attitudes just like they resented my arrogance for assuming I knew what they could do better than they did.

One CEO who had a likeminded approach to me was Sauro Mambrini, who led Champion Europe. The two of us butted heads at first but came to respect and like each other a great deal. He began working for Champion the same year I joined Coach, in 1979. He also loved brand building, and he appreciated that having high standards in every part of a business is necessary for consistent quality. We shared the view that without operational discipline, processes get diluted and a brand can lose its essence. Continuity builds value forever, Sauro would say. As we grew closer, he began to call me Luigi, which I found endearing. Whenever Sauro came to New York on business, I insisted he stay with my family rather than in a hotel. The kids and Bobbie loved him. The closeness of our relationship, which still exists, was an exception among those I worked with at Sara Lee.

The long and the short of it was that I had earned little influence over the executives I managed, having failed to win their hearts and minds. Maxine believed the cards were stacked against me from the get-go because certain people at Sara Lee weren't fond of me. But it wasn't that clear-cut. We were different types of people who ran different types of businesses, and I didn't do much to adapt. Rather, I rolled in, assuming everyone would welcome my input given my track record at Coach and my understanding of brand building. And I mistakenly assumed that the rigor of my thinking—the logic—coupled with my persuasive ability—dare I say, part of my magic—could also win people over.

The businesses under my remit didn't all perform poorly. Playtex did well, and the group's combined revenues grew. But one company, Aris Isotoner, one of the largest glove makers in the United States, had a particularly bad run due to unseasonably warm weather in the winter of 1994 that hurt sales. Also, its longtime CEO and founder chose to retire rather than work with me. The new CEO also moved production from the Philippines to China, which took longer than expected. A *BusinessWeek* article in September 1995 quoted people who blamed me and others at Sara Lee for the problems. It was a high-profile embarrassment that didn't help my reputation inside Sara Lee.

All in all, I was struggling to be effective with a lot of different people across a range of businesses, and I had to come to grips with the fact that I wasn't suited to being a group officer. No longer was I grappling with a fear of failing in the future: now I was grappling with the reality of failing in the present. The consequences were several. For starters, my future was less certain because my damaged reputation meant that advancement inside Sara Lee was now unlikely. A few years earlier, that personal growth trajectory had seemed like a possible career path. Now the prospect of Lew rising through the ranks wasn't an option either Sara Lee or I wanted. I also felt disappointed in myself because I was letting down people whose opinions mattered to me.

Experiencing the first substantial failure of my career not only felt awful, but the failure manifested physically. I had trouble sleeping. At night, I'd fall asleep fast then wake up at 3 a.m., often in a sweat, with my sheets soaked after dreaming our house was falling off that cliff. My mind raced as I ruminated on being fired and losing my income. I'd lay there fixated on things I couldn't control, or what was going wrong. Lack of quality sleep took a toll, and I didn't wake up with my usual gusto. During the day I started to move at a slower pace, my energy sapped. My body felt heavy, and it took everything I could muster to show up to meetings as the leader I wanted to be. My mental bandwidth also narrowed, and I found it difficult to maintain the single-minded focus that's so critical for people in leadership positions. Effective leadership requires an ability to be in the present moment, meeting after meeting. There's no allowance for distractions.

I felt worse when I wasn't working. At home or on a family vacation my brain was free to dwell on problems. I was able to relax a little on Saturdays, playing games and running errands with the kids, or going out with Bobbie and friends on Saturday night. But inevitably I tensed up on Sundays. Unfortunately, I didn't have any real hobbies or interests to distract me or bring me fulfillment outside work and home life. I began to question my worth, as if the present moment was the sum total of my life's work. I had few tools at the time to quiet my mind.

Thankfully, I did exercise. Jogging, sometimes with Bobbie or my kids by my side, helped lift my mood.

Still, I'd never felt this low. Bobbie, who knew me better than anyone, was of course aware that I was unhappy. We talked about work, but I didn't want to burden her with just how terrible I felt, and I didn't want to cause her to worry about my mental health or our finances. She had her hands full with our three kids and her business, Sandbox, which was doing quite well.

I think I was also embarrassed that I couldn't handle my situation better. And who was I to complain about feeling low given that l had a degree of success behind me, a beautiful home, and a close, healthy family? I certainly didn't expect anyone to feel sorry for me. I largely kept my thoughts to myself.

What I did not realize was that I was having my first depressive episode, in part triggered by the extreme lack of control I had in my role, and heightened by the experience of feeling like a failure. Because I did not know the clinical term for what I was experiencing, I would refer to this as my first dark period.

At work, I confided in a few of my closest colleagues, including Maxine, about how unhappy I was. Seeing a therapist was not something I did, and I am not certain why. After all, I was a fan of executive coaches, so why not therapy? There was more of a stigma around mental health issues back then; it was not part of the national dialogue like it is today. But I do not think it was that. I'd always been pretty open-minded since my college days, when I went to Bethel, Maine, and sat in those group sessions at National Training Labs. In hindsight, I can see how beneficial it would have been to make therapy part of my life.

Long, solo plane rides, especially overseas, gave me a chance to sit back and process what was happening. I realized I was in the wrong role. And I missed being in the right one. I derived so much pleasure from working with my teams at Coach on the day-to-day operations, executing campaigns, strategizing, and building road maps for growth. I was a big-picture guy who also loved the work of the work. I missed the culture, too, and felt myself longing to be back in the more familial environment. Other brands didn't capture my imagination like Coach did. It also was hard for me to get enthused about brands in mature categories where there was less room for growth, and especially where people just wanted the cheapest price.

Maxine and I began to discuss the option of my returning to Coach. I knew I could, but I worried that doing so would be seen as a demotion—an admission that I'd failed at Sara Lee. Those were stigmas that would be hard for me to bear. What I didn't realize was that most people already knew that I wasn't succeeding in the role. Could I go back to Coach and be respected? Would they welcome me? Maxine, thankfully, convinced me that going back to Coach was a recognition of my strengths. Eventually I mustered the wherewithal and the courage to extricate myself from a professional situation that I never should have been in in the first place, and I asked John Bryan to please let me go back to Coach. He agreed. Sara Lee and Lew may not have been a fit, but I do believe that John saw me and Coach as a perfect match.

Removing myself from a bad situation, even if it meant admitting I'd been unsuccessful, helped me regain a sense of control over my life, and only then did I begin to feel better.

• • •

My years as a group officer managing a portfolio of brands were a period of self-reflection and contemplation. I realized how much of my success running Coach was a combination of three things. First, and most importantly, my genuine passion for our products and customers, which I'd had since day one and that was now part of me. Two, my ability to inspire and influence people to build something that had never been built before. And three, the authority that comes with being a CEO, which allowed me to make decisions I believed were correct.

At Coach, I had a passion, the requisite knowledge, the influence to win hearts and minds, and the control I needed to actually lead.

More broadly, I also realized that vision and opportunities play different roles in entrepreneurial, early-stage cultures than at established corporate workplaces. A founder's enthusiastic startup mentality can easily imbue excitement among people. Being an underdog who is out to bring something new to the marketplace is inherently exciting. David up against Goliaths is a mission in and of itself that brings people together with shared passion for the undertaking. There's also a scrappiness to the endeavor, an all-in mentality and a driving purpose that bonds people. The communal energy and ambition can be addictive. The intensity is also not for everyone.

Different stages of a company's growth require different attitudes, and different leadership. I was learning this now, and I would learn it more in years to come. The trick is knowing your own strengths and preferences so you can work where you thrive and can be effective.

The discomfort of my years as a Sara Lee group officer forced me to face what I liked and didn't like to do. And what I was and was not good at. All in all it was painful, clarifying, and humbling. As such, it was not a loss. We often discover our best destinies by pursuing the wrong ones. My best destiny was to lead a business with a group of talented, passionate people committed to working together to build an enduring brand.

My move back to Coach was not just for my benefit. The company's sales were beginning to slow and a radical pivot was going to be the only way forward. It needed my undivided attention. The good news was that being away from Coach day-to-day had given me a fresh perspective of what needed to be done.

In 1996, I returned as Coach's full-time CEO, and almost everything changed.

PART THREE

Reinvention Years

CHAPTER 10

Elevating Creative Expression

Several months after returning to Coach full-time I was alone on a stage casually sitting on a stool wearing gray slacks and a white dress shirt with my sleeves rolled up. No tie. I was in an auditorium at our New Jersey factory with about 100 people from our retail division, mostly store managers and field leadership. It was a two-day off-site to discuss what it would take to grow Coach from $500 million in sales, a milestone we'd recently hit, and stalled at, to an ambitious $1 billion level I had previously set for the year 2000, which would require nearly 20% growth in annual revenue.

I'd give a formal presentation the next day, but first I wanted to have an informal conversation. A way to introduce myself to new employees who'd joined Coach while I was ensconced at Sara Lee, and to confirm my commitment to anyone skeptical about my return. In the past we'd called these unfiltered Q&A sessions Lew Unplugged, and it was the first one I'd held in a while. I fielded about a dozen questions. Three stood out because my answers were reasons why Coach had thrived for decades, and hopefully would continue to thrive in the future.

"What is one aspect of Coach's history you feel needs to be remembered daily for our continued success?" someone asked. I considered it for a good minute.

"That anything is possible," I finally said, recalling the innovative step Coach took when we began selling direct to consumers by starting a mail-order business, and then, in 1981, opening our own retail stores when almost all bag brands sold only in department and specialty stores. I didn't tell them about my hallway conversation with the CEO of Bloomingdale's, which was still a secret.

"I continually remind myself not to be limited by tradition," I said, not yet knowing just how difficult this goal would be in the coming years.

Another person asked, "If you had to select one thing that makes Coach a premier retailer, what would that be and how can we take that to the next level?" For this one I was quick to answer:

"One of the biggest challenges for us is to maintain the balance between accessibility and exclusivity."

My passion for democratizing luxury was as strong as it had been during my early years at Coach. I knew that exclusivity was the terrain of luxury brands like Louis Vuitton, and it was not who Coach was or wanted to be. But accessibility was not about being available everywhere to everyone.

For one, it was about pricing our products right so Coach would be a brand that was affordable to the middle class. Accessibility was also about offering convenient ways to purchase, wherever our target consumer wanted to shop. We needed to sell our products in image-enhancing sales channels that were easy for the customer to access.

"But if we're too accessible, we risk becoming commonplace," I said, "and not aspirational." That's why I wouldn't let Sara Lee sell Coach bags in JCPenney. Growth without ubiquity was essential, as was maintaining our position between mass and luxury, which would forever be core to our identity. Both could be sources of friction as we tried to find the right balance.

A third question was trickier: "What do you think is the number one key to your professional success?"

"That's a tough question," I said. Since my stint as a Sara Lee group officer I still didn't see myself in the most successful light. Whatever success I did have was tied to Coach's performance. I answered the question in terms of what was true for me as the CEO of Coach:

"Being able to walk between dreaming about what's possible and execution."

Again, that crucial blend of magic and logic. And at that juncture in Coach's history, we lacked the level of creativity we needed to grow. As a result, that growth was stalling.

• • •

Every morning I checked our sales numbers for the prior day, and the downward trend line was concerning as well as frustrating because the market for handbags was growing and the opportunity remained huge. Women in general were buying more bags than they once did. As workplace attire continued to be more reflective of personal style, women gravitated toward lighter-weight and less-structured bags for work, like choosing totes instead of briefcases.

As for competition, mass brands like Nine West were imitating European bags and offering them at low prices but made from cheap materials and with a lack of detailing. Fashion-editor-turned-designer Kate Spade had introduced her boxy, nylon monotone totes at prices similar to Coach's, and they were compelling to stylish younger women. European designers were becoming more important factors in the American marketplace, too. Coach was being squeezed from above and below.

Our sales slowdown was also of our own making. We still had credibility as an authentic American brand, but too many people only thought of us as that maker of dependable handbags. For decades Coach had been the most significant investment many people ever made in a bag, in part because it lasted so long that it never needed to be replaced. Customers still talked about "my first Coach." Those of us inside Coach were fiercely protective of that heritage and felt a sense of responsibility to uphold Coach's attributes so people's experience of the brand validated their early Coach experiences.

With these thoughts in mind, I had set Coach's design boundaries too narrow. Someone would occasionally remind me that we had permission to offer more fashionable products and could do so without compromising materials and craftsmanship. Indeed, the success of Sonoma's relaxed silhouettes, without unessential hardware, proved we could push the bar on design. But we weren't pushing far enough in large part because I had not been ready. We'd built a very strong foundation based upon classic products that never wore out or went out of style. But style, which has an enduring quality, is different than fashion, which reflects trends of the moment and creates for consumers a perceived rather than a practical need. Your life might not require a new carrying vessel, but you desire one because it's the color for summer, or because it makes an older outfit feel fresh. In short, Coach's appeal was not what it used to be.

My distance from Coach's day-to-day operations while at Sara Lee had given me a wider perspective, which was a good thing. Sustained, long-term growth would not come from making more of what we had, which worked for apparel staples like underwear and pantyhose but would not work for handbags, which were moving further away from sheer utility to more emotionally based buys. As the *Wall Street Journal* would put it, Coach's reputation for quality was a big asset but also a big dilemma because our bags lasted so long that they didn't need to be replaced. More than ever, we had to attract repeat buyers and appeal to new women by evolving our personality and expanding our emotional equities—that top layer of the brand pyramid.

As an American brand, we also had to do what America did, adapt to accommodate new generations, without losing the underlying and fundamental equities that underpinned our success and made us special.

How had we gotten here? I could now see that we'd been operating more like a classic consumer packaged goods business, safe and predictable, than a brand in the fashion business by invoking curiosity and imagination, a problem I needed to urgently address. I'm not sure why I didn't tackle it sooner. Maybe because I was more comfortable with the logic side of our business. Or, because I knew it would be a battle to get Sara Lee on board. Through the early 1990s, there had been a methodology to everything we did, driven by consumer-centricity. Collecting and analyzing data for insights we could act on was something we could control—that *I* could control. The logic that we had employed to get Coach to $500 million certainly included some magic, which was how we creatively interpreted insights and knowledge into how we designed, branded, and marketed products. But artistic expression and fashion were not my innate sensibilities. I appreciated beauty and knew it when I saw it, but I didn't naturally summon it from within myself. I also didn't have an artist's bold imagination. As a result, Coach was missing people who engaged with fashion.

Having over-indexed on logic, we had to bring more magic back into the equation.

• • •

After more than 15 years at Coach, I had developed my own philosophy about branding. As I defined it, brands are images, associations, and emotions that people consistently hold in their minds about a particular entity. I was also starting to think about brands as people, because the images and associations must evolve, but without losing their essence. In our youth, we're imprinted with foundational values, similar to a product's foundational equities. Over time we discover and develop our distinctive skills and passions, as well as layers of personality, as we blossom into adolescence and adulthood.

Similarly, a brand's personality can emerge and even evolve with time. But it has to be authentic, because people are smart, and they will see a brand as an impostor if it tries to be something it's not. It's a fatal mistake to think you can leave your current customers behind and replace them with new ones. You must bring them along with you.

Coach's brand was no longer blossoming—sort of like a kid who peaks as a teenager. We had strong roots, but we had to get out into the world more, because the world around us was changing! We had to evolve and strengthen our identity, without losing our foundational equities or our product codes. The time had come to offer an updated, more relevant impression of Coach.

For the first time in our history, we were intentionally in fashion.

To proceed, I had to force myself not to be limited by tradition. In the magic-plus-logic framework, I had to adapt my thinking as circumstances warranted, but I had to trust the instincts I'd honed.

The luxury market informed me once again. Gucci was being revitalized by a partnership between its business-minded CEO, Domenico De Sole, and the young designer Tom Ford. Their partnership was about more than product design. It was about dramatically recasting Gucci's voice from your grandmother's plain, patrician brand to an avant-garde, sexy, youthful vibe. I wasn't looking for an equally dramatic departure from Coach's past, but something intangible had to shift at Coach, too.

I needed a confident, creative storyteller who could make Coach more compelling by expanding its personality, and expressing it through products but also through advertising, public relations, catalogs, store design, and in every way that Coach connected with consumers. More than a chief marketing officer or chief designer, I wanted a creative thought partner who believed in Coach the brand and felt passionate about evolving it, but who also respected the intersection of design and commerce. Someone who could be fashion-forward to make Coach more enticing to a wider segment of consumers, while bringing loyal customers along with us. Someone as interested and capable of building a business as well as a brand. I went in search of a person who could add magic but respect the logic, someone who could fill a position that didn't exist at Coach or at any company that Sara Lee owned: a chief creative officer.

• • •

Reed Krakoff was a talented young designer who was leaving a senior role at Tommy Hilfiger and planning to join the Milan fashion house Trussardi as its creative director when a friend of his called and said, "I really want you to meet Lew Frankfort."

Reed and I first met for breakfast in Florence. He was quite tall, and had a clean-cut, discerning way about him. He'd grown up in Connecticut, studied economics and art history at Tufts University before studying fashion design at Parsons School of Design, then worked alongside Narciso Rodriguez at Anne Klein. He spent several years at Ralph Lauren before joining Hilfiger. It was my understanding that Reed had little if any experience in accessories, but he could sketch details, and more important, he already admired Coach as an American brand that people had a personal attachment to.

The rapport was instant and mutual. I liked that he had a point of view but an open mind. That he was clearly talented and possessed a sincere desire to make products that people wanted, not just designs that pleased the artist within. In Reed I saw someone with deep respect for the customer. His commercial sensibility would keep us a consumer-led company.

I implored Sara Lee to let me hire Reed at a salary his history and the marketplace warranted, which was on par for the fashion business but higher than what Sara Lee paid most of its division CEOs, me included. Sara Lee couldn't fathom why I would give a designer so much creative control, which was a rare move for any existing brand, and pay him so much. When Reed went to Chicago for his final interview with John Bryan, John unapologetically asked him, "Why would a man want to design purses for a living?" Further proof that Sara Lee and Coach were a mismatch.

I put Reed in charge of all consumer-facing creative. He came up to speed, experimented, and began to make bold moves. When he updated our logo, some people gasped. For years our logo was the word *Coach* in an upper- and lowercase serif font inside a box shaped like the lozenge tags that hung from our bags. It had a traditional feel. For the most part Reed kept the bag tags the same, but for everything else—store signage, advertisements, catalogs—he removed the box and put *COACH* in all uppercase letters in a slim, sans serif typeface with more air between the letters. It was a clean, modern, open aesthetic that felt right.

The nature of our relationship was as important as his talent. Reed took the creative lead, and I was the business end. We understood each other, and we gave each other room and respect, despite differences in our age, backgrounds, and skill sets. Reed was a creative person who could speak the language of business, as he described it, and I was a business person who understood the language of a creative. We could disagree, then go into a closed-door meeting for a candid conversation, and emerge with a decision. I felt as if we were equals, but I also felt paternalistic toward Reed. In those early years nothing Reed did went out without my reviewing it, and he didn't begrudge me for it. I initially joined him at some photo shoots and together we edited copy for catalogs and ads. Over time I became more hands-off as he built a team that could translate what I wanted and what Reed wanted into something that worked for both of us, and most importantly for consumers.

The creative progress was exciting, but results were not immediate. You could see and feel Coach's voice begin to elevate but it wasn't yet something either Reed or I could quite yet verbalize. We both saw and felt the opportunity ahead; we just had to have patience and give the creative process the time, experimentation, and even the failure it required. This was something I was willing to do because I trusted Reed.

Then something unexpected happened, and it became clear to me that revamping Coach's creative was not going to be enough to lift the business out of its rut.

• • •

Within several months after I recruited Reed, I received a call from Victor Barnett at Burberry. The then-141-year-old London-based apparel company was looking for a new CEO. I was surprised, and also a bit flattered.

Burberry was and remains a rare example of a legacy brand in that its product and brand imagery have transcended lifetimes. Despite ups and downs in popularity and financial performance, generations of people have associated Burberry with the image of the tan, belted, double-breasted trench coat that, according to Burberry heritage, is made from a shower-resistant, breathable fabric invented by Thomas Burberry. In a history similar to Coach's, Burberry sold the company to a conglomerate, which had its own saga. In the early 1930s, during the Great Depression, Great Universal Stores (GUS) was a struggling, family-owned mail-order business in the United Kingdom when Scotsman Isaac Wolfson joined as merchandising manager. Isaac rose to take control, acquire the business, and through acquisitions turned it into a retail, manufacturing, and financial conglomerate. Victor was Isaac's nephew, and he had just been named executive chairman of Burberry when he called me in 1997. The brand was floundering and he wanted a new CEO to reinvent it.

I made my way to London to meet Burberry's managing director, and I remember thinking it was crazy that I could be in charge of an iconic English brand. I was committed to Coach but continued the conversations with Victor for my own learning, and to see whether an actual offer would pique my interest.

I went far enough in the recruiting process with Burberry that Victor offered me twice my current compensation.

My boss at Sara Lee was Don Franceschini, and he found out that Victor was trying to recruit me. He and his colleagues assumed that I'd pursued Burberry and was looking to leave Coach, and so I soon found myself at a three-hour dinner in San Francisco with Don. He was among those at Sara Lee who genuinely liked and respected me, and the feelings were mutual. Don was a savvy, relationship-oriented executive who thought people did their best work when they were in the right role for their skills and personality, when they have the right kind of support, and, in his words, when they are left the hell alone. He always took an interest in me and my career—and for the most part let me do my thing. That night he urged me not to accept the Burberry offer, and he made it clear that he and John Bryan agreed that I was the best and only fit for Coach. As he put it, there was no Coach without Lew.

"Be patient," Don said. "Sara Lee is going to sell Coach at some point."

This was music to my ears.

I used the Burberry job offer as leverage to speed up the process. If I could find a buyer willing to pay at least $1 billion for Coach—a number Sara Lee arbitrarily came up with—they'd let Coach go.

I was fired up. If I pulled off finding a buyer, the Burberry offer would be the serendipitous catalyst that got Sara Lee what it wanted, a superior return on its initial $30 million investment in Coach, and got me and Coach what we wanted, our freedom.

• • •

To help me find a buyer, Sara Lee's corporate development office paired me with a young banker in mergers and acquisitions at Goldman Sachs, Jide Zeitlin, who was a protégé of Hank Paulson, the future Secretary of the Treasury during George W. Bush's second term. Sara Lee was Goldman's client, so Jide understood the politics of the place and our incompatible natures. He also had a remarkable background. He was born in Nigeria, the son of a single mother who worked as a housekeeper, who had agreed to let an American family adopt Jide when he was five so he could access a good education and hopefully a better life. Jide eventually moved with his adopted parents, a university professor and a journalist, to Cambridge, Massachusetts. He attended Amherst College, got his MBA from Harvard, and had been working in investment banking for about 10 years when we met.

Jide was invaluable in my attempts to liberate Coach. Steely minded, unflappable, a champion of the underdog, he coached me through what questions to expect before we walked into a room. A six-minute miler, he was also a formidable jogging partner, and I have vivid memories of running with him along the Seine in Paris, pigeons taking flight around us, as we prepped for our next meetings.

I also remember arriving in Paris with Reed and armloads of Coach products to show potential suitors. I wish I could say that having so many meetings was exciting, or even gave me satisfaction. But I was preoccupied with a concern that even if we got an offer, Coach's profitability was in the midst of decline, so getting any deal across the finish line was going to be next to impossible.

A meeting with Gucci was interesting but quickly went nowhere. The most compelling opportunity was with the one brand I'd admired since my earliest days at Coach, Louis Vuitton. LV was a cornerstone of Bernard Arnault's publicly held conglomerate LVMH Moët Hennessy Louis Vuitton, which in 1997 was on its way to amassing what would one day be more than $80 billion in sales from a collection of some 75 brands, many luxe, including Tiffany, Dior, and Veuve Clicquot.

I recall little about the LV conversation other than that it was with its then CEO, Yves Carcelle. I knew him to be a visionary, although we'd never met in person, and I found him thoughtful and gracious, without a trace of elitism. We developed an easy rapport. And Yves sent a team of analysts to Coach's offices in New York, where they set up camp for a week or two, poring through our books and files as due diligence for a potential offer.

It was a smart move on LV's part, but not so smart on mine. I basically gave them permission to mine our business practices, including our market research methods and the consumer insights we'd so diligently amassed, especially in the United States and Japan. In retrospect, it was naive of me not to be concerned that their due diligence might reveal information about Coach that we would not want a competitor to have.

LV made a soft offer to buy Coach in the ballpark of $800 million. Sara Lee would have welcomed such a marque buyer, but not for $200 million less than the $1 billion it wanted. I felt disappointed yet also relieved. I wasn't enthusiastic about becoming a minor piece of LVMH's empire, or any other corporation for that matter.

The whole exercise of peddling Coach had echoes of trying to sell the business with Miles in 1985. Now as then, the most palatable path for me was not an acquisition, but identifying a private equity option.

I had an acquaintance, Dan Doctoroff, a managing partner of Oak Hill Capital Partners in New York, who appreciated the global opportunity for Coach, so I asked Dan to come to Chicago with me and meet with John Bryan to scope out if John was even willing to consider the private equity option. But John had no interest. As he saw it, being backed by private equity was essentially selling Coach to me, which Sara Lee feared set a dangerous precedent that could trigger a stampede of other high-performing CEOs to unhitch their companies from the mother ship, too.

"We can't have a revolt," John said. Dan backed away, but he would become a dear and trusted friend.

Not long afterward, the financier Tom Lee and his firm, THL, provided Goldman with a written offer of $850 million, with an upside that could have gotten the price up to $1.2 billion based on future performance. I thought John might go for it.

Unfortunately, he still wasn't interested. The private equity investment option was off the table.

By mid-1998 Coach had no offers. I was disappointed but not deterred. I believed in Coach. So I took a breath and reassessed.

Shopping Coach had been an unexpectedly edifying, illuminating experience that got me thinking about the company's situation in a more comprehensive, realistic light. Sitting across the table from executives of several heralded brands was an incredible opportunity to learn about what Coach could do differently. In essence I also conducted my own diligence, asking questions about their operations while fielding their inquiries about ours. Getting a peek behind the scenes into their strategies and operations revealed to me that Coach had so much more to change than just hiring a chief creative officer. As talented as Reed was, he was necessary but not sufficient to reverse our decline and take Coach to a place where we could sustain long-term growth. New bag collections, a fresh logo, a new advertising campaign, and updated collateral were essential but not sufficient.

Elevating creative expression was going to affect every operational aspect of the business—from how we sourced raw materials, how we developed new products, and how often we introduced them, to how and where we manufactured. As a manufacturer, Coach had become constrained by the limitations of our technical know-how as well as capacity. If we were going to allow the brand to reach its potential and not fade into irrelevance, we needed to reinvent ourselves, without losing ourselves in the process.

A lot had to change, including me.

• • •

Sara Lee and I had crossed over into a mutual acceptance that our companies were incompatible. Having failed to find a strategic buyer, and with private equity not an option, there was only one path forward, and it wouldn't be easy. We had to try to take Coach public.

With Coach's sales down 3% in 1998, from $540 million the previous year, and profits waning, we were nowhere near ready for an IPO. To go public we'd have to show potential investors revived vitality in the Coach brand by improving sales and profits, as well as presenting a well-articulated road map for growth. Internally, we also had to be functionally prepared to operate as an independent public entity. Sara Lee was tough on results. Wall Street would be brutal.

Coach was at another crossroads. I recall being nervous but also optimistic that we could do it if we kept our standards high, didn't limit ourselves by tradition, kept the right balance between accessibility and exclusivity, and walked that fine line between dreaming about what's possible and execution.

I, too, was necessary but not sufficient to take Coach forward.

Transforming the company meant I also had to transform myself and go from thinking that Coach could keep succeeding as a house of American leather goods, to realizing that was just a foundation on which we had to build and become a true lifestyle accessories brand. I did believe I was the right person to lead us forward—after 19 years, Coach ran through my blood—yet there was still a lot I didn't know. Plus, I'd never run a publicly traded company.

As CEO, I didn't have to know exactly what to do, I just had to recruit people who did.

COACH
LEATHERWARE
THIS IS A COACH BAG. IT IS MADE
OUT OF A COMPLETELY NATURAL
GLOVE TANNED COWHIDE. THE
SCARS, SCRATCHES, VEINS
AND WRINKLES ARE NATURAL
MARKINGS CHARACTERISTIC
OF FULL-GRAIN LEATHERS.
MADE IN NEW YORK CITY, U.S.A.

Early Years

I grew up in the Bronx, the son of a policeman and a mother who wanted me to be the first in our family to go to college. After graduating, I spent 10 years in government. By the time I joined Coach, in 1979, founder Miles Cahn and designer Bonnie Cashin had developed a collection of distinctive bags that had a cultlike following.

> My parents taught me to respect but challenge authority. Fixing NYC's Agency for Child Development taught me to make tough choices for the greater good.

Clockwise from top right: 1. Traveling in Greece, 1973; 2. With Mom at my Hunter College graduation; 3. Speaking at a publi hearing as Commissioner, Agency for Child Development (credit: Associated Press); 4. Bobbie and me at our small wedding 1975; 5. Next to my mentor Herb Rosenzweig *(left)*, listening to Mayor Ed Koch (credit: *New York Times*/Redux); 6. Visiting daycare facility; 7. My father, a proud New York City policeman.

May 29, 1979

Lewis J. Frankfort
165 West End Avenue
New York, New York 10023

Dear Lew:

This letter will confirm our agreement t
employment by Coach Products, Inc. will
October 1st, 1979; that your title will
President-Marketing and Special Projects
that your salary will be $800.00 per wee
agreement may be terminated by either pa
thirty days notice to the other.

Will you please sign and return this letter acknowledging that this is the entire agreement between us and that it may not be modified except by a writing signed by both of us.

Very Truly Yours,
COACH PRODUCTS, INC.

Miles Cahn, President

Accepted and agreed to:

Lewis J. Frankfort

Miles opened a store on the Left Bank in Paris in the 1970s. Our first US store opened in New York City in 1981, a space so small shoppers had to line up outside.

Clockwise from top left: 1. New York City, Coach's heart and home since 1941 (credit: Angela and Marcello Bertinetti); 2. Classic Shopping Bag, 1963; 3. Designer Bonnie Cashin; 4. Entrance to our factory and offices on West 34th Street; 5. Our first US store, on Madison Avenue; 6. My letter of employment; 7. Lillian and Miles Cahn in Paris.

A Commitment to Craftsmanship

It could take more than 100 steps to create a single bag. Our artisans came from all over the world and had specific roles: pattern maker, cutter, stitcher. I can still hear the familial banter and whir of sewing machines from the factory floor.

Clockwise from top right: 1. Hot stamping our horse-and-carriage logo; 2. and 3. Tools of the trade; 4. Attention to the details; 5. Bolts of leather await pattern cutting; 6. Carrying finished products (credit: 2., 4., and 6.: Jeremy Salz Lezin); 7. Drum dyeing at the tannery (credit: SteveLadner.com).

Anatomy of a Coach Bag

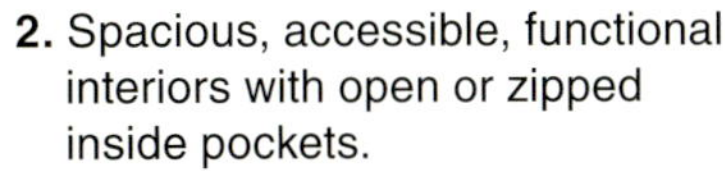

2. Spacious, accessible, functional interiors with open or zipped inside pockets.

1. Embossed hangtags on beaded chains confer authenticity: "It's not a Coach bag without a Coach tag."

3. Functional hardware, such as adjustable stirrup buckles and trigger snaps for removable straps.

6. Our full-grain, "glovetanned" leather was inspired by the supple texture and unique patina of a worn baseball glove.

4. External, double-stitched bindings for distinctive, durable construction.

5. Easy turn-lock closures in burnished brass for safety and style.

Willis Bag No.9927

1993

Bags through the 70s, 80s, and 90s

The original "Coach look." A strap. A flap. A pouch without lining. Simple. Sturdy. Functional. An enduring symbol of classic American style.

Basic Bag No.9455
1974

Stewardess Bag No.9525
1975

Compact Pouch No.9620
1981

Embassy Briefcase No.5090
1986

City Bag No.9790
1987

Bucket Bag No.4075
1988

Soho Bag No.4082
1991

Darcey Drawstring No.4229
1993

Backpack No.0529
1994

Anderson Zip No.9976
1995

Saddle Bag No.9988
1997

Bridle Hobo No.6708
1998

Innovating with Signature

Our first logo collection launched in 2001 as we were transforming Coach into a lifestyle brand. The "twin Cs" broadened Coach's appeal and ushered in a period of exponential growth.

Clockwise from top left: 1. Signature Mini Tote; 2. "Moose" from the TV show *Frasier* brings a smile to people's faces; 3., 4., and 7. Catalog photos show a lifestyle brand (credit: 2., 3., 4., and 7.: Steven Sebring); 5. Signature Embossed Leather Small Daphne; 6. Olivia Boot and Bibi Boot; 8. Signature Mini Skinny with Keyring; 9. Poppy Signature Satin Lurex Spotlight Shoulder Bag.

The Product Is the Hero

The bag was at the center of storytelling, from our 1970s tombstone ads to our late 1980s lifestyle marketing. In the early 1990s, the Legacy Campaign paired descendants of famous Americans with their favorite Coach.

Straightforward taglines highlighted popular style numbers or usage occasions.

Clockwise from top left: 1. and 4. Lifestyle advertising; 2., 3., and 5. Tombstone ads appeared in newspapers and Playbills. *Right page*: 6. One of many ads from the American Legacy Campaign (credit: Kirshenbaum & Bond).

Mark Twain's great great great great grandnephew, Clint Clemens, with his Coach Metropolitan Brief Bag.

COACH

AN AMERICAN LEGACY

The Metropolitan Brief Bag, No. 5180, $324. Enduring style, made of fine natural leather that becomes more beautiful with time.
To order, or for a complimentary catalogue, call 800 262-2411. Also available at Coach stores, select department and specialty stores.

Leading with Magic Plus Logic

During my 35 years at Coach, we strove to blend creative thinking and disciplined execution. I also developed frameworks to guide my approach to different aspects of leadership.

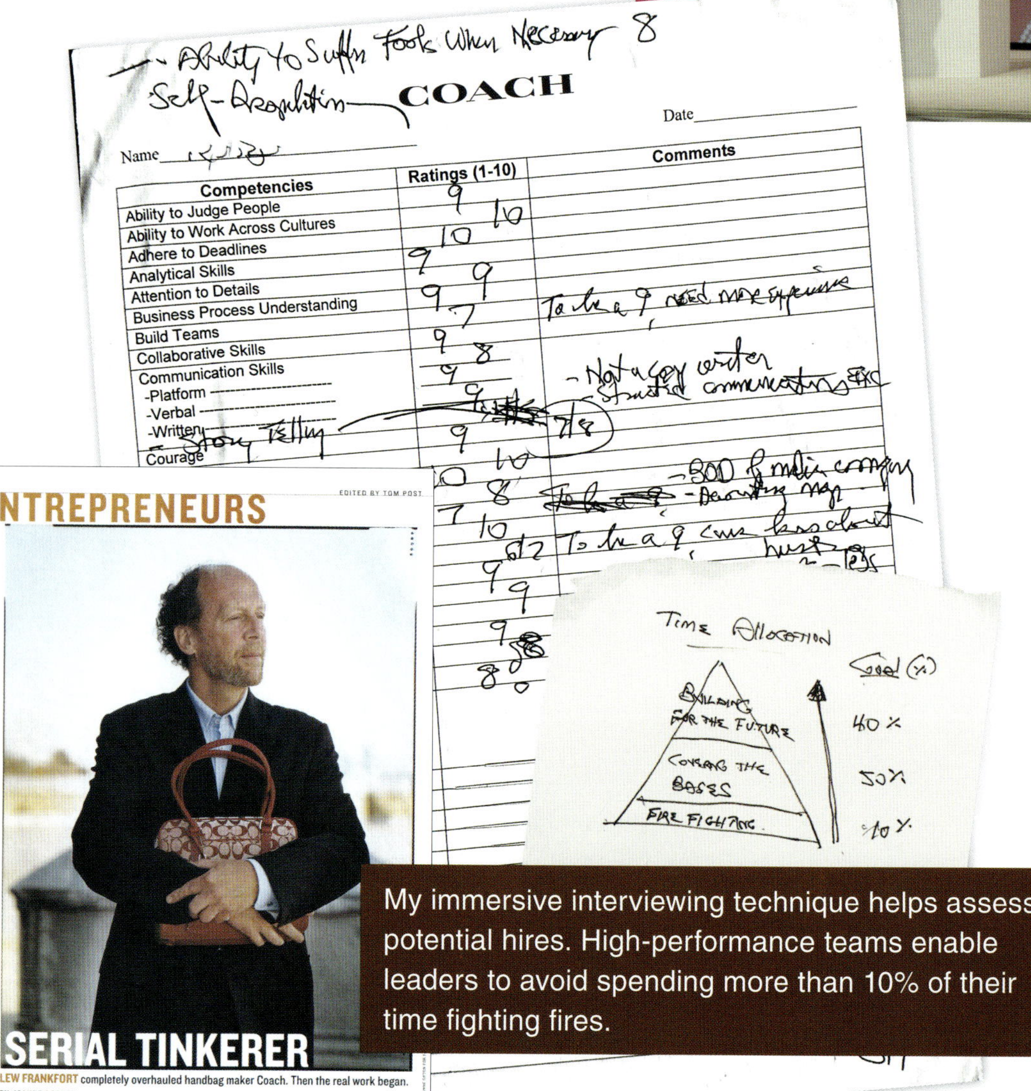

My immersive interviewing technique helps assess potential hires. High-performance teams enable leaders to avoid spending more than 10% of their time fighting fires.

Clockwise from top right: 1. On stage at an internal meeting; 2. A sample of the competency screen from an interview; 3. My time-allocation pyramid; 4. *Forbes* article from 2001 (credit: Suzanne Opton).

Accessible Luxury Goes Public

Coach was owned by the Sara Lee Corporation for 15 years prior to its IPO in 2000. Our leadership team was still busy transforming every part of our business when we gathered in October to ring the bell at the New York Stock Exchange.

We coined the term "accessible luxury" to help investors understand the market opportunity Coach created.

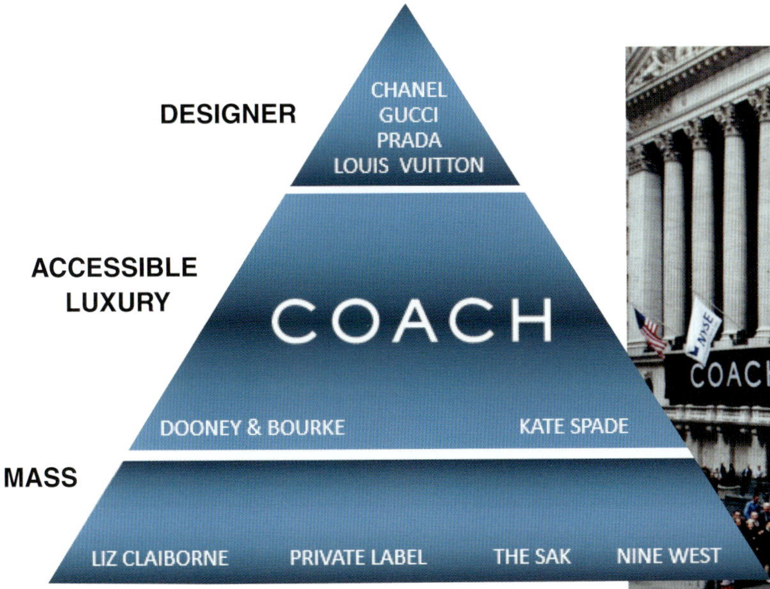

DESIGNER
CHANEL
GUCCI
PRADA
LOUIS VUITTON

ACCESSIBLE LUXURY
COACH
DOONEY & BOURKE
KATE SPADE

MASS
LIZ CLAIBORNE
PRIVATE LABEL
THE SAK
NINE WEST

Clockwise from top left: 1. Coach leaders and my family gather for the milestone; 2. Standing outside the NYSE; 3. The diagram we created for investors to explain Coach's market position.

Retail Is Detail

Coach was among the first US brands to open its own stores. Our original "library look" was an intimate environment. Brighter, more playful spaces in the late 1990s showcased our broadening bag styles and product assortment. In every store, we strove to treat customers like guests in our own homes.

Clockwise from top right: 1. and 2. The interior and exterior of our first stores; 3., 4., and 5. The interiors and exterior of redesigned stores in the late 1990s and early 2000s (credit: 3. Haruyoshi Yamaguchi/Bloomberg via Getty Images).

Appeal Abroad

Coach's early popularity with Japanese travelers led us to start selling Coach in Japan in 1988 through a partnership with Mitsukoshi department stores. We finally entered China in 2005, where Coach was popular with the burgeoning middle class.

Coach confident of taking China share

LUXURY GOODS

By Raphael Minder in Hong Kong

China's development of native luxury brands will have no impact on the continued expansion of western
es
ef
JS
so-
he
w-
ur-
its rate of expansion in North America, reducing the number of annual store openings there from 40 to 20, Mr Frankfort said he was likely to accelerate development plans in China.

Speaking at the end of a visit to China, he said: "I am leaving this trip with a view that our numbers might be conservative . . . We see sophisticated [Chinese] consumers shopping and international brands thriving."

Coach estimates that China will represent 10 per more than 100 cities that have populations of more than 1m, and "all of these cities will be candidates for Coach one day", said Mr Frankfort.

China has not escaped the global downturn, but Mr Frankfort insisted Coach's own performance so far provided evidence of the robustness of Chinese consumerism in the face of a broader economic slowdown. In the quarter that ended in March, Coach posted an increase of about 30 per cent in same- for the big western companies because "their positioning will typically be below the positioning of the luxury European brands and Coach".

He drew a comparison with the Japanese market, where western brands have thrived alongside domestic ones, and where Coach now has about 20 per cent of its sales.

Mr Frankfort added: "I believe that new [Chinese] brands will generally not be able to obtain the perceived

lockwise from top left: 1. Opening our first shop-in-shop at Mitsukoshi in Nihonbashi; 2. The *Financial Times* covered our China xpansion in 2009 (credit: *Financial Times*); 3. Our Hong Kong flagship store on Canton Road; 4. Interior of the Hong Kong flagship.

Legacies

Legacy brands are those that capture people's hearts. They create indelible images and lasting associations and can withstand periods of ups and downs. Legacy brands are rare, and not indestructible. They must be nurtured and loved—just like family.

At Coach's new headquarters in New York's Hudson Yards, CEO Todd Kahn and Creative Director Stuart Vevers continue a legacy of authenticity and excellence.

Clockwise from top right: 1. View from our vertical campus; 2. The Brooklyn bag, 2024; 3. Wall of bags in the Coach lobb (credit: 1. and 3.: Related Companies); 4. Tabby bag, 2019; 5. CEO Todd Kahn, Creative Director Stuart Vevers, and me, 202 (credit: Billy Farrell/BFA.com); 6. Honoring employees with the Lew Awards.

Clockwise from top left: 1. Bobbie and me with our parents on our wedding day, 1975; 2. With my mom, 2005; 3. On vacation with Tamara, Bobbie, Sam, and Alana, 1988; 4. The family, 2024.

COACH
COACH
LEATHERWARE
COACH
LEATHERWARE

CHAPTER 11

Transforming the Ecosystem

After returning to Coach full-time in 1996, I had assumed that restoring growth by reinvigorating our product assortment and strengthening our brand image might take 18 months, maybe two years. I now understood that it would take five times the effort that I originally thought. Not just more time and more money, but more reach. It had to be comprehensive, which meant we had to transform so much more—production, supply chain, retail operations, and store design.

The dual goals of transforming the business *and* being IPO-ready required an investment-grade leadership team, which I defined as a collaborative group of seasoned professionals with a diversity of experiences, including growing brands and businesses through adversity. I wanted to surround myself with domain experts who had knowledge I lacked. They also had to fit our Coach smart culture.

Selecting a senior team is one of a leader's most critical roles. There had been times in the past when I didn't adequately screen a candidate or think critically enough about the job's requirements. As a result, I had sometimes mistakenly recruited the wrong person for a role in which they were not successful. I blamed myself for such failures. To reduce the chances that I'd fail at the critical task of hiring the right people, and increase the chances that I'd succeed at hiring great people, I had been refining my interviewing technique. I wanted to be more interactive so I might have a complete view of a person.

Specifically, I wanted to hire people with two foundational characteristics: values and capabilities. If someone isn't wired right from a values perspective, then no matter how capable they are it's going to be impossible for them to thrive. Similarly, if you have good values but lack the skills and drive for a job, you also won't succeed. When we understand someone as a full person, we can increase the likelihood of their professional success in a given role, and the role after that.

I called the technique I developed immersive interviewing. The approach I used in the 1990s is similar to what it is today.

If you were applying for a leadership position at Coach, you likely met with many people who vetted your technical skills and expertise before you sat down with me. For my direct reports and select others, I met candidates both at the beginning and at the end of the process. Either way, my goal was to get a handle on your less tangible abilities, such as whether you can build effective teams and how you make decisions.

I usually divided the interview into three phases. First, I eased in by asking about your background and most recent work experiences. This biographical line of inquiry was somewhat personal. I had already reviewed your résumé and other background materials. Now I wanted to know a bit about where you grew up, and events that were life changing, or life shaping. I wanted you to tell me about your family. What you liked most and least about your last job. What were your interests and hobbies? What achievements were you most proud of? I was trying to get at your life's journey, listening for who you are as a person, not just as a professional. I would jot down some highlights and takeaways, then set them aside to come back to later. After about 15 or 20 minutes, I would transition into the next phase.

For the second part of our time together, I'd ask the name of your current or a recent boss, whoever knows you best. Then I'd ask you to rate their emotional intelligence, or EQ, from a low of 1 to a high of 10. Most likely you would rank them at a 7, 8, or 9, but if you ranked them lower I'd ask you to share more so I could better understand the lens through which you gave this rating.

Next, I'd want to know what this person would identify as your strengths and opportunities for growth, regardless of whether you agree. If you said that your boss thought you could be more incisive, I'd ask for an example. In my experience, asking you to consider your strengths and weaknesses from your boss's perspective enhanced your reflections. Many people don't have the language or the inclination to describe themselves in full dimension, so this angle would help you express yourself more precisely. It would also force a level of honesty, especially if you knew that your boss was a reference I might talk with. To ensure I understood exactly what you meant, I might paraphrase some of your answers back to you. Again, I would never want to assume. And I would ask you to use only a few words to describe each strength to ensure we covered all three phases of the interview within our allocated time together. For an undisciplined interviewer, it would be easy to get sidetracked and run out of time before you had covered all the areas you wanted.

The third part of the interview was the immersive screen. I turned to a long list of competencies I'd amassed over the years, and for each I would ask you to rate yourself on a scale of 1 to 10. The numbers enabled me to see how you perceived your strengths relative to each other. My list of more than 80 competencies included these:

The ability to judge people professionally. Adherence to deadlines. Analytical skills. Attention to details. Build teams. Collaborative skills. Communication skills—verbal and written. Courage. Curiosity. Creativity. Decisiveness. Facility with technology. Financial acumen. Get the job done. Incisiveness. Investigative skills. Juggle multiple tasks at the same time. Lateral thinking skills. Learn quickly. Multitasking ability. Numeric dexterity. Persistence/ability to get the job done. Relationships with peers, subordinates, and supervisors. Self-awareness. Self-motivation. Sense of integrity. Sense of strategy. Situational leadership. Street smarts. Team-building skill. Tenacity. Work ethic. Working under adversity and pressure. Working with ambiguity.

I would first ask you about traits that had already emerged as strengths in our conversation, as well as easier ones like work ethic or juggling many things at once. Individually and collectively, your rankings would offer insight, telling me where to lean in for more information and clarity. I was looking for clusters of similarly rated competencies—for outliers that might suggest a concern, and for dichotomies that reveal where I needed to probe to get to a deeper truth. If you gave yourself a 7 on decisiveness, I would ask what it would take to get you to a 9 so I could understand if this was a deficit that could be overcome with coaching, or one that could be offset by others. If you told me your financial acumen was a 9 but your dexterity with numbers was a 5, I'd push you to be more specific; I wanted to understand why there was a gap, or whether you had assessed yourself accurately.

Overall, I was also looking for deal breakers and caution areas. If you rated yourself a 6 on making tough decisions, that rating would concern me. I would not ask you directly if you have gravitas, but if I sensed that you lacked it you probably weren't the right person to lead a business unit, which requires someone with a confident presence.

In my head, I was also triangulating your responses from all three phases of the interview to understand your level of self-awareness and your ability to grow. For example, did your life experiences and self-assessment suggest that you would perform best in a structured environment like Sara Lee, or at a more entrepreneurial place like Coach?

The questions I asked did not have right or wrong answers. They were more about determining whether you had the skills, personality, and values for the role. Were you the real deal, ready to be a VP? And were you Coach smart?

If we did hire you after this thorough interview, we would also have a better sense of how to help you become your best self.

My immersive interviewing framework routinized my natural curiosity about people and helped me avoid the trap of making assumptions about skills and overlooking major weaknesses. Immersive interviewing is an imperfect science, and there's no correct way to interpret a candidate's answers. Anyone who adopts the technique brings to it their own filter of experiences, bias, and intuition.

The best way I've found to describe the method of inquiry and assessment is "grokking," from a concept coined by Robert Heinlein in his 1961 science fiction novel *Stranger in a Strange Land,* which I'd read during college. In the book, grok was a Martian practice of trying to understand something or someone so thoroughly that "the observer becomes part of the observed." Heinlein's definition was literal as well as figurative. To drink water, for example, was to "grok it" because water becomes part of you, physically. But you could also "grok" a society or a religion, coming to understand it so fully that you merged with it. I found this concept profound as well as pragmatic, and I adopted it for my own purposes by grokking potential hires to see if they had what it took to work at Coach.

For all my rigor, I could still hire someone not right for a role—and not right for me. I could get so captivated by someone's reputation or impressed with their prior experiences that I assumed they possessed certain abilities and values. I might overlook shortcomings or not take time to thoroughly grok them.

I was, and remain, especially susceptible to people who exhibit a high degree of confidence and even charm. Not until I work with them do I realize that they're incapable of collaboration and being open to other people's points of view. They are so sure that they're the smartest person in every room that they're incapable of considering any idea other than their own. I call these types of individuals hardwired narcissists, and they are toxic. Unfortunately, we can't always see them coming.

Despite my own blind spots, immersive interviewing helped me throughout my career at Coach, especially in 1998, when the most important thing I needed to do was recruit an investment-grade leadership team to help me transform the business.

• • •

The first hire I had to get right was a chief operating officer, whose responsibilities would include migrating Coach from manufacturing in our own company-owned factories to independent facilities abroad.

Trying to sell Coach had confirmed for me that the only way to broaden our product assortment with sufficient margins without compromising quality was to diversify our factories to lower-cost countries while maintaining strict controls. Introducing new bag styles with different materials, features, and detailing—extra zippers, linings, ornamental stitching, and added pockets for more functionality—would require more time to construct. We couldn't continue to manufacture in the United States at the same price points with the same level of profitability. Our facilities lacked the capability to perform more complex work on the larger scale. Coach now needed to compete and grow at a cost structure that could keep our prices accessible.

By 1998, many apparel brands made their products in China, but few if any premium accessory brands did. Coach would be among the first, and some people in our industry doubted we'd succeed, given our high standards. We also wondered if making products in China would cost us customers. High-profile revelations about poorly made products and abusive labor practices in China had begun to surface. Chinese workmanship and facilities had improved, but they were hardly uniform.

We did our usual market research to assess if having "Made in China" labels on our handbags, a legal requirement, would encounter some resistance. The results were surprising. People said that where products were made did matter to them. But when asked to rank a dozen factors likely to influence their purchase, "country of origin" ranked near the bottom. Quality, however, was still a top factor. Ultimately, we decided that "Made in China" wasn't a problem, at least in the North American market. However, in Japan, a product's country of origin did matter more, particularly to our sales staff. So we'd have to provide training and education to ensure they understood that the Asian factories we contracted with met our quality standards. That onus was on us, and I had to recruit someone who delivered on it.

That summer the COO of Timberland, Keith Monda, flew to New York from his home in Portsmouth, New Hampshire, to interview for the role of Coach's COO, a position I created to migrate our manufacturing abroad, as well as oversee finance, supply chain, administration, and legal. Keith had been involved in a number of apparel company turnarounds, most notably with Timberland, another US brand with an iconic product: the chunky mustard-yellow work boot. Timberland's origins dated back to 1918, when Russian-born shoemaker Nathan Swartz started making shoes in Boston. Swartz and his son, Sidney, used a new technology, injection molding, to bind the bottom of a shoe to its upper body, creating an insulated, waterproof boot revolutionary to the footwear industry. The unique construction held up to the region's wet, cold conditions better than other footwear. The company introduced the Timberland boot in 1973.

Prior to overhauling Timberland's supply chain and manufacturing, Keith had worked in the pharmaceutical industry, then J. Crew. He had the confidence of someone who'd been on this journey before, and as he put it, knew how to do the dance.

He appreciated the respect and affection I had for our North American factory workers, but he also made it clear that he'd only accept the position if

I was willing to close the factories where most of them worked—except for our sample-making facilities in New York, which we agreed were essential to maintain. I paused for a moment, processing exactly what it would mean to let so many workers go. I was well aware of the economic hardships many would undoubtedly face. But I also knew this migration was necessary for the company to grow and flourish, so I assured Keith that while painful, I was committed to building an efficient supply chain. At the same time, I said that we would treat employees that were let go the way we would like to be treated in their position—with ample notice, substantial severance, and making every effort to help them get new jobs, including encouraging other manufacturers to hire them. Keith responded with what would be his mantra throughout his tenure: "At the end of the day, everybody's got to be okay."

We took each other at our word, and Keith moved his family to New York.

Keith's methodology was designed to give Coach maximum control in any factories we worked with in Asia, and to meet and even exceed labor standards set by the United Nations and other organizations. We'd only select facilities with track records for producing quality leather goods. We wouldn't do business with any outfit that didn't abide by local labor and environmental laws. We also held manufacturing partners to our own, often higher standards and stricter rules for worker pay, treatment, conditions, and living accommodations. Many Chinese workers traveled from rural areas to work in factories for a period of time so they could send money home to their families.

Keith's plan also called for Coach to provide everything a facility needed to make our products, such as technical packets with the exact specifications of thread, hardware, colorations, and construction—essentially, instructions for each handbag or belt, down to the amount of space between stitches. We'd also control the sourcing and negotiate the pricing of all raw materials and hardware. Anything factories did buy, even spools of thread, required our approval.

Keith's team would also hire and train teams of engineers to work in factories full-time, monitoring workmanship and conditions so problems were addressed before products were shipped and costs incurred. Keith didn't call the facilities "factories," but "finished goods suppliers" to reflect the degree of control Coach would retain. Frequent visits by Keith, me, and members of our manufacturing and legal teams made sure the facilities and their managers were in compliance while meeting our standards.

I would come to know Keith as a self-styled character who did things his own way. Prior to starting at Coach, he had wanted to run the New York City Marathon but avoid the crowds, so he mapped his own route in his hometown in and around Portsmouth, starting his solo run at the exact time the regular marathon began. He approached his work with the same renegade mindset, determined to forge a custom path that preserved Coach's high standards for less cost.

I was reassured that I'd hired the right person when one of the first things Keith did was write the word *QUALITY* in large white chalky letters on the blackboard in his office. He didn't erase it during his entire tenure with Coach.

• • •

Another crucial role I needed to recruit for was someone to lead operations and growth of all Coach stores in North America.

Visiting Coach stores had always been one of my favorite things to do. I might stop by our Manhattan stores two or three times most weeks. I spent the most time at our flagship store, where the full world of Coach products was on display. Some afternoons I might also head to our smaller Rockefeller Center store to talk with tourists and the smattering of business customers, and then go to our Upper West Side store which catered to local residents. I knew many of our store associates' names, and we greeted each other with a handshake or hug. There was camaraderie and a sense of family in our stores that mirrored our office's culture. I loved walking the floor, talking with managers, sales associates, and customers.

Regular store visits also helped me to toggle between the high and the low of the business. I could be in an annual planning meeting in the morning, then head to some store visits in the afternoon, where I could witness the transactional details of retail. The strategic and the tactical were equally important, so no matter how much I relied on data, there was no substitute for listening to customers and our store teams.

Our standalone retail and factory stores had become our most crucial sales channels as department stores began to decline in popularity throughout the 1990s. The library aesthetic we'd pioneered in 1981 still existed in most of our full-price stores, and we'd remodeled several stores a while back in an ad hoc effort to spark sales, but the arts-and-crafts interiors we chose weren't a dramatic enough departure to generate excitement.

Basically, our stores craved a makeover.

Bright, happy, and *sexy* were not words I associated with Coach, at least not yet, but for Dave DeMattei, that's what Coach stores needed to become. Dave built his retail career at the Gap, where he started as an accounting manager and spent the next 15 years in different operational roles, rising to CFO before becoming president of Gap-owned Banana Republic. Throughout, Dave worked closely with two master retailers. One of them was Don Fisher, who founded the Gap in 1969 by opening a store with his wife, Doris, in northern California that only sold men's Levi's jeans—yet another iconic American brand—in every style and size, unlike department stores, which carried limited inventory. The concept took off. They opened more stores, started making Gap-branded jeans, and diversified with the purchase of the upscale Banana Republic in 1983 and the founding of value chain Old Navy in 1994. Dave also worked with Mickey Drexler, who led the Gap's rebirth and exponential growth in the 1990s, in part by modernizing stores and creating Gap-branded sportswear and lifestyle clothes, including men's khakis that hit the decade's business-casual trend.

After the Gap, Dave joined J. Crew and ran the catalog business's burgeoning retail division, alongside its creative visionary, Emily Woods. He left after helping sell J. Crew to a real estate operating company, and he was planning a move from New York to California in 1998 when Jane Ramsey, who had joined Coach to head HR for a bit after Maxine had left, reached out to him. He hesitated.

"You claim to be a premium brand but you have a thriving factory store business," Dave said, not yet understanding Coach from a multichannel perspective. Fortunately, Jane persisted.

"You have to meet Lew," Jane told him.

Dave was an emotional force of conviction with a well-rounded background. He had finance, merchandising, and leadership experience, plus a product-centric ethos he'd gleaned from Don, Mickey, and Emily. He also had a singular view about how profitable retailers should organize and staff stores.

In his view, the role of stores was straightforward: showcase the right product.

When I told Dave that we were launching a travel collection with different pieces of luggage, he frowned. "Lew, where's it going to go? Your stores are too small." Filling Coach stores with more products, he said, wasn't how to boost sales. We had to make the stores more productive, in part by showing less product in a more enticing environment.

Dave's husband, Patrick Wade, a designer and visual merchandiser, also joined Coach, and together they set to work revamping store environments and retail operations.

About a year in, Dave and Patrick invited me to the existing Coach store in Westchester. I arrived to discover the traditional brown wood interior—every shelf, every table, every wall—painted white. The 1,900-square-foot space looked twice as big. Only about half the number of handbags we typically displayed populated shelves and tables so they were easier to see, reach, and try on. Bags were also positioned more sparingly, some on pedestals, like precious art in a museum, which made them appear special, even rare. Our small leather goods and apparel collections were usually clustered in corners of the store. Now, wallets, belts, and raincoats were also interspersed with bags, like small scenes that told a story: The color yellow is big. Straw is perfect for summer. Match this handbag with that scarf.

The Westchester store's staff was energized by the brighter look and feel. Their enthusiasm coupled with the new merchandising had already translated into sales, which were up 10% since the revamp. For me, seeing the store in person was rejuvenating.

"Do 10 more," I told them, and off they went.

Dave was a magnet for talent and recruited relentlessly to get the field operations and merchandising expertise he knew Coach desperately needed. He wooed many former J. Crew colleagues and other top industry talent, like Jody Kuss, who had been schooled as a merchant, first at Federated Department Stores, then at Barney's New York, the men's clothing store founded by Barney Pressman in 1923 and converted by his son, Fred, into a high-end fashion retailer for men and women. For 13 years Jody worked with Fred, walking store floors, talking to shoppers, watching trends. She had traveled the world scouting hot designers and the best mills to curate custom garments. Jody jumped from luxury back to mass retail when she joined the Gap to help transition Banana Republic from safari-themed attire to modern sportswear. From there, four years at J. Crew added to her breadth of knowledge about specialty retail.

Dave convinced Jody to interview at Coach for what he described as "the opportunity of a lifetime." Thankfully, Jody saw the same future potential for Coach that Reed saw by revitalizing our products—if we could embrace fashion. She also saw the same operational benefits that Keith predicted from a revamped supply chain—if we could maintain quality. Plus, she had a personal love for Coach—Jody's mother had some of Bonnie Cashin's original handbags—and a professional respect for our consumer-centric, knowledge-driven approach to business.

I met Jody and saw her as someone who understood product, consumers, brand, and the business side. She had a fiery energy, and she was insatiably curious. I also liked that she was a lateral thinker who used data, experience, and intuition to reach conclusions, and I thought she would have the courage to change course if doing so was right for the business.

As Coach's first chief merchant, Jody's job was to refine and enhance what Coach had been trying to do for years: understand people and translate their needs into products. She brought additional depth and dimension to this calculus, and she worked in strong partnership with Mary Grace. For all her experience, Jody had not yet been at a company with such strong consumer research. We began to more thoroughly examine our luxury competitors to see what they were doing that their customers liked. Luxury brands didn't yet sell online—and we were just beginning to—so we had to comb through their catalogs and visit stores. The intent was never to mimic, but to better understand why their customers engaged with the brands.

Jody was also insistent that we identify what consumer segments Coach was missing so we could decide who else to target, and how. She was a powerful presence who became the link we needed to bridge consumer insights and design, as well as the front and back end of the business. And like Keith, Jody tapped her network and brought on more merchandising expertise.

Francine Della Badia, who had worked with Jody at the Gap, came on as Coach's lead merchandiser for handbags. Fran quickly established herself as an astute merchant. She too was a right- and left-brained thinker, creative and analytical. Her mother was a sculptor, her father an engineer, and her grandmother and aunt were dressmakers. Fran grew up appreciating the beauty and technicalities of design. She had a sixth sense for the commercial value of fashion products, and was curious, methodical, and adept with numbers. She also was thoughtful and rarely dismissed a new idea out of hand but dug in to understand it and advance something if it had merit. She earned my respect as well as Reed's, and people gravitated to her wide, easy smile.

Seasoned talent like Fran Della Badia, Jody Kuss, Dave DeMattei, Keith Monda, Reed Krakoff, and others joined Coach for similar reasons: They respected our authentic heritage of quality. They saw the untapped potential of our positioning between mass and luxury in the bifurcated and burgeoning bag and accessories market. And, as a team, they knew what to do operationally to move the business from a manufacturer of leather goods to a marketer of fashionable products.

By the end of 1999, I'd filled most of the spots of our senior team, and they hit the ground running. I was aware, however, that such a rapid influx of strong personalities with similar yet diverse backgrounds risked overshadowing the intangible values that made Coach Coach. Our new team was missing an essential player—a keeper of the culture.

• • •

Between 1991 and 1998 our workforce ballooned from 1,500 to 5,000. Our culture had emerged organically over time, first with Miles with his emphasis on quality products, then with me with my consumer-centric focus, and even from Sara Lee with its added discipline and rigor. During Maxine's tenure as our head of HR, she had done a tremendous job shaping a Coach smart workplace that valued people as well as performance.

Many employees described Coach as the smallest big company they knew. A bustling, friendly energy permeated the loft-like space of our New York offices as we expanded to every floor in the building, where once we occupied just two of the 12. The white brick walls emanated a charming warmth.

Most people at Coach were passionate about being part of a company with such a rich heritage. Everyone arrived with respect for the brand, many with personal affection for it because Coach had been their first real handbag or briefcase, or their mother's favorite bag. There was a shared commitment to preserve and nurture what people loved about Coach. Our employees' belief in the Coach brand was not something you could measure but it was steadfast and real, and frankly rare. Being surrounded by bright people with such a strong work ethic, as well as integrity, bred a mission-driven camaraderie that was refreshing in an industry that could be superficial and dominated by egos.

Almost without exception, people at Coach were not only committed to the growth of the company but also to their own individual growth. We attracted aspirational professionals who sought more from a job than just a paycheck, but also fulfillment and satisfaction. Beyond excellence, they were likely after self-actualization, the highest level on Maslow's hierarchy of needs. This distinguished Coach as a place where smart people could get wiser about their particular area of expertise and about themselves. I think that's among the reasons why so many people loved working at Coach and stayed so long—and once they left they recalled their years there as among the best of their career. It was and still is a special place.

Although our employees had similar values and drive, we were hardly a cookie-cutter organization, but a collection of self-styled individuals who marched to our own beats. We prided ourselves on being open to people of all backgrounds, races, sexual preferences, ages, and genders. It truly didn't matter where you were from. People had their share of eccentricities that could be endearing and gave the workplace a colorful, at times playful flavor that softened the seriousness of the work. But some also had quirks that probably would have prevented them from thriving in a straitlaced corporate environment, or proclivities that could have interfered with their jobs and kept them from becoming the best version of themselves.

A big part of my role was to shape a group of highly motivated, independent leaders from diverse backgrounds with different personalities into a cohesive, high-performing team. I considered myself a situational leader, and I could vary my communication style to fit someone else's and a given situation. Because I was such an immersive interviewer, I had a pretty good idea of how you were wired, as well as where you needed improvement. Coaching was one of the most important parts of my job, but I was not a trained executive coach, nor did I have a clinical background that equipped me to address deeper, internal challenges some people faced.

Early on, I'd brought in the Center for Creative Leadership to conduct 360-degree assessments so people could identify their development opportunities, like I had, and work with a professional to strengthen their performance. I also championed personal development and an open environment where people regularly provided constructive feedback to each other. Coach was not a place that let things slide or allowed something that should be better to go unnoticed, so you needed to be able to accept that constructive feedback, and the intent behind it. I had low tolerance if you weren't open to coaching, or didn't learn from your mistakes in a reasonable amount of time. Accountability was paramount and, naturally, execution mattered more than good intentions. Ultimately, if you did not perform, you would be asked to leave.

Of course, some of my own traits could endear me to people or be tough to tolerate. In addition to being genuinely interested in helping you to develop professionally, I was also curious about who you were outside of work, and I was interested in your well-being. In one-on-one and small group meetings, I often spent five or 10 minutes at the onset asking about your weekend, your kids, even your health. If you seemed especially stressed, I might suggest you see Edgar Pena for a massage session.

Among my less-appreciated traits was the fact that I liked the office cold. Whenever I felt energized or stressed, which was most of the time, my heart rate went up and I tended to sweat. Because my body also ran hot, I needed a cold environment to work in. Some people on the 12th floor, where my office was located, complained that they were too cold. At one point Keith had his team install an air conditioner on the roof above my office so I could control the temperature in my space and the rest of the floor could warm up a bit. Keith kept a parka in his office for when he came to meet with me, and I am sure others made similar accommodations. I also kept extra zip-up sweatshirts in my office closet for visitors and others who came unprepared for the chill in the room.

Just like I ran hot, I also tended to run late, even though it would often be disruptive to other people's schedules. I was always intent on finishing a meeting's agenda so whoever I was with could leave with the answers they needed to advance their work and the business. I was willing to go over our allotted time too if we hadn't yet identified next steps or answered critical questions, especially if it might be weeks until we were scheduled to meet again. Pat Cherry, my executive assistant, did her best to give people a heads-up when I was running late. People often waited in a quiet room I had built next to my office, with low couches and soft chairs, so they could work in peace while they waited. I'd patterned the room after Zen-like spaces I'd experienced while traveling to executive offices throughout Japan. People got used to waiting for me, and most knew it was never personal to them, or out of disrespect.

More broadly, Howard Guttman and his organizational consulting firm, Guttman Development Strategies, became somewhat embedded at Coach, helping us develop into a high-performance culture and address challenges most growing companies face: for one, scaling high performance. You can have people who are technically strong in their areas of expertise but lack the ability to lead teams and departments. Howard helped us define competencies that people needed to advance, and be what we called "a player," as well as determine who had, or could develop, those multidimensional skills in addition to their technical orientation. A lot of those traits became competencies I looked for in my immersive interviewing process.

Howard and his team also helped us institutionalize certain practices and mindsets. We became a true learning culture that actively taught people how to strengthen their interpersonal skills and adopt common methodologies and language to better collaborate with peers and manage conflict, so people throughout the company approached problems in similar ways. We had courses and modules that taught people to become better listeners, assert themselves, and hone influencing skills.

We had our dysfunctions, of course, and our share of politics—although nothing like Sara Lee—in which case one of our consultants might come in to mediate difficult conversations between teams to resolve differences.

We also used compensation as a tool to reinforce our values and encourage excellence. Our HR professionals, like Laura Booth, took a great deal of pride that Coach didn't let industry standards or even Sara Lee dictate our policies, and that we were willing to buck convention or create our own programs to meet our objectives. "We're all in this, and we all matter," was how Laura put it, and she believed we had to prove it with "programs and our pocketbook, not just with words."

Almost all employees were eligible for a bonus when the business hit or exceeded goals. During the years when we soared, payouts were substantial. The plan was so unique that Sara Lee had us speak about it to other companies' HR departments.

In stores, we asked how compensation could help sales associates feel valued and also provide excellent customer service and meet sales targets. To that end, they had to know our products and make genuine efforts to engage people who walked into a store, but without being pushy. We created a team incentive bonus program at the store level to reward superior performers. Maintaining our collegial vibe meant sales associates couldn't compete with each other for customers, so unlike many other retailers I didn't want us to have individual commission programs, but a team-sharing approach to reinforce a collaborative atmosphere.

These tangible and intangible aspects of our culture were developed throughout the 1990s as we tried to blend creativity and business. Elements of magic and logic were at play in all sorts of ways. You had to listen to your instincts about people and adapt your own style so you could collaborate with people across functions and roles even when their styles were different than yours. You had to be respectful, while at the same time asserting your own opinions and holding yourself and your teams accountable to high standards of behavior as well as results. You had to think imaginatively and laterally by being open to new, even contradictory ideas, and then being willing to pursue a path for the greater good of the business.

Making decisions through the lens of the greater good was a very important aspect of Coach's culture. It had long been one aspect of my drive for excellence. At Coach it translated to considering the consequences of your actions on the entire ecosystem, overriding self-interest for the benefit of the whole. I was always saying to people that it was never too early to do what was right for the business.

A company full of passionate, talented high achievers that come together—despite their quirks and eccentricities—can achieve remarkable things when mixed with a rigor, accountability, and a commitment to a greater good. And as we entered a new chapter at the end of the decade, all these aspects of our culture needed to be preserved and elevated by a chief of human resources who could succeed Maxine for the long term.

In October 1999, the last interview I had with Felice Schulaner was in a booth at the Empire Diner, near Coach's offices. She told me she'd had more than a dozen interviews with people at Coach and Sara Lee.

"Lew, when are you going to make this decision already?" Felice was straightforward, wicked smart, and seasoned, with seven years in a variety of HR executive roles at American Express and four years at Macy's. Like Keith, she knew how to dance, and she had a definitive point of view.

Felice believed that four things make people love their job. One, a sense of accomplishment. Two, a sense that they have influence over their work. Three, that they feel recognized and rewarded for their contributions, and four, they believe their values are aligned with the organization's values. Her intent as head of HR was to maximize the chance that all four things existed for most employees on most days.

Just as I had known that Coach needed Maxine, I now knew that Coach needed Felice, who would serve as the truthful thought partner I wanted in the role. Sitting across from her in the diner, I told Felice that I'd already decided to offer her the job. I just had one last question: "Are you joining Coach, or Sara Lee?" I wanted to make sure her loyalty and interests were with the right business, especially since Coach was likely to go public. I didn't mention it at the time because I didn't want her to be disappointed if the IPO never materialized. She didn't hesitate. "Coach," she said. When she'd left Macy's back in 1990, the last thing she'd purchased with her employee discount was a black Coach Bucket bag for $90, the most expensive bag she'd ever owned because, as she recalled it, "she had to have a Coach."

I'd found the keeper of our culture.

• • •

All in all, 1999 was a tense year with layoffs, new faces, and internal change. By fall—a few months before Felice joined Coach—quarterly sales were edging up, but the prevailing mood was uncertainty. Most people at Coach didn't yet know we were hoping to go public. Even if they did know an IPO was a possibility there was no guarantee we'd actually do it. Sara Lee wouldn't initiate our public offering unless there was enough investor confidence to get them their $1 billion. That meant we needed to achieve positive metrics that showed evidence that customers were embracing Coach's transformation.

Everyone needed a morale lift, including me, so we threw a Halloween party in our showroom. People went all out, and I have to say it was a welcome moment of stress release as we all showed off our costumes to applause and laughter. I came as Batman. Black mask, boots, cape. The full head-to-toe ensemble. I'd certainly come a long way since being the only kid without a costume at the tail end of the elementary school parade!

Now my job was to lead the team I'd hired, which meant I had to be willing to listen, learn, collaborate, delegate, let people do their job, and hold them accountable. I hoped I'd grokked well.

CHAPTER 12

Going Public

In the beginning of 2000, everyone was in high gear while some of us quietly prepared for a public offering. Some days an IPO seemed likely. Other days something unexpected threatened the possibility.

In February, the NASDAQ hit its peak after five years of unprecedented growth. Widespread embrace of the internet had spurred entrepreneurs to start online businesses that attracted many billions of investment dollars. But just because you had an idea didn't mean it would translate into a viable business. Undisciplined tech founders had burned through cash, which was starting to reveal weak business models behind many companies' bloated valuations. The dot-com bust, as it would be called, chilled investors' appetite for IPOs starting in the spring of 2000, especially for companies that investors couldn't easily understand.

The significant market downturn was a mixed blessing for us. A profitable business like Coach that sold tangible products you could see and touch was appealing. But accessories are also discretionary items, and the economic downshift also weakened consumer spending just as we were doing all sorts of things to woo more customers.

A year earlier, in fall 1999, we'd redesigned our multistory, 6,400-square-foot store on 57th and Madison Avenue in New York with architect Peter Marino to showcase our expanded vision with the full range of Coach merchandise in one place for the first time. When the flagship store opened, the *New York Times* ran an article headlined "Something's Glittering Among the Leathers at Coach."

"Customers are in for some surprises," the piece began. "Oh, there will still be bags, but there will also be leather jackets and pants, shoes, watches, bracelets, scarves, hats, luggage and furniture." We'd had Coach-branded extension products for years, of course, but the flagship's relaunch was an attempt to publicly reposition Coach as a lifestyle accessory brand, not just a bag business. Reed had collaborated with our various licensees, including Jimlar, to design new shoe styles, like black Mary Janes with chunky rubber soles, and Movado, for stainless-steel watches engraved with *COACH.*

"Fashion is what drives our business now," Reed told the *Times.*

I gave Reed due credit for imbuing Coach with a fresh perspective, "in tune with our changing consumers' expectations."

The *Times* article concluded that while Coach was indeed updating its image, we'd "broken no new ground in terms of design." I didn't like seeing this in print, and wasn't sure customers agreed. Based on strong sales volume that first week alone we increased future sales projections. But it was still early days of our metamorphosis, and I remained optimistic we would go beyond hitting singles and doubles and eventually hit it out of the park. Still, the *Times* was right that we faced many challenges in our bid for global recognition as a fashion force, including a balancing act many classic brands face: "how to attract a new breed of shopper while continuing to cater to the old faithfuls."

I placed a lot of trust in Reed because he was a visionary thinker and a pragmatic marketer with excellent taste who understood that the brand couldn't abandon its history in the pursuit of pure fashion. We were still a consumer-led brand. Reed got that. If something didn't sell, or if the women we surveyed felt lukewarm about a new style, he wasn't precious about altering it and didn't blame people for not getting our vision. He'd agree to alter it or stop selling it. At the same time, he listened to his gut. He wouldn't, for example, force Coach to succumb to every trend if it wasn't right for us. This, too, was part of the logic-magic balancing act, and for Reed it was second nature.

He also could straddle past and present across all aspects of creative, not just product design. For example, he was injecting more spirited language into our marketing lexicon, without losing our voice. In catalogs, classic descriptors like *well-crafted, dependable, functional,* and *enduring* appeared alongside new words like *sleek, slim, crisp, relaxed,* and *easy.* A new marketing campaign used photographer Mario Testino to shoot portraits of multigenerational celebrities with our bags and apparel. The young, statuesque model Alek Wek, actresses Julianne Moore and Katie Holmes, even Moose the dog, who played Eddie from the hit television show *Frasier*, appeared in print ads, catalogs, store windows, and outdoor displays. The campaign was upbeat and approachable while exuding the understated sophistication of our first breakthrough legacy advertising campaign, which was intended to reinforce Coach as a classic American brand by tying us to the nation's heritage. The new campaign tied us to living legends, which placed Coach more firmly in the present, and it felt modern.

Reed's designs also experimented with a juxtaposition of familiarity and surprise. The Mercer Collection was meant to be functional *and* more stylish. The Hippie Flap flat crossbody in our cowhide leather was a streamlined vintage look, an ode to Bonnie Cashin's 1960s design. There were also compact shoulder bags in bright paisley and straw bags with zebra prints. All sold moderately well.

An early disappointment was the multipurpose Neo Collection for "modern moms and glamorous grads," as our 1999 Mother's Day catalog asserted. Women responded well to the more sporty look, but when someone in our offices punched a pencil through its lightweight, structured neoprene material to test its durability, we realized Neo was a fabric-quality miss and discontinued it.

Meanwhile, Jody and her merchants worked closely with consumer insights to develop a more comprehensive approach to market segmentation to help further broaden the brand's personality. Coach already categorized our customers into classic, functional, and aspirational personas. Now we were going beyond that to represent a fuller consumer landscape, and identify archetypes by people's ages, geographies, personal interests, styles, shopping-channel preferences, and more. Like me, Jody was interested in how to move our current customers forward, while pushing us to recognize that the biggest opportunity was to give women who didn't engage with Coach a reason to purchase by understanding *why* they didn't. By now, most women were aware of Coach, and we went after non-buyers with renewed gusto.

Our stores' refresh and expansion were happening in tandem. Dave also was professionalizing our retail operation with new training and incentive programs for sales staff, while modernizing our retail fleet. The bright white spaces and gleaming fixtures displayed fewer products. Their layout created a sense of exploration. We didn't want people to see everything all at once, nor did we want them to assume that the most compelling products were in the front of the store, so the combination of store layout, product mix, and merchandising had to encourage people to stop, pick up products, and meander. All of these factors informed how products were positioned throughout the store, given that, in the United States, shoppers habitually entered stores and turned to their right, especially browsers. (In Japan, they tended to walk to the left.) Renovated stores continued to drive more sales. Eventually, the team would renovate our factory stores with exposed-beam ceilings and an open minimalism that made the spaces more inviting to a more cost-conscious yet discerning customer.

Dave, Jody, Fran, and Reed were also working together to accelerate the flow of new products into stores monthly by applying a cadence of routine newness and seasonality that was common in ready-to-wear fashion apparel retail stores but not accessories. In department stores, bag selections changed only every few months, giving people little incentive to browse.

Prior to 1998, our product development cycle took 24 months. Now we were reducing it to 12 to 18 months, with multiple new product streams happening at once. Products in various stages of development overlapped and informed each other. We constantly toggled between what we had learned and what we had planned, a delicate balance that required a routine of listening, analyzing, retooling, and tweaking.

All these efforts came together in spring 2000 when we hit a triple with a wildly popular new collection called Coach Hamptons. This collection reflected women's growing preference for lighter-weight bags to carry for work, as well as outside the office when they shopped and traveled. Our multi-sized Hamptons totes, handbags, satchels, backpacks, and zippered pouches—named after the sophisticated beach towns where New Yorkers went to relax—came in a custom, sturdy, double-faced cotton canvas with a rubberized layer in between. We produced them in neutrals and an array of pastels like pink and light blue. The bags had contrasting black leather trim and turned-in instead of externally bound edges, which gave the more casual bags a polished look. The vibrant collection popped in our bright stores and window displays and immediately won people over. The Hamptons Small Book Tote was $198. The most popular, a carryall we called Hamptons Weekend Tote, was $258.

The Hamptons Collection was our first breakthrough attempt at fashion, and a eureka moment inside the company. It was like a light went on. Suddenly more people saw what else Coach could be. And they liked it. Coach was starting to feel fresh because the story was new, and the product was still the hero.

• • •

All these creative initiatives were possible because the back end of the business was also changing.

Keith and Jody were starting to establish small, cross-functional, collaborative teams for each product category. The women's handbag team, for example, included a merchandiser, a designer, and representatives from supply chain, retail, and marketing. The teams worked with our business units—retail, wholesale, factory stores, international, and online/catalog—to create a more matrixed organization that improved information flow and decision-making so we could take advantage of the biggest business opportunities, which were becoming clear. As one person put it, people from different departments and reporting relationships felt unofficially tethered because they knew that their work didn't happen in a silo but impacted everyone else's.

Openness was part of the logic of how we operated, and it wasn't new to Coach. I'd always thought it was essential that people share knowledge and views across business units and disciplines. I encouraged people to talk with each other, and I routinely had skip-level meetings with someone's direct report, who might know more than their boss in certain areas, and whom I liked getting to know. When Coach was smaller, it was easier for me to walk through our offices and spark conversations with people at all levels. But as we got larger and opened more facilities, I was more intentional about it. We all had a responsibility to listen to each other. Now we were doing it in more systematic ways, which the increasing complexity of our business required.

Simultaneously, Keith's controlled efforts to globalize manufacturing and diversify suppliers was giving us access to new types of craftspeople, as well as the nimbleness required to expand product offerings at greater speed and scale. That let us get new products into stores and replenish bestsellers more quickly. He rejected five manufacturers for every one we selected. There were bumps, of course, like when we discovered the brass-plated zippers we were sourcing had arrived tarnished after being transported. The culprit was oxidation, so we solved the problem by having the supplier apply a lacquer coating to prevent it.

On the whole, our quality standards were being met and the overall shift to a lower-cost, outsourced manufacturing model was resulting in significant cost savings and margin improvement that would prove critical to our future success.

Wall Street was going to love our double-digit margins—if we went public.

On May 31, 2000, Sara Lee publicly announced that it was reshaping its own business to narrow its focus on a smaller number of consumer packaged goods segments. Among its many changes, it would divest two companies via public offerings by year-end. One was a food service business, PYA/Monarch. The other was Coach. The plan called for Sara Lee to float just under 20% of its ownership in Coach and sell the rest of its stake within 18 months. As part of the plan, Coach would form a board of directors, with Sara Lee controlling four of the seven seats until it fully divested.

Despite the announcement, though, an IPO was not guaranteed. Sara Lee still wanted $1 billion and could cancel or delay the initial offering at any time if Coach didn't keep its financial momentum and garner enough investor support.

• • •

The dual efforts of preparing the company for a likely public offering and a high-profile attempt to reinvent the brand were exciting but also uncertain. There were a lot of levers that needed to be pulled to stay in control of both endeavors. Every day I was aware how much could be lost if we failed to pull the right ones. At stake was the future of Coach to finally be on a path to realize its full potential. I doubled down on a bevy of techniques I'd been developing that together enhanced my endurance and allowed me to work through my fears and remain optimistic.

For one thing, I began occasionally taking brief naps during the workday. At the office, a power nap for five to 15 minutes helped me reset. If I was getting tired and losing my edge, I knew I needed to check out and clear my mind, so I might ask a group to start without me or ask everyone I was meeting with to "take 10" and then regroup. I'd go into my office, shut the door and sit in a chair until my alarm went off or Pat knocked. Afterward I felt more energized and ready to focus.

On weekends, I took refueling naps for longer periods in the late afternoon, up to 90 minutes, telling my family that I was "going under the covers" and would return in about two hours. I would turn the room's temperature down so it was cold and cover myself with heavy blankets. Inevitably I fell into a deep sleep, and I usually woke up feeling refreshed, sometimes like I'd had a full night's sleep. Not everyone can take the time to nap in the middle of a workday, or even on a busy family weekend. But for me, finding just a few minutes in the day to stop, close my eyes, and reset was a powerful tool to clear my mind and reenergize.

I also became aware of when my blood pressure and heart rate spiked, which often happened when I got frustrated in a meeting. Rather than get angry and express my feelings, I'd try to acknowledge to myself what was happening in my body, and ask myself, "Okay, Lew, how are you going to deal with this right now?" I'd attempt to slow my breathing, which calmed me down.

As long as I can remember, I was mindful that I had to manage my time effectively. In the early 1990s, I'd devised a simple triangular model allocating my time across three categories: Building for the Future, Covering the Bases, and Fire Fighting. Of course, it applies to all senior leaders, especially in early-stage businesses and sometimes during times of transformation.

At the top of the pyramid was Building for the Future, because it was my most important responsibility. I tried to consciously spend nearly 40% of my time here by envisioning, strategizing, and iterating how we would grow the business over the next few years. This would include roadmaps for growth, as well as developing and recruiting talent.

Covering the Bases, the middle section of the pyramid, referred to the regular day-to-day operations that were also other people's responsibilities. This usually required about 50% of my time. I needed to work collaboratively with teams in all parts of the business and delegate to my most senior leaders in those areas where they were domain experts and were able to work independently.

Fire Fighting, or dealing with routine problems, was the least valuable way to spend my time. It could be tempting to get involved in everything that went awry, like shipment delays or tech issues. However, putting out regular fires was someone else's job—unless they were extraordinary circumstances—and I had to trust that people could handle them. If Fire Fighting required more than 10% of my time overall, I probably didn't have the right people in the right roles.

If I started to become obsessed and distracted by something that wasn't urgent, I invoked my compartmentalization strategy of "parking" it. Visualizing myself putting the problem in a proverbial mid- or long-term parking lot, like at an airport, to be retrieved and dealt with at a later date gave me immediate comfort and permission not to agonize over it in the present. It was a simple mind game that allowed me to let go and move on to the myriad other issues on my plate.

• • •

While everyone was running fast to rebuild operations, Felice focused on strengthening the foundation, our culture. Without it, the rest was futile.

One of the most important things Felice would do for Coach was institutionalize our workplace values by crafting language to articulate them in more succinct, memorable ways: "The brand is our touchstone." "Customer satisfaction is paramount." "Integrity is our way of life." "Innovation drives winning performance." "Our success depends on collaboration."

The essence of these values was not new to Coach, but now they were being codified.

Felice also helped me express myself better than I was doing on my own, creating new vehicles to share my voice with more frequency and scale. Together we wrote quarterly letters to employees about the state of the business. She also arranged monthly sessions in our boardroom called Lunch with Lew. Any office employee could sign up to eat sandwiches and salads while asking me questions, and the 20 or so spots usually filled fast.

Both the letters and the lunches were also a chance to articulate competencies that made people successful at Coach—and thus made Coach successful:

Don't think of your job as narrowly defined.

Your role is whatever is needed to advance the collective agenda.

Leadership is an attitude, not a title.

Be tougher on yourself than you are on others.

Your job isn't done after you tell someone what to do; you must follow up, have milestones, make sure they deliver.

And one I emphasized often: empowerment or delegation without accountability is abdication.

As the keeper of the culture, Felice had us course correct if we strayed. If my passion and frustration flared up in meetings when I thought someone was not adequately prepared—a habit I never fully kicked—she might slip me a note to tone it down. When we planned a celebratory boat ride around Manhattan for our corporate employees, Felice came to my office upset that the janitorial staff had not been invited. She was right, of course, and I told her to make sure they were welcomed. At another point, a person important to our operations was accused of inappropriate behavior. We were close to the IPO date, and I was inclined to reprimand him instead of letting him go. Felice was appalled and told me I had a choice: "You can fire him or me." Felice stayed and would work with Coach and me in some capacity for more than 15 years.

One of Coach's most important programs, the annual Chairman's Award, was also a way to reinforce our values. For many years this award was given to employees below director level who exemplified excellence. It was a way to celebrate more junior workers who went above and beyond to make extraordinary contributions. Managers could nominate anyone, and I handed out the awards to winners at a luncheon. The highlight was when each manager stood up to tell everyone about the winner they'd nominated. The traits they called out were always more about a person's character and attitude than their expertise. The award luncheon amplified the qualities that made Coach special. People left feeling good about themselves, their colleagues, and the company.

• • •

During fiscal 2000, all of our efforts continued to come together to achieve the financial results we needed. Year-over-year sales were up 8%, to $549 million. Net income was up 130% to $39 million.

We could now also show a solid trend of quarterly same-store sales growth, a comparison of sales in one period to sales during the same period a year prior. Comps, as same-store sales are also known, are the best measurement of a brand and retailer's health at a given moment, as well as a leading indicator of near-term future performance. Our renovated stores were delivering almost double the comps of unrenovated stores. Overall, Coach's comps indicated we'd continue to grow at a compelling rate. With another 50 new stores planned for the next three years, we had a strong story to take to investors—assuming Sara Lee let us get that far.

In August, Sara Lee canceled PYA/Monarch's planned IPO and instead sold the company to a Dutch supermarket chain. Speculation began about whether Coach would meet the same fate, with at least one analyst insisting it wasn't a matter of if Sara Lee would sell us, but to whom. There were even rumors that crystal glassmaker Waterford Wedgwood was interested in buying us. I'd been down that road, and assumed it was still a dead end. Then again, our business had improved since Jide, Reed, and I had made the rounds to LVMH and others, so anything was possible now.

Another potential problem arose in August, when Coach's comps dipped. I worried Sara Lee would halt the IPO if they gained wind of it, so I focused my team on bringing sales back up to show a strong quarter. Putting products on sale was not an option for Coach despite being an easy tactic many retailers use to boost sales fast. Philosophically, Coach didn't put products on sale in our own full-priced stores even to liquidate excess inventory. Selling at full price maintained brand cachet and reinforced Coach as a value 365 days a year. We also didn't want to set a precedent and create pent-up demand for anticipated sale periods. This was the right strategy at that time, so I refused to deviate. To combat the dip in same-store sales, we leveraged our now nimbler supply chain to speed up product delivery so new merchandise scheduled for October and November arrived at stores in September. We also accelerated deliveries to factory stores and increased promotional activity.

As these tactics played out, I forged ahead, assuming an IPO was imminent.

• • •

My only direct interaction with Wall Street had been my ill-fated stock pick as a nascent analyst. Indirectly, I'd been part of a public company with rigorous performance standards that taught me how to operate on a quarterly cadence. I knew what metrics to measure, and I had the discipline required to set and meet performance goals. I also knew how to pivot in response to market shifts to shape near-term results. Fifteen years at Sara Lee gave me and thus Coach a head start compared to companies that go straight from being private to public. Still, I'd never been a public CEO and I had to learn how to communicate with analysts, portfolio managers, media, and the greater investment community.

The challenge was defining Coach to investors at the same time we were redefining it for consumers. I leaned on three people. First, Joe Ellis, a top analyst from Goldman Sachs, the firm leading our public offering. I'd asked Joe to join me on Coach's board because I wanted his knowledgeable, outsider's voice in the room when I was sitting there with four of Sara Lee's executives. I'd also asked Keith Monda to fill Coach's third seat because he had become a thought partner, and someone whose counsel I valued. I also relied on our new head of investor relations, Andrea Resnick, who joined us a few months before the IPO.

When Andrea and I first met, she thought I looked familiar but couldn't peg how she knew me, and she didn't ask. During our second interview, I stopped midway to take a call.

"It's my daughter Tamara," I said as I picked up the phone. The mention of Tamara's name jogged Andrea's memory. She'd babysat for her and Sam in the mid-1970s when our family lived on West End Avenue and Andrea attended Barnard College in Manhattan. Andrea kept this revelation to herself until a few years later when she told me and a few others. We were all shocked and got a good laugh that Coach's head of investor relations once babysat for Lew's kids.

At the time of our interview, though, all I knew about Andrea was that she'd had a successful 15-year career on Wall Street, first as a research analyst for Oppenheimer & Co., then as a portfolio manager at HSBC. I remember being impressed with her from the start even though she'd never worked in investor relations, which made her the least seasoned leader I would hire. But Andrea knew how the Street functioned, and she became integral to helping tell our story, sell Coach to the investment community, and prepare us for our 10-day roadshow to pitch investors on Coach's value proposition.

A big challenge was how to accurately define Coach in the context of the marketplace. There was no widely embraced term for the white space between mass and luxury accessory products. Terms I'd relied on for years to differentiate us, "premium" and "democratized luxury," didn't do it justice.

I distinctly remember sitting at the round table in the executive conference room with a group of people when Joe Ellis told me that Coach needed to declare a position.

"Lew, you can't have one foot on the dock and one on the boat."

This spurred hours of discussion in our offices, with whiteboards full of words. I'm not sure anyone knows the exact moment someone paired the words "accessible" with "luxury," or when we circled that term, realizing that it covered every dimension of who we were, doing the work we needed it to do. Price made Coach more accessible, as did our distribution. We were accessible wherever our target consumers chose to shop. For me, the term "accessible luxury" seemed to fit my long-held vision of Coach as a microcosm of what I liked most about America, a country where so many people had access to better lives and lifestyles. Coach gave more people access to a quality product that became a beloved companion.

The term accessible luxury stuck. It would become part of the fashion industry's lexicon, with Coach credited for coining a term that also jumpstarted an entire market category with the same name. It's possible the term appeared in print for the first time in our roadshow presentation, on a page that showed a pyramid that depicted the overall US handbag and accessories market. The pyramid was divided into three sections. The peak we labeled "Designer." The flat base was "Mass." The space in between we labeled "Accessible Luxury." For us, that included any handbag between $100 and $300—prices that were just within our target consumers' reach. We estimated the overall market to be $6 billion.

Still, it would take more than two words to win over a skeptical, and predominantly male, investment community that didn't intuitively appreciate the emotional connection that exists between a woman and her bag.

• • •

In late September, seven of us, including Keith, Dave, and Andrea, and me, flew around the country to meet with potential investors in Chicago,

Minneapolis, Milwaukee, Houston, Denver, San Diego, Los Angeles, San Francisco, Baltimore, Boston, and New York. It was a heavily orchestrated, grueling 10 days as we tried to sell Coach to potential investors.

"How many bags does a woman really need?" was a frequent question we were asked, implying Coach had a limited runway for long-term growth. Andrea fired back that they were thinking about it wrong.

"Look, a man buys a new wallet when his bills start coming out the bottom. Not because red is in, or because you love suede, or because you want something in straw for spring." She had to explain that the reason women bought new bags had less to do with actual need and more to do with perceived need and desire. We also made a point to show them Coach was creating needs women didn't yet know they had. We showed them sports bags with built-in zip pouches shaped to fit the head of a tennis racquet, and small leather cases to hold electronics in the pre-smartphone era, mainly Blackberries or Palm Pilots.

Another frequent question analysts asked was why someone would buy another Coach bag if the one they already owned was meant to last for years. Again, Andrea explained it was not about needing a new bag but desiring it.

We also told potential investors that unlike designer-dictated bag brands, Coach was consumer-centric. No other fashion and apparel company used this language. Our products reflected input and insights gleaned from consumer research. For example, a designer didn't just randomly decide to add a roomy interior pocket to fit an HP 12c calculator. Instead, women in our focus groups told us their bags didn't have pockets big enough to fit the bulky calculators they carried to and from the office. We took learnings like these to our designers, who didn't balk that a larger pocket ruined the bag's aesthetic. Instead, they figured out how to add it because functionality was part of our brand's ethos.

We also got a lot of questions about why Coach was modernizing a classic. Wasn't it a tremendous risk to start changing it up? Again, Andrea shined. Her background as a portfolio manager helped her answer in terms that made sense to Wall Street.

"If you had an investment portfolio of only consumer staples and those stocks suddenly went out of favor, the best thing you could do is add to it and diversify, right?" Coach's expansion into fashion was about mitigating risk. This they understood.

Some investors got why Coach was unique, but for the most part they didn't want to hear about how we blended magic and logic. They were more interested in nailing down our market position, which also wasn't easy. Was Coach a specialty retail stock? A manufacturer? There was no accessories sector of direct competitors to easily compare us to. When the Street tried to lump us with apparel manufacturers like Tommy Hilfiger, we said no, we're a marketer and a specialty retailer. But there was no retailer quite like us, either. Our integrated, multichannel model, with its direct-to-consumer and wholesale distribution, was a bit of an anomaly. The closest comparison was Tiffany, even though its jewelry wasn't sold in wholesale channels or through outlet stores. Ralph Lauren was multichannel, but like Hilfiger it was considered an apparel brand.

Coach was different in that we were an American accessory brand that operated its own full-price and off-price stores *and* sold at department stores *and* specialty shops, *plus* had direct mail, and almost 200 sites outside the United States, including duty-free shops and department stores. We'd also started selling online.

It would be 10 years before "omnichannel" became a popular way to describe companies that integrated distribution channels and marketing communication like Coach had for many years.

The October date of our IPO approached, and I was feeling ready and eager to have the type of accountability required for the CEO of an independent company. I believed I had the right team, and I'd become increasingly confident that the initiatives we were putting in place would provide a runway for accelerated growth with higher rates of profitability. I also knew that once we crossed that threshold, the stakes would be much higher.

• • •

October 5, 2000, was a cool, cloudy Thursday in Manhattan. A massive chocolate-brown banner with *COACH* in huge white letters hung from the marble facade of the New York Stock Exchange.

Coach was set to offer 7,380,000 shares at $16 a share that would trade under the symbol COH. We'd settled on the price the night before, despite my preference for $15. Every full-time Coach employee—from our leadership team to hourly store staff to unionized workers—was granted five-year stock options as part of a program Felice titled No Employee Left Behind. We also created a way to extend the program to our employees in Japan. If the company did well, this unexpected benefit could help our employees buy homes, pay for their kids' college, or save for retirement. I remember people clapping their hands and even crying when they learned they'd be getting grants. We wanted every employee to feel part of the changes underway. Their buy-in and participation would be a critical success factor, and we'd be asking people to work hard and get out of their comfort zones in the years ahead. Stock options tied to the company's performance were a powerful incentive to rise to the challenge. I wanted to maximize employees' future payouts with a lower vesting price, but our bankers insisted we price the stock at the top end of our initial \$14–\$16 range because there was so much demand.

Some analysts were recommending Coach as a good "old economy" stock. But not everyone was bullish. Astute readers of our prospectus noted that our fundamentals had only recently improved, and that we had a history of misreading market trends and could do so again. Also, we were saddled with a \$190 million debt to Sara Lee, which all proceeds from the IPO would be used to pay off, instead of being invested back in the business, further challenging our growth prospects. The analysts weren't wrong; these were real challenges. But that was tomorrow's worry. Today was a moment to celebrate a milestone. And for once, I did.

A large, exuberant contingent from Coach arrived at the stock exchange early Thursday morning to ring the opening bell. I remember standing on the elevated platform overlooking the chaotic exchange surrounded by my Coach colleagues and my family: Alana, who at 16 was still in high school, and would soon be contemplating college; Sam, at 22, had graduated from college and started working in sports marketing. At 23, Tamara was working in publishing as she contemplated getting her MBA. And, of course, Bobbie. She was the heart of our family, caring for the kids and the house while also running Sandbox Industries and leading a nonprofit called New Jersey SEEDS. Bobbie was still passionate about education, and New Jersey SEEDS was an incredible organization that gave young people from lower-income families access to leading high schools and colleges through scholarships and other supports. Bobbie played a significant role in growing the organization. More personally, she was my most trusted advisor, and she was more important to achieving this milestone for Coach than any single person who worked for the company.

I know my father would have been proud of me, as he always was.

As for my mother, who was 87, she was thrilled watching it all unfold on CNBC. I doubt she was thinking about the day in ninth grade when the two of us walked out of my guidance counselor's office. Only in retrospect do people tend to recognize pivotal moments in their lives, and I'm certain that if my mom had acquiesced to Mr. Schmutter's vision of her son's future, I would not be standing in the New York Stock Exchange taking a bag business public. A lot had happened in between, of course, but it only takes one bold decision to make a lifetime of other decisions possible. I owe my mother a debt of gratitude.

After several media interviews, I returned to Coach's offices to celebrate with newer employees as well as long-timers including Pat Cherry, Fred "Mr. Leather" Friesenhahn, and many others. We toasted with champagne to the beginning of a journey that we knew had the potential to unleash possibilities for all of us. Now that we were public, the financial by-product of Coach knocking it out of the park could forever change many lives, especially Coach's senior leaders. As CEO I owned about 570,000 shares of Sara Lee stock that converted to Coach shares.

We closed the day with an $860 million valuation based on a closing price just over $20 a share, on a non-split adjusted basis.

For the second time in 20 years I felt liberated. Once again, Coach and I had more control of our destinies, free of constraints to grow. But beneath the joy was a question: Were we truly free? I'd traded a hierarchical, conservative conglomerate for the scrutiny of Wall Street. I welcomed it, but now we would answer to investors with their single focus on financial performance and their insatiable appetite for short-term growth. The fallout from failing to meet expectations was more than a black box drawn around my photo, being disliked by colleagues, or even fired. Now at stake was the financial health of hundreds of employees and investors, and the future of a company I loved as much as any founder loves a business they built from the ground up.

From the moment I woke up each morning I was intent on getting out of the house early enough to beat traffic so I'd arrive at the office in time for my daily 8 a.m. meeting. Some days I was up at 4:30 a.m. so I could exercise, which I made time for because it was so crucial to my physical and emotional health. After working out with a trainer at a small gym I'd race home to shower and dress so I could reach the George Washington Bridge by 7 a.m. before tens of thousands of other commuters. The GWB was the world's busiest suspension bridge. A massive steel structure that spans the Hudson River, connecting New Jersey and Manhattan with two multilane decks. As I approached the bridge, I would often recall my father. During World War II, when President Franklin D. Roosevelt crossed the bridge in his motorcade, my dad was among the sharp-shooters assigned to climb the bridge's suspension towers where he was stationed with a rifle to help protect the president. Just approaching the bridge on the New Jersey side and seeing those towers in the distance could make my heart beat faster if I saw a lot of cars. Unless I crossed the GWB early enough, I risked getting stuck in crawling traffic, which would give me too much time to think, and excessively ruminate about the day ahead.

The nightmare that began before the IPO also hadn't stopped. Many nights I still awoke drenched in sweat after dreaming that I was walking down Madison Avenue, terrified that I was destined to show up to a crucial meeting in a suit but with bright blue woolly socks and no shoes. Now that Coach was public, being unprepared in any regard was not an option we could afford or tolerate. We had to be on our game every single day. The stakes were higher, and they were also personal. If Coach failed, Lew failed. In my mind, our identities were inextricably tied together, for better or for worse.

PART FOUR

Growth Years

CHAPTER 13

Breaking Through

Shortly after the IPO I told my executive team we were running a marathon. We had just run the first mile, and we had 25 more to go. Each quarter of the fiscal year was equivalent to a mile. There was no stopping and no goal other than to keep moving, keep improving. Each week and each month were as vital as the next.

I felt confident in the team I'd assembled, but I couldn't allow that confidence to stop us from being maniacal about making sure nothing slipped through the cracks. That included how we communicated with the Street, which was as crucial as how we executed internally. From day one we treated our credibility with investors as paramount, and thanks to Andrea we began public life by managing Wall Street with the same rigor that we managed the business.

The two of us diligently prepared for every earnings call and analyst meeting, writing and rewriting slides and scripts, sometimes changing sentences the night before only to change them back the next morning. Words mattered as much as our financial guidance. Coach never projected a number we believed we couldn't make, and almost always gave ourselves enough latitude so we wouldn't risk missing expectations. It was no accident that Coach became known on the Street for predictability and consistency.

Being surefooted on every analyst call meant coming armed with the same depth of knowledge that I expected people to have in our internal business review meetings. Andrea would prepare detailed answers to dozens of questions that she thought an analyst or reporter might ask. She and her investor relations (IR) team also created fact books for each call, a practice that began with our roadshow. These thick binders were full of data points about our business and the business of accessories, handbags, and specialty retail. Over time we triangulated our data with data from competitors' public statements and industry groups like NPD, which tracked department stores' sales. We'd connect these disparate pieces of information to develop new knowledge about, say, the actual size of the handbag category and Coach's share of it. For Wall Street to understand Coach, we had to proactively educate the Street about the industry. No other company undertook this kind of education, and over time Coach was also perceived as a market expert. And yet, the better analysts would put some facts together in ways we had not, asking questions in a way that advanced my own knowledge, or got me thinking differently about certain things.

Putting together those Q&As and fact books required input from people throughout the company. Andrea was smart about that, too, and made a point of educating managers about the vital role of IR. Since every Coach employee had stock, they also felt a sense of ownership and responded quickly when IR needed their input. It helped that we had a collaborative culture where people already knew how their role and other people's roles fit into the business. All of these activities strengthened our effectiveness as a public company.

Inevitably, our share price became like a daily report card, and it was hard for me to accept that there was a lot we couldn't control. External events moved the market overall, and a sharp decline in our share price could sink my stomach. I took any recommendation to sell the stock almost personally, and I didn't hesitate to call an analyst who issued a "sell" to find out why and tell them I thought they were wrong. It rarely made a difference. That's just how Wall Street worked. People had their opinions and reasons. After a heated conversation, Andrea might call an offended analyst back to smooth any feathers I'd ruffled.

"You have to understand," she'd explain to the party who was either annoyed or even hurt by my call, "you've downgraded his baby."

Learning to live with the scrutiny of Wall Street and vagaries of the market was not easy, but it was necessary. It also made me tighten my grip on what we could control.

• • •

Because I loved a good analogy, I also started to tell people that we were turning Coach into a superhighway. After occupying a single lane since our early days, we were now focused on enhancing the brand's personality with additional traits to bring in new consumers and increase our share of existing customers' closets. But what traits? And which consumers? That's what we were figuring out.

One of our biggest aha moments was that fewer younger women—roughly between the ages of 18 and 30—were buying Coach, and those who already owned a Coach bag weren't compelled to buy another. For this younger cohort, Coach was what their mothers carried. We knew our customers skewed older, but recent research revealed the growing appetite that younger women had for fashion. Here was a massive market we were missing. But what did a fashionable Coach bag for younger generations look like? And how was it different from what we'd already tried?

We would never bet the farm on any one market at the expense of others, especially our core consumers. I could recall the time in the mid-1990s when I'd visited a Coach store in San Juan and met a woman shopping with her teenage daughter, her mother, and her grandmother. All four generations loved Coach. Unfortunately, we'd lost some of that multigenerational appeal. Could we get it back by tapping into a particular zeitgeist that crossed demographic and psychographic archetypes, and create something relevant to the widest possible group of consumers?

There was another thing we were learning. When we asked women in focus groups what attributes they wanted in a bag, the term "fun to be with" kept coming up. Anyone from Coach listening to the group from the other side of the one-way glass would roll their eyes because Coach was many things, but fun wasn't one of them. We were a serious brand. Not much fun since Bonnie Cashin delighted people with her whimsical shapes 30 years earlier. This was consistently confirmed on surveys that asked people to rank more than a dozen attributes that they associated with different brands. Coach came back as earnest and hardworking. Kate Spade was the one you took to a party. "Fun to be with" became an inside joke as well as a business imperative.

Could we create products that brought a smile to people's faces?

Yet another clue emerged from our enhanced scrutiny of luxury brands. European designers had long been famous for so-called logo products that used their monograms as design elements. Louis Vuitton's overlapping *L*s and *V*s wallpapered its bags and luggage. Chanel had its interlocking *C*s,

Gucci its hugging *G*s. This logo treatment had gone in and out of style over the years, but its popularity was surging again during the 1990s and early 2000s, especially as the European brands moved into the United States. But no American accessory brand had anything equivalent in recognition or mass adoption. What really intrigued us was the immense popularity of luxury logo products in Asia, especially Japan, where conspicuous consumption was a cultural phenomenon. Coach was already a player in Japan, with a growing presence.

Was the logo treatment right for Coach? We'd never shouted our identity. Our lozenge tags dangled from bags with modesty; the chain could even be detached if you preferred the anonymity. The idea of Coach declaring itself so boldly with a blatant monogram seemed inconsistent with its understated nature. But what if we embraced the logo concept in a way that preserved that heritage? What would that look like? Could we execute it so it conveyed a dramatic departure from "mom's handbag" to capture the interest of young, fashion-oriented women but without alienating their more classic moms?

We began developing a Coach logo collection during 1999. By then I'd expanded my mindset to think beyond our narrow lane, because I understood the necessity of taking more dramatic departures from our status quo. I trusted the data and the collective judgment of the team, and I agreed that there was an unmet need for logo-like products at more affordable prices, especially given our planned expansion into Asia. And I was comfortable taking the leap because by now we had the capability. In fact, we never would have arrived at this conclusion without the knowledge and structural changes that our new team had brought to Coach.

Inventing a logo platform became a business necessity, and we immediately started to develop what we called Coach Signature.

Reed felt strongly that our logo be the letter *C* in the original font, even though he had changed it to be more modern. The original *C*, with its thick curved spine that tapered to thinner upper and lower strokes, was authentic and recognizable, providing a visual anchor to Coach's history. The familiar font also avoided the risk of Coach coming off like we were imitating other brands that began with *C*, like Chanel or Celine. Reed began to visually manipulate our *C*—upside down, sideways, interlocking—to come up with a graphic that was scalable and adaptable to different products.

At the same time that we designed a pattern, we also searched for the right material. I set strict guidelines to ensure that whatever we chose held true to our DNA: It had to be durable—you shouldn't be able to punch a pencil through it—as well as stain-resistant and waterproof. For functionality, it had to be lightweight and usable year-round. Ultimately, the team landed on jacquard, a fabric that had designs that were knit or woven into it. Jacquards are complex to produce, requiring special looms that alternate horizontal and vertical threading. Italian mills produced the best woven fabrics, although rarely at costs that would keep Coach's pricing affordable. Eventually we found a mill in Italy, Limonta, that could help us develop a custom jacquard within our cost constraints. Collaborating with the mill, we produced dozens of fabric samples with the *C* in different dimensions, sizes, scales, and colorways.

Finally, Reed landed on a base pattern that incorporated variations of two *C*s next to each other in some way: facing one another, their tips connected; stacked, with both *C*'s facing forward or both facing backward; side-by-side, with both facing up or down. Alternating the images of twin *C*'s created various patterns that both hid and emphasized the logo, and felt modern yet classic.

Once we landed on the fabric and a base pattern, we had to find a facility to construct the bags. Our current stable of fabricators specialized in leather, so we cast a wide net to find factories in China that worked with other materials and met our quality standards. We'd send contenders the jacquard fabric with our technical specifications to make prototype bags, which we rejected or refined.

We also had to take pricing into consideration when sourcing suppliers and fabricators. We intentionally priced our logo bags modestly lower than most of our leather bags because similar styles *not* made of leather didn't convey as high a value to people.

All this iterative, overlapping work was a massive effort shepherded by a small group that routinely convened at our sample-making facility in Florence, where bags were handcrafted, reviewed, tweaked, and remade—sometimes all in the same afternoon.

Two photos of early sample Signature bags appeared in the presentation we'd prepared for the IPO roadshow. If you weren't looking closely you'd barely notice them. And if you did notice something different amid our monotone leather products, you probably would not have guessed that the bags with the twin *C*s were going to be such a game changer. Even we couldn't predict what was coming.

• • •

It's hard for people to imagine a product that does not yet exist. You can describe it and show drawings and do your best to explain it, but until people have a physical thing to touch and feel you just can't predict how something new will resonate.

For all our reliance on research, we had no way to confirm the degree to which people would embrace Coach Signature. All we knew for sure was that it checked multiple boxes of what our new target consumers and current Coach customers wanted: It was fashionable, durable, lightweight, even fun. And it was priced right.

Initial focus groups in the United States came back lukewarm. But in Japan the response was so enthusiastic that we knew we had a hit with Japanese consumers. Inside Coach, some employees raised eyebrows, worried that such a deliberate attempt at fashion would tarnish our brand's authenticity. Felice was among those who wasn't a fan of Signature—she preferred her more understated Hamptons tote—but her mother loved it! For most others inside Coach, logo products brought a smile to their faces. We hoped they would do the same in the marketplace. But the truth was we really didn't know just how big Signature might be, and because we took measured risks, we were conservative with initial production.

We began an eight-week pilot, shipping thousands of Signature bags to 30 stores in the United States and Japan, with the intention of tracking daily sales. The results would tell us how broadly to launch the collection. One week in, I had a meeting with Fran to go over various ways we might proceed based on the pilot. Fran walked into my office with a thick stack of PowerPoint documents she'd prepared for me. She just stood there, threw up her arms with a sense of joy, and flung the presentation into the air. Dozens of pages wafted to the floor.

"Well, this is out," she said, going on to tell me that 80% of the Signature products had already sold. In just one week! Whatever projections were in her presentation were no longer valid. Most of our inventory was now gone. Like vapor. We had no back inventory and not nearly enough fabric on order. And once we did order it, the mill could only make so much at a time. We also had no suitable distribution plan to meet what was clearly a demand we had grossly underestimated.

"There's only one thing to do now and it's one word," Fran said. "Lew, do you know what that word is?" She answered before I could respond. "Chase," she said. "We have to chase product." Which basically meant that we had to move faster than we ever had and not let demand outrun us.

In any consumer business, it's truly rare for a new product or collection to catapult the trajectory of the company. So it was thrilling for us, but the overnight sensation was also a bit of a shock. Mind-boggling even for an industry veteran like Jody, who couldn't believe the sales numbers. To figure out just how much we should actually produce, I insisted we depth test it, so I told Fran to pick 10 stores—three of our highest-performing and at least three with more average sales—to track how the bags sold.

For the next months and even into the next year, we scrambled to catch supply up to demand as we splashed the Signature pattern on hats, umbrellas, shoes, key chains, even dog sweaters.

In early 2001, the same year we turned 60, Coach had the most successful product launch in the company's history. By December, Signature bags and accessories accounted for 20% of sales in the United States and 40% in Japan.

This breakout collection wasn't the result of luck, serendipity, or an accident. Nor was it the result of one person's creative vision. Inside Coach, the creation of Signature was, in many ways, the ultimate manifestation of magic and logic. Our merchants' immersive curiosity and instincts about where consumers were and where they were going, paired with the insights gleaned from methodical research, revealed that we were missing women who were hungry for fashion and logo products. Especially Japanese women who primarily bought logo bags from European luxury brands. We needed our designers to boldly imagine what a Coach logo might look like, but they had to do so in conjunction with our merchants to ensure the designs they came up with would resonate in the marketplace. Extreme collaboration across functions and roles was also imperative to produce Signature products at prices our target consumers would be willing to spend.

The undertaking also required a belief that such an unconventional creative move was the right thing for the greater good of the business, even if it felt uncomfortable to some. It also demanded a willingness to hold past and present in our minds at the same time—being open to a different look without forsaking Coach's recognizable product codes and equities.

The market's explosive response to Signature hearkened back to one of my favorite descriptions of Coach's magic-plus-logic approach: When various elements come together to strike the right spot and catch fire, in a kind of spontaneous combustion that creates a product whose spirit matches users' personal values and actual lifestyle.

It's worth noting that, as CEO, I more than anyone else, had to welcome and embrace dramatic change, in my mind and in the company, while insisting that we not abandon the past. I am not sure a CEO new to Coach would have had such fidelity to our heritage. There's a bigger lesson for incumbent CEOs and founders of discretionary consumer brands who want to grow their businesses: embrace change within the boundaries of your brand.

Signature's launch was a seminal moment for Coach. The ultimate interplay of magic and logic resulted in fashion innovation that became a cornerstone of our rejuvenation. Millennials gobbled up Signature bags and accessories in different versions. Black on white. White on tan. When we added Signature bags in soft pink, they flew off shelves. Many older customers loved Signature totes, and we incorporated the twin *C* pattern into the popular Hamptons collection of bags and countless other products.

Signature's business dividends went beyond sales and profits. We attracted and hired younger professionals now that the brand resonated with that demographic. The rapidly growing sales of Signature, with its higher margins, gave us unexpected infusions of cash so we could more quickly build out our infrastructure, with better IT and reporting systems. Keeping up with the success of Signature forced us to become a more fine-tuned business more quickly. Signature also catapulted Coach's popularity in Asia. An early poll of 400 women in Japan who'd recently bought handbags revealed that 37% of those who'd bought Signature were first-time Coach buyers, and 30% were under 26 years old.

Coach ended fiscal 2001, our first full year as a public company, with net sales up 8.5% to $600 million, and net income up 73%, to $67 million. As predicted, Wall Street loved our performance, particularly our significantly improved margins.

That fall a *Forbes* journalist did the first profile of Coach since our IPO. It was a chance to tell our revival story, and we invited Joanne Gordon to sit in on some meetings, see our sample-making facility, and interview me, Dave, Reed, and others. The piece had a full-page photo of me standing on Coach's roof, my arms wrapped around a red Signature handbag with the headline "Serial Tinkerer." Not a term I particularly liked but that I had to admit was true. The piece was generally positive. "This is what the aftermath of a makeover looks like," it read, which in retrospect seems like a premature declaration, considering what was yet to come.

A *Worth* magazine article, "Growth in Store," contended that there was no other company out there quite like Coach because we gave upscale shoppers good value and were a chance for mass-market buyers to splurge.

Our momentum continued into fiscal 2002, outpacing our stated goals and analyst estimates. Sales increased 20% to $719 million, substantially faster than the industry's overall sales growth of about 5%. Sales at full-priced retail stores that year were about $865 per square foot, almost five times that of traditional retailers like the Gap. A UBS analyst told *Fortune,* "No retail chain like this in the U.S. has this kind of sales" for its article, "How Coach Got Hot: The Maker of the Indestructible Purse Finally Considers Style."

Our net income soared 31% to $88 million, in large part because of our ongoing migration to lower-cost manufacturing. The *New York Post* compared our earnings to a runaway train.

Behind the numbers was a brand with increased relevancy and recognition, with *Lucky* magazine naming Coach the most "splurgeworthy luxury brand."

Consumers and the media got us, and by now many in the investment community also got the logic of Coach. A Morgan Stanley retail analyst told *Fortune* that what differentiated Coach from other fashion brands was "a tremendous amount of testing." That year we spent about $2 million just on consumer surveys and studies, and our database was up to 7 million households. He also credited Coach with inducing people to buy more handbags in general, "changing the way our particular market worked." That market was now being called accessible luxury by people outside Coach. It seemed as if Coach had officially made a market.

Coach's stock rose more than 300% between the IPO in October 2000 and November 2002, while other brands struggled in the languishing economy. *Women's Wear Daily,* the fashion industry's business bible, asked, "What's Coach's secret?" in an article headlined "Frankfort's Coach Approach." Of course, Coach's success was not *my* approach, but a team effort by many people who made countless collaborative decisions for the greater good of the business. When another reporter asked me how Coach would be able to maintain our "sizzling" growth rate as we got bigger, my response was the same I'd given for years—by balancing magic and logic. The reporter's response? "Keeping that balance over the long term would be a neat trick indeed."

In fiscal 2003, Coach's sales growth accelerated, increasing 32% to $953 million. Comparatively, the rate of growth was quite remarkable given that the retail industry was up just 7.5%. Our earnings that year skyrocketed to $146 million, up 67%. For context, these kinds of results are rarely achieved unless a company is firing on all cylinders.

Overall, Coach's first three years as a public company truly felt like the marathon we were on, as we opened more than 40 new US stores, expanded our most productive stores, and renovated the full-priced fleet. We continued to innovate and diversify our product mix to increase Coach's share of our existing customers' wardrobes and bring in stylish, younger women. Store traffic and conversion rates were rising, and our 18- to 24-year-old consumer segment had doubled, representing 11% of sales, up from 5% in 1996.

Beyond big strategies, every corner of the company paid attention to details. Of course, we continued to respect and listen to women, and what we heard informed our actions. We knew, for example, that giving Coach products as gifts accounted for 40% of all purchases, so our integrated marketing campaigns emphasized gifting at major holidays. We also displayed prewrapped items to make gift buying easier for shoppers. Many bags also came with protective cloth coverings, a signal of precious cargo. In stores, we put catalogs that looked more like coffee-table books into millions of customers' shopping bags, and placed sales receipts in Coach-branded envelopes.

Behind the scenes we were refining our manufacturing and supply chain while diversifying our supplier base and tightly managing inventories, processes that drove gross margins higher. Our global office and retail workforce had also ballooned to 3,500.

The granularity combined with the fast pace could feel grueling, but there were always moments of levity, like when a meeting started to feel overwhelming and Jody would throw open her arms and declare, "Relax, people. It's only handbags!"

A lot of positive articles ended with the same caveat: Could Coach maintain its pace of growth? Every day was a new chance to prove we could, as long as we didn't stop running the marathon.

By mid-August 2003, I was elated but exhausted, and I was desperate for my scheduled two-week vacation with Bobbie and the kids. But instead of going to the beach as planned, I found myself stuck in a hospital bed, and plunging into my second dark period.

• • •

In July I'd gone for a routine prostate cancer screening that returned a higher than normal antigen reading of 4.7. My doctor thought it was an anomaly, but to be safe we scheduled a biopsy. It was a routine procedure, and I remember inquiring what percentage of patients reacted adversely to it. I was told that one out of 200 get an infection, and I did the math. Half of 1% didn't seem like a huge risk.

Two days after the biopsy, on Thursday, August 14, I was in an afternoon leadership meeting in our 12th-floor executive conference room. It was the last one before most of us took time off before what was sure to be our busiest holiday season yet. We were likely going over plans for holiday when I started feeling dizzy, and woozy in my lower torso.

"Let's break for five minutes," I said, and excused myself.

In the men's room I saw enough blood in my urine to know something was wrong. I put my hand to my forehead. I was burning up. Suddenly the bathroom lights flicked off and I was standing in near-total darkness. As I made my way back to the conference room someone told me we'd lost power. Apparently, so had around 50 million people in seven nearby states and parts of Canada in what we would soon learn was the start of a massive, multiday power outage.

I adjourned the meeting and told Pat I was feeling lousy and needed to leave. With the power dead and the elevator not working I walked down 12 flights of stairs. Outside, the streets were crowding with people filtering out of their powerless buildings. It had to be at least 90 degrees in the city, yet I had chills. I got my car out of the parking lot and headed toward the GWB, weaving through clogging intersections as I talked with Bobbie on my car's cell phone. She was home packing for our family vacation. The next morning we were scheduled to drive to Sagaponack, Long Island, where we planned to spend two weeks in a house we'd bought the prior year. It had been a substantial purchase, and Bobbie and I had taken a deep breath before committing. Affording it required selling some of my Coach stock for the first time since the IPO.

The pain was much worse as I turned into our driveway in Tenafly to see a worried Bobbie and her sister, Ellen, waiting for me with my niece, Leslie, a resident in medical school. She took one look at me and insisted I go to the ER. Bobbie drove me to nearby Englewood Hospital, where backup generators were keeping lights and essential equipment running. It was a zoo. Every curtained room in the emergency room was full, so after being admitted I spent the next few hours in a dim hallway on a rolling bed in excruciating pain, the shooting sting in my groin escalating.

Despite my high threshold for pain it was all I could do not to pass out before finally seeing a urologist who'd been called to the hospital to assess my condition. He said I had all the signs of an *E. coli* infection, likely from the biopsy. It would clear up with medication, but I couldn't be prescribed anything until the lab cultured the bacteria, and complications from the power outage were preventing the lab from doing anything other than life-and-death work. There was no way to treat me until the tests came back. I had to wait it out.

Instead of going to the beach to relax I spent the next several days hooked to a morphine drip and a catheter. Quite literally tethered to the bed, I couldn't easily get up and needed assistance just to turn over. All I could do was lie there while the infection played itself out and we waited for the hospital's power to be restored. The days were a blur as family and friends trickled in and out. I felt trapped, because I was. I also felt my mind and emotions descending to that dark place I hadn't experienced for a long while.

After five days my *E. coli* was officially diagnosed and I could go on antibiotics. When another urologist from Columbia Presbyterian finally arrived, he told me that I did indeed have prostate cancer. Thankfully we'd caught it early, and with the right treatment I believed I would beat it. If anything, I felt grateful that my prognosis was not worse, and that I had the financial means to get to an outcome millions of other cancer patients would never experience. So I had faith that I would ultimately be fine. I was very lucky, and it was just plain bad timing that the *E. coli* infection and the Northeast power outage had hit at the same time.

During that week in the hospital, my emotional and mental states started to slip into another depressive state. It was triggered by the pain and uncertainty, as well as, I would later ascertain, the overall experience of having such little control from the moment I arrived at the ER. The lack of control I felt was similar to how I felt when my situation was deteriorating as a group officer at Sara Lee. The circumstances were also quite different, of course. But now I realized I couldn't just muscle my way through my emotional low without more support. There was too much at stake at work if I couldn't function at my best.

Since the IPO, Coach's growth had been like a rocket ship. The faster we grew, the more everyone's expectations rose. Especially Wall Street's. Any significant misstep could cause us to slow our momentum and miss a quarter, hurting the stock and dampening morale. Everyone inside Coach was executing beautifully against a strategy that was delivering. We were working hard and enjoying the success it brought. I didn't see how I could give any less than I was, so I wanted to prevent myself from sliding further into a dark place.

Unlike years ago, however, I had developed an appreciation for antidepressant medication after witnessing its positive effects on people I knew. From the hospital, I called a close family friend who was also our doctor to ask him to suggest a therapist who could prescribe medication, as well as some form of therapy. I reached out to the psychiatrist he recommended, and I scheduled a visit.

I left the hospital having lost almost 15 pounds and feeling like a shell of myself. From a governance perspective I had a fiduciary responsibility to share my cancer diagnosis with our board, and once I was home I called each one individually. I remember writing notes about the points I wanted to make so I was clear about my condition and instilled confidence that I would get through this. I informed Irene Miller and the rest of the board that I'd already told members of my senior staff, including Felice, Keith, Andrea, and Reed. Bobbie and I were researching treatments, and I'd let the board know when we chose a path. I did not explicitly mention my mental state, but I reassured them that if at any time I felt my performance was lagging, I'd discuss with the board what actions to take.

After Labor Day weekend I returned to the office determined not to let anyone else know or suspect what I was dealing with. I couldn't distract the business from the roll we were on. I also didn't have the energy to address people's concerns for my health. It was all I could do to keep my back-to-back meeting schedule and summon my usual energy despite my diminished zest.

Over the next several weeks Bobbie and I decided radiation was the best path forward—I just had to wait a few months for the infection to completely leave my body for treatment to begin. Meanwhile, at the office, I kept up a strong front, fearing what might happen if I didn't bring my A game to work every single day.

I was grappling with a reality that many people faced as their careers progressed and they took on ever higher roles and more responsibility. The bigger and more successful we became, the more was at stake when we didn't perform. Like most leaders, I served multiple stakeholders. Knowing that many people would be affected by my decisions was a mental load I carried, even more so since Coach went public. I was always conscious of its weight, and in some ways it was a motivator. Not until now, when my performance risked being compromised, did I feel the potential for it to overwhelm me.

In response to all this stress, I tried to influence what I could. I began taking an antidepressant to reduce the depths of my lows. Medication takes a while to make a noticeable difference, but it did make me feel better just to know I was taking some control of my mental health. To keep my energy up and prevent negative thoughts from distracting me day-to-day, I called on various coping techniques I'd used to manage previous periods of low energy and high stress. I took power naps. I ran and exercised as often as possible. I saw Edgar, our masseur, who redirected my energy to ease physical tension. I also tried to catch myself if I became unduly impatient with people.

When I felt my heart rate spike in a meeting, I tried to slow my breathing—four seconds inhale, four seconds exhale. I might even call a 10-minute break to close my eyes and reset.

My radiation treatments began in January, so for 13 weeks I left the house at 5:30 a.m. four days a week for an hour of treatment at Sloan Kettering in Manhattan before going into the office to make my usual 8 a.m. meeting. Similar to how I was caring for my mental health, just knowing I was taking steps to eradicate the cancer gave me a sense of control and a little more peace of mind.

My weekly therapy sessions began as soon as I returned to work, and the effects were more immediate. Talking with a trained clinician about what was on my mind and how I was feeling was invaluable. Our sessions were a safe place to put burdens I didn't even realize I needed to release. My therapist was a pragmatic thought partner. We mostly focused on my daily struggles so I could move through them a little easier, and with new perspective. We might discuss how to alter my schedule to keep up at work while going through radiation. And just having her reassure me that depressive feelings were normal, even if they weren't comfortable, helped me relax. It became a confidential place to work through a difficult conversation I might need to have with a colleague, and I was able to air emotions before they became overwhelming or debilitating. As time went on and she got to know me, she offered insights into my behavior patterns.

Unlike working with an executive coach, therapy was longer term. And more about me as a whole person, not primarily how I showed up professionally. We began to talk about how I could strengthen my relationships and communication with the kids and Bobbie, which my family would agree was beneficial for all of us. Despite my fascination with the human condition, it was new to dive so deeply into myself. I frequently left our sessions feeling lighter, musing about what we'd discussed.

By April 2004, the radiation ended and I was now in remission. My emotional health was also stabilized, and I was back to feeling like myself. I continued taking my antidepressant medication, and I kept up therapy, with regular sessions that became essential to my self-care regimen. Having time planned to unload whatever was troubling me usually allowed me to park my worries because I knew I'd revisit them soon. It was not always easy to pull myself away from work earlier than usual for my late-afternoon appointments, but I made sure I made it to her office.

Of course, misfortunes can make us stronger. The difficult period that followed my *E. coli* infection and cancer diagnoses ended up introducing me to therapy as a valuable life tool that I wish I'd taken advantage of a decade earlier. And not just for periods when I was really struggling, but also during long stretches when my stress felt less heavy and more routine. It was an opportunity to reflect more broadly and gain insight into my own motivations and patterns. Therapy also helped me identify what, exactly, I feared and how I defined failure. Like many people, I had fears that ranged from the tangible to the existential, from the bottom to the top of Maslow's hierarchy of needs. Just talking about the specific fear helped me address it. Tame it. Disaggregate it so I could understand its components and see what I had some control over. I could also take time to feel it. I also learned it was important to let the emotion of a negative thought run through me—I had to allow myself to feel the feeling—so its energy didn't get stuck, and build up in my mind and body.

I would also begin to accept that my fears would never disappear. Regardless of how Coach performed, or how I performed, no amount of accomplishment or success would somehow heal me. The fear-drive-failure-excellence connection was a continuous cycle that fed itself, and it was part of my human condition. The best I could do was try to manage its many manifestations—and I still had a lot to learn on that front.

Did these and other epiphanies and benefits happen all at once? Of course not. It took time for me to be able to articulate much of this about myself. Therapy is an ongoing process, and I would see the same therapist for the next twenty years. To this day we still have sessions as I continue to learn more about how to more peacefully exist in the world, for myself and for others.

Being in therapy is not, as some people still perceive it, an admission of weakness. It's a strength. Caring for our mental health is as empowering and productive as caring for our physical health. And like exercise, its benefits are both short- and long-term. Sometimes we see them immediately. Others we trust are taking root. Frankly, I firmly believe that regular opportunities for self-reflection and self-knowledge with a trained practitioner are vital tools, especially for those of us in leadership roles. Any senior leader who doesn't feel the weight of their responsibility is kidding themselves. Fear is normal and, as I knew from Coach, it can have positive benefits especially when paired with a drive for excellence.

There's no doubt that my experiences seeing a therapist made me better equipped to lead, especially as we continued to expand beyond our US borders, and as the stakes kept getting higher.

CHAPTER 14

Building the Brand and Business Away from Home

In early 2005, a senior executive from the Japanese department store Mitsukoshi unexpectedly flew to New York City and asked for a private meeting. Mitsukoshi had been Coach's most important distributor in Japan for almost two decades, and I welcomed the exec into my office and closed the door. He'd come all this way to inform me that Louis Vuitton had halted construction of one of its in-store boutiques. They were refusing to resume unless Coach stopped expanding its own space in the same Mitsukoshi store. Coach, he said, had to cease our planned renovation. He hoped I understood. Of course I did not, and I told him we'd continue with our plans. We had a contract.

This wasn't the first time we heard that LVMH was making similar threats. I had a sense of how Bernard Arnault, the CEO of LVMH, felt about Coach. I believed he saw us as an impostor. I even heard secondhand that he once called Coach "the McDonald's of luxury." Although likely intended as an insult, it actually struck me as a compliment: I saw it as evidence that he considered Coach a formidable competitor. LV was by far Japan's bestselling imported bag brand, with an estimated 28% share of the market. By our own estimates Coach was number two, at 8%. We knew we were taking market share from LV—between fiscal 2001 and 2005, Coach's sales in Japan had grown from $45 million to $370 million, an astonishing 800%—and we had every intention of continuing to expand our presence in Mitsukoshi and other department stores.

On March 9, 2005, we filed a complaint in Tokyo against LVMH with the Japan Fair Trade Commission (JFTC) accusing LVMH of harassment and anticompetitive practices in Japan. Our complaint, which JFTC considered a private document and never made public, described a pattern of conduct over the past year in which LVMH engaged in inappropriate or threatening behavior by exerting pressure on department stores where Coach was also sold. We alleged that LVMH threatened department store management with either not going forward with development plans, or pulling the LV brand out of certain locations entirely, if Coach was allowed to open or expand their in-store shops. LVMH's efforts didn't yet have a material impact on our sales, but we believed they would if we didn't act. We wanted to challenge their behavior in the public forum to stand up for fair play and consumer choice, and to protect our own interests abroad. We announced the complaint in our own press release, which the *Wall Street Journal,* the *New York Times,* and other media picked up, perhaps intrigued by the David-versus-Goliath tale that Coach intentionally played up.

There was a good chance the complaint would go nowhere, but we filed it nonetheless to try to deter their bullying and frankly embarrass LVMH, compelling them to at least be less overt about their efforts to thwart Coach's growth. We also hoped department stores would be less prone to accept their demands.

The Japanese commission launched an investigation, which ended six months later with no action or conclusion. Our hope that the increased scrutiny that the complaint brought would end LVMH's interference seemed to have worked, given that we never again heard of any similar demands.

LVMH had played many roles throughout my Coach career. I'd admired and learned from its practices. I'd invited the company to study our business, and I was relieved when Sara Lee declined their offer to acquire us. Now we were fending off their attempts to strangle us. How had we gotten to the point that this esteemed global brand saw Coach as a threat? Understanding the answer requires going back in time to consider the knowledge- and insight-driven ways Coach went about its international expansion—primarily in Asia, which was essential to our overall success.

• • •

Coach's first foray abroad was in the early 1970s, when Miles and Lillian opened the Coach store in Paris. That store had closed by the time Miles sold

Coach to Sara Lee in 1985, and at that time I was ready to begin to strategically expand outside the United States.

I was keeping an eye out for someone to lead it when, in 1986, our Madison Avenue store received an unusual request. A British retailer of women's clothing, Alexon, was opening its first US store near ours. Someone from Alexon asked to "borrow" a few bags to accessorize the apparel in Alexon's window display. Flattering, but our store associates declined. I didn't know any of this when Alexon's US head, a dapper man named Peter Emmerson, walked into my office in his tailored suit and tie, and in his British accent respectfully asked to borrow some bags. I said no because I knew they should and would pay, which Peter did. We got to talking. Peter was looking for someone to help him understand the US retail market, and I was intrigued by his expertise in Europe.

Eventually Peter left Alexon to develop Coach's international business. We didn't have office space for him on his first day of work, so the two of us lugged a desk for him into a quieter hallway space.

"What else do you need?" I asked him.

"A phone," he said. So I found him one.

Peter wondered whether he'd made a dreadful mistake, joining such a scrappy little leather manufacturer, but that would turn out not to be the case. A big-picture, logical thinker with a visual sensibility and an amazing work ethic, Peter would be with us for 20 years.

• • •

About a year after Peter joined us, in 1988, he was with me in Tokyo when we first convinced Mitsukoshi to become Coach's sole distributor in Japan, which opened the door for us in that crucial market, where a cultural shift was underway.

A new generation of Japanese women were starting to live independent of their parents, not marry, and work outside the home. One of my favorite memories from that period is standing with Peter in front of Mitsukoshi's flagship store, located at the prime intersection in the middle of Tokyo's Ginza district. For about 15 minutes, the two of us watched the sea of pedestrians crisscross the wide streets. I'd never seen such a massive flow of people, and I remember how we scanned the crowds that passed us to catch a glimpse of the bags women were carrying. At most we saw five Coach bags. We also observed many younger women wearing professional attire, something that wasn't unusual at that time in America but in Japan was a sign of the times as more emancipated, college-educated women joined the workforce. Millions of them needed bags they could carry to and from work with pride, but most couldn't afford the European luxury bags that dominated Japan's branded bag category. The country had no significant indigenous brands close to Coach in quality and price, so we very consciously—and logically—insinuated Coach as a value-based alternative to international luxury bags. The product-market fit for us was close to perfect.

The original deal we'd struck with Mitsukoshi in 1988 called for them to purchase inventory from us and distribute it to their respective locations, at their expense. They also put in 100% of the capital to build Coach shops in their department stores, which were usually next to or near Louis Vuitton, Gucci, Prada, and other luxury brands. Coach was the only American handbag brand among the European designers, a fact that Mitsukoshi believed would drive more traffic from current customers and attract new customers loyal to competing department stores.

Coach wasn't a passive supplier; we were hands-on in how our brand showed up in stores. In turn, Mitsukoshi sent its representatives to the United States to examine our facilities and make design suggestions to enhance our chances of winning over Japanese shoppers. A few reps had worried that our glovetanned leather wouldn't appeal to people who were accustomed to European leather that was coated to resist stains and scratch marks from wear. They urged us to put a finish on our bags so they wouldn't look aged. But we held firm, explaining that our leather's natural beauty got softer and more personal over time, like a well-worn saddle or baseball glove.

We were selling Coach as an American story, and we were inviting the Japanese to be part of it. We couldn't depart too far from the narrative.

In a sense we were experiencing a challenge that any consumer brand has when it expands beyond its geographic borders: how to respect and reflect regional tastes while staying true to equities that make its brand original. We wouldn't coat our leather, for example, but we did make additional styles with top handles for Japanese women who liked to hold bags in their hands, and we added a petite version of popular US styles to cater to the Japanese proclivity for smaller bags. In general, we were willing to customize product development to meet some preferences of international consumers, but not at the expense of our brand identity.

Of course, there were snags. In the early days Mitsukoshi often sent purchase orders too late for us to fulfill by the desired date. It was frustrating, and even several years later we were once again trying to plan ahead for the holiday season but had yet to receive an order from Japan. For some reason we couldn't seem to fix this problem.

In 1993, Peter had hired someone to help him oversee our international growth. Ian Bickley had lived and worked in Europe but had zero experience in Japan and didn't even speak Japanese. Like most new members of the leadership team, Ian went through a cultural boot camp as he grasped how Coach operated, and while I decided how much to trust him. Only after a year of Ian's proving his worth did we ask him to go to Japan.

He arrived determined to solve the logistical delays that were plaguing us. Ian gathered a group from Mitsukoshi in a room, and in a plodding effort, he spent hours mapping out the coming year's procurement plans on a whiteboard, forecasting sales projections and inventory levels through the coming holiday season. The common-sense approach to problem-solving worked, and Ian returned to the United States with a $3 million purchase order that allowed us to fulfill Mitsukoshi's supply needs in time to meet the expected seasonal demand.

Ian's ability to get things done became critical to our success abroad. He was nimble and adaptable, and his strong interpersonal skills translated across cultures. His operational proficiency complemented Peter's strengths, and the two made an effective team.

Our first five years selling Coach exclusively through Mitsukoshi were wildly successful. But contracts are not set in stone, and over time we learned things that compelled us to keep modifying our original agreement.

First, we realized just how loyal Japanese shoppers were to their favorite department store. As a result, Coach wasn't reaching shoppers at those that competed with Mitsukoshi, like Takashimaya or Seibu. When our contract first came up for renewal, we told Mitsukoshi that if it wanted to continue as our sole distributor they had to agree to introduce Coach into other department stores, and build our in-store shops. Mitsukoshi reluctantly agreed and in 1991 set up a separate import business, Pacific Distribution Company (PDC), a generic name that made working through Mitsukoshi more palatable for their rival stores. Coach compromised, too, at first agreeing to target only department stores in cities where Mitsukoshi did not have a presence. As our success became apparent, and our profits benefited Mitsukoshi, they began opening Coach shops in more places.

Elements of magic and logic played into our success in Japan, of course. Extreme collaboration with Mitsukoshi allowed us to creatively design bags for Japanese women and jointly plan production. We were ceaselessly curious about people, we studied the market, and we knew the trends. As a result, we could see the void in the marketplace we could fill if we positioned and priced our bags right, which we did.

The next time our contract with Mitsukoshi came up for renewal, we were ready to open our own freestanding stores. This practice was uncommon for individual brands in Japan, other than European luxury, in large part because the economics of operating a standalone store usually made it prohibitive. But as the Japanese economy began to cool in the 1990s, many banks abandoned their buildings, which opened prime real estate to retailers. There was a land grab as luxury brands rushed to sign leases. Mitsukoshi wasn't pleased with our plans and threatened to end our relationship. But we held firm and told them we'd already found a partner, J. Osawa, to own and operate Coach's standalone stores. Thankfully, Mitsukoshi remained our exclusive department store distributor, retaining the lion's share of our business in Japan.

From the start, our focus was never solely on Japan, the country, but on Japanese consumers wherever they chose to shop, and a significant number shopped outside their country. Each year in the early 1990s about 17 million Japanese traveled overseas, and when they did they bought a lot of luxury goods at department stores, full-priced retail stores, factory outlet malls, and duty-free shops.

We'd been doing business with Duty Free Shoppers for a few years before Coach went to Japan, and that experience helped us shape Coach's global pricing strategy. Our products were priced substantially higher in Japan, at an amount that research told us that Japanese consumers were willing to pay for the value they received. In other Asian countries and in Hawaii, where Japanese frequently visited, we priced bags between what we charged in the United States and Japan, which positioned Coach as an even better value for travelers. A $200 bag in the United States could sell for $360 in Japan and $300 in Hong Kong—all were still less than half the price of luxury brands.

Younger Japanese women especially realized the value. If an LV bag cost ¥100,000 in Japan and a Coach bag cost ¥40,000, she knew the ¥60,000 cost differential could pay for a roundtrip flight and a hotel stay for a weekend away in Taiwan or Korea. For the cost of one LV bag she could get a Coach and a mini-vacation.

Despite the contracting economy, Japanese women were still spending four times per capita what American women spent on bags. The opportunity for Coach was still huge.

Peter and Ian believed the best way for Coach to grow revenue and profits was to end our partnerships with Mitsukoshi and J. Osawa so we could take even more control of our Japanese business. We'd expand more quickly by running all retail, distribution, and merchandising ourselves. And we would implement more of the operational efficiencies and customer service tactics we employed in the United States. Operating our own business in a foreign country where we had no infrastructure was risky. We'd have to buy out our distributors, plus take on various expenses that Mitsukoshi and J. Osawa currently shouldered. And we knew that it would upset Mitsukoshi. They had been a great partner, and we still valued the relationship.

Inside Coach, we had many discussions about how to proceed, and I admit I was hesitant. Partnering with local companies gave me a sense of security. Eventually I agreed that it was wise to take control, but I was only comfortable going forward on two conditions. One, that Ian agreed to stay in Japan for at least three years, overseeing it on Coach's behalf. And two, that we have a joint venture partner, which would give us some operational know-how and access to talent, and allow us to leverage its existing relationships with department stores, landlords, and government officials, as well as banks so we could secure lines of credit to run the business.

The way I saw it, a local Japanese partner was a short-term insurance policy to mitigate risk. We just had to negotiate a contract that gave us that security without losing control.

In June 2001, we announced the formation of Coach Japan, a 50/50 joint venture with Sumitomo Corporation, one of the country's largest trading companies. Thankfully, Ian had agreed to stay and lead our expansion as Coach Japan's president and CEO, reporting directly to Keith. Ian by now spoke nearly fluent Japanese, and he had a rich network in the country and a deep understanding of the culture. As expected, Mitsukoshi was terribly upset when we informed them prior to the public announcement. After the initial shock we came to an agreement that showed our deep respect for the company, giving them preferential terms in their stores. Coach also agreed to acquire PDC, the subsidiary Mitsukoshi had formed when we decided to expand Coach's wholesale distribution.

After that, Coach Japan's growth would be meteoric, with sales increasing by double digits quarter after quarter in constant currency as we opened new locations, expanded the best-performing ones, and flowed new products into shops monthly.

I'll never forget when we opened our flagship store in Tokyo's Ginza district in 2002, and over 100 people were lined up before the doors opened at 11 a.m. I introduced myself to almost everyone in line, asking some of them how they knew about us, and if they already owned a Coach bag. One woman said she'd waited more than six hours in line, which meant she had to arrive before sunrise.

Unlike in the United States, Coach did not grow revenues in Japan because the accessories market grew, but rather by taking market share away from European luxury competitors, eventually becoming Japan's number-two imported accessories brand, second to Louis Vuitton.

It's no surprise that LVMH went to such extremes to keep Coach at bay.

• • •

We were maniacally focused on the Japanese consumer, and I wasn't giving much attention to the other Asian country that was certain to become the world's biggest luxury market, one day surpassing Japan and the United States: China.

Coach's directors, especially Irene Miller and Ivan Menezes, had been urging me to enter Mainland China for some time. So what was holding me back from grasping the obvious opportunity?

We'd had stores in Hong Kong for years, but I had no familiarity with Chinese consumers, and I worried I didn't have the bandwidth to learn about and focus on such a massive market. I told myself that China's billions of citizens weren't going anywhere, so starting a year or two later wouldn't make a material difference. Looking back, I realize that I simply found the project too daunting since so many other things were going on at Coach.

The board finally insisted we move ahead by articulating financial performance goals for China, and tying international performance to part of the leadership team's bonuses, mine included. We made our intentions public, telling investors in August 2005 that Coach was looking at greater China in a more serious way. We made it clear, however, that significant revenue wouldn't come for several years. It was all a bit vague, but the goal was no longer optional, compelling me to fully embrace it. The board was right, and I took no umbrage with its decision. China's rapidly growing middle class would eventually become Coach's largest opportunity in Asia.

Entering China was also a wholly different proposition than entering Japan, where we knew we'd be profitable from day one. The vast majority of Japan's egg-shaped economy was middle-class, and culturally handbags were already a coveted expression of oneself and a symbol of success. Japan was also a mature accessories market, and if anything, shoppers were willing and ready to trade down. In contrast, China had an underdeveloped accessories market, with a population interested in trading up. In that sense, China's population at the beginning of the 21st century was akin to the United States into the 1960s. Back then, the rise of median incomes produced many millions of people who strove to live a better life than their parents, an achievement marked by the ability to afford well-made goods beyond basic necessities.

Coach's democratized luxury brand played well with emerging Chinese consumers, who embraced us for our American heritage and New York roots. Symbolically, Coach the brand began to mark an arrival to the middle class for many Chinese. Most Chinese had little if any exposure to luxury accessory brands. At this point, the European designer brands were only available in the biggest, most cosmopolitan cities, like Shanghai and Beijing. Coach opened stores in those cities to build brand awareness, create trial, and learn about the Chinese consumer. But our real opportunities were in China's secondary and tertiary markets, the 100-plus cities with more than 1 million people. In those locales, spending on any luxury product was nascent, and for years limited to cosmetics. Beauty brands like Estée Lauder and Lancôme were the first higher-priced brands available in China's version of department stores, which were housed in mixed-use retail and office buildings. There were no Chinese versions of Bloomingdale's or Mitsukoshi.

The up-and-coming Chinese consumer had no preconceived notion about what a quality bag could or should be. They were neither compelled nor equipped to compare Coach to, say, Gucci or LV, which gave Coach a sort of first-mover advantage in China's swelling middle class, even though we'd arrived in the country later than we could have.

A downside was that we had no obvious data of competitive bag brands in China to inform our plans or track progress. In Japan, sales from other bag brands supplied to us by department stores helped us set strategy. With no equivalent benchmark in China, we turned to China's imported beauty products. Their success was proof that Chinese people appreciated quality brands, so we began asking department store owners to share beauty brands' performance with us, which they did because they wanted Coach as a tenant. We used that data to decide where we'd have the best chances of success. Once we opened a shop, we continued to track cosmetics' sales relative to ours. Soon we were seeing high levels of correlation between Coach's sales and those of Chanel, Dior, and Lancôme. If those products did, say, $1 million a year, we could comfortably predict that Coach would do $1 million to $1.5 million. If we were considering opening in a location where those brands only generated $500,000 a year, we might hold off to see if their performance improved before we invested in a store.

This triangulation of cosmetics' data influenced location strategy for the majority of our China stores over the next 10 years.

Our experience in Japan did give us confidence that we could operate our own business abroad. In China, we also contracted with local distributors, but unlike in Japan they had no equity. The Chinese distributor ImagineX bought Coach products wholesale, ran our Coach shops, and handled back-end operations like payroll and logistics, similar to a US franchisee model. It also helped Coach establish relationships with other retailers, landlords, and the all-important Chinese government.

As always, Coach kept contractual control of how the brand showed up in the marketplace. We controlled store designs and staff training content, and we approved marketing materials.

After about two years we understood the China market well enough to end our agreement with ImagineX, and in 2008 we began a phased buyout to transition to full ownership. We built a distribution center in Shanghai in a duty-free zone and close to our manufacturing facilities to optimize for timely product flow and profitability, and we installed a tech platform for planning, financials, data warehousing, and customer relationship management.

We also took a big swing by opening a flagship on Hong Kong's famed Queen's Road, in a prominent, highly trafficked location that exposed the brand to Chinese consumers living in and traveling to the city from the mainland. Whenever the famous Queen's Road intersection was photographed or broadcast on local or international media, the Coach store was almost always visible, raising our awareness. Our store got so much exposure that it became a preferred meeting point for people in the crowded city, giving Coach a certain gravitas.

In 2008, we boldly told Wall Street that our goal was to become one of the top three imported handbag and accessory brands in China.

• • •

For all our success in Asia, we could never quite break through in Europe, in large part due to the nature of the region and the category Coach was in.

During that first foray in the 1970s, Coach had low brand awareness, which continued into the late 1980s, when we opened a store on Sloane Street in London and a few stores in Germany.

A visit I made in the fall of 1989 coincided with a monumental global event. I'd arrived at my hotel in West Berlin late at night on November 9, and when I turned on the TV the first thing I saw on CNN International was live coverage of jubilant people swarming the Berlin Wall, many using sledgehammers and mallets to knock through sections of the graffitied concrete. Since 1961, the 12-foot-high, 9-inch-thick wall had separated West Berlin from East Berlin and the communist German Democratic Republic. The wall was a symbol of the broader cold war and its ideological divides. I realized, of course, that history was being made, and there was no way I was going to miss it. I called my Coach colleagues and we jumped into a car and drove to the Brandenburg Gate, and then walked to a less crowded section so we could actually touch the wall. In the dark, we came across a group of people who had chiseled a small, ragged opening that was wide enough to walk through if you hunched over. So that's what we did. When we emerged on the East German side it was pitch-black, and all I saw was a lone soldier pointing a rifle at us telling us we were trespassing, and that we needed to go back. Twenty-four hours later, my colleagues and I returned to the same spot to find that the break that we'd crawled through was now big enough to fit a car. Once again we walked through to the east side, and this time were greeted not by a guard but by effusive East Berliners. I'd never experienced such a palpable, collective hope for the future. It was intoxicating.

The next morning I was up early to begin our scheduled day of meetings, our purpose for being in Berlin. The timing of the business trip with the fall of the wall had been coincidental, and it was a moment in history I was lucky to witness and would treasure.

Despite shared values, however, German and European consumers in general had little interest in an American bag brand back then.

Another challenge we faced in Europe was the continent's diversity of countries. Between their cultural variances in fashion and language barriers, to logistical complexities and government regulations, each country required different business and marketing models. And unlike an emerging economy like China, European consumers were a mature market, and quite loyal to a number of mid-priced and luxury, local, and pan-European brands. Overall, there was less white space for Coach to insinuate and distinguish itself between mass and luxury.

And, of course, there was a clear preference for French and Italian brands, two countries that were virtually impossible for Coach to crack.

Our only positive presence in Italy wasn't a store but our sample-making and sourcing facility in Florence that we'd opened in about 1990. A funny memory involved a local Italian manufacturer that we used to produce some of our bags as we experimented with using different materials. One day a group of us went to visit a factory outside Florence and have dinner with the company's founder and his wife. The factory was in a building that must have been hundreds of years old, and at one point during the tour the owner asked to meet with me privately. I went into his office, where he shut the door and handed me a wrinkled brown paper bag, the kind you'd get in a grocery store. The top was rolled up, its bulky contents unclear.

"What is this?" I asked.

He said, "It's for you." I opened it and peered inside, shocked to see a bundle of 100-dollar bills.

Again I asked, "What is this?"

"It's $38,000, and it's for you."

"What's this about?" I was still baffled.

"You paid our bill, and then paid it again. When a company does that, I know that the second payment is actually for the owner." I quickly handed the bag of cash back to him.

"That second payment was a mistake," I explained. "We'll account for it on future payments." He laughed, and that was that.

I may have been one type of bag man, but I was definitely not the other.

I did have the chutzpah to open a Coach store in Florence, in a building formerly occupied by a bakery, but it was barely open two years before we shuttered it.

Despite our respect for Italian craftsmanship, Italian consumers did not have much interest in Coach.

And yet, we never ignored Europe. It was important to have stores in major tourist cities like London and Paris since we marketed ourselves as an alternative to European brands. We'd been selling in England's famed Harrod's department store since the 1980s, but during my years at Coach the United Kingdom barely exceeded 1% of our global sales.

When expanding internationally, it's important to know where your brand has legs—and for Coach during my tenure, that was in Asia.

One of my other favorite memories is being back in Tokyo's Ginza district about 20 years after Peter and I first stood at the bustling intersection outside Mitsukoshi, trying to spot the rare Coach bag. Once again I watched the crowds of pedestrians crossing the wide streets every which way. I'm not exaggerating when I say that this time every fourth or fifth bag I saw hanging from a woman's shoulder or clasped in her hands was a Coach.

It's rare moments like that when I was reminded of my original hopes for Coach, and almost in awe, if not disbelief, of how far we'd come. I might think back to my first year at Coach when I began to understand why so many women loved our bags, and the emotions that can make a handbag feel like a beloved companion. So for me to stand on a corner a world away from where my journey with Coach began, and to see with my own eyes that the product traits that had first endeared Coach to customers had transcended time and place, was incredibly gratifying.

The United States, however, would always be Coach's home and largest market, so it was there that we needed to continue to grow—and we did exactly that between 2000 and 2007, at such a rapid pace that some people referred to it as Coach's Golden Decade.

CHAPTER 15

Following Our Four-Strategy Playbook for Five Years

A dynamic tension exists between a brand and a business, and there are times when a brand is bigger than the business. When I first joined Coach in 1979, it had a cult following but an owner who was reluctant to make more products to meet rising demand, making the Coach brand larger than Miles's business. We began to grow the business, and for about the next 15 years the health of our brand and our business were generally in equilibrium. Then, when sales hit a wall in the mid-1990s, I realized that the Coach brand had been losing its luster and for the first time I felt that the business was getting bigger than the brand. So, we began to change creative course and revamp operations. This allowed us to reinvigorate sales and earnings, go public, and arrive at the game-changing brand evolution that was Signature, which catapulted our business throughout the decade by expanding our appeal.

Going forward, I was intent that Coach build its brand and its business together, a destiny that was tied to growing the US handbag and accessory category and our share of it.

In June 2003, when we closed the fiscal year with sales just shy of $1 billion, I told investors Coach would grow by sticking to the four strategies that had already been keys to our success for years:

One, focusing on our core product, the bag, by building on our unique position as an American accessible luxury lifestyle brand.

Two, expand the footprint and productivity of our full-priced and factory stores.

Three, aggressively grow market share with the Japanese consumer.

The fourth strategy was to increase margins and our rate of profitability.

Products. Stores. Japanese consumers. Margins.

Sticking to these four strategies with equal effort and attention was how we'd build our brand and business in tandem over the next five years. Each strategy was finely tuned, with nuances and tactics that ensured excellence in execution.

In retrospect, they served as a 360-degree playbook for extraordinary growth.

• • •

As always, the product stayed the hero.

Brands that stand the test of time innovate to stay relevant and build upon the product imagery that first captured customers' hearts. So-called legacy brands and their associated images include Timberland boots, the Burberry raincoat, Tiffany diamonds, and Levi's jeans. Even Disney, whose fantasy characters remain central to the customer experience. Each consumer-facing brand expanded its appeal while staying true to its foundational equities. Conservative Burberry got sexy by putting its tartan pattern on bikinis. Tiffany signed Elsa Peretti to design more accessibly priced silver and gold jewelry that was still distinctively elegant. Traditional Disney acquired Pixar's more modern storytelling. By definition, legacy brands can also survive a spate of bad management, bad economies, even bad luck—but not in perpetuity.

Was Coach a legacy brand?

We first put our distinctive glovetanned leather bags into people's hands back in the 1960s, and they not only used them, they also cherished them. Now, as we entered a new decade, we were striving to create products people loved by embodying our brand's fundamental equities—quality, function, durability—but also by expanding our brand's personality to be more fun, fashionable, and feminine. To that end, our Signature *C* logo products were a grand slam, and a rare game-changing achievement in the fickle fashion business. But one blockbuster innovation isn't enough to maintain sustainable growth, or achieve legacy status. Coach had to keep innovating by offering exciting products, anchored in bags, with aesthetics and prices that appealed to a larger cross section of consumers.

One safe, predictable way to innovate was to build on prior product successes.

We did this in many ways, like iterating upon our most popular bags, which we dubbed power styles. We turned the bestselling Hamptons Weekend Tote into its own collection, with new shapes and materials, like nylon instead of cotton, and top corners that folded in, but could also expand out for more interior space. In stores we filled the tote with beach towels and Signature flip-flops to alert people how they might use it, and sales staff made sure you knew that the nylon was water-resistant, perfect for the beach. The Hamptons Weekend Collection sold 60,000 units when it launched in 2003, bringing in about $10 million in sales. The next year we iterated on it again, and sales tripled.

Our obsession with what made consumers tick remained a competitive advantage. Analyst Dana Telsey from Bear Stearns would tell *Women's Wear Daily* that our momentum was unique for the industry. "I think the fact that Coach knows so much more about its customer helps them keep that customer." She was right. In 2004, we spent about $3 million on market research and surveyed some 14,000 people as we divined new collections that leaned into lifestyle trends, including products that filled usage voids.

One of the best examples of how we paid attention to what made consumers tick came about shortly after the IPO. We observed women using bags-within-bags, mainly their small cosmetics cases, to hold more than lipstick but also keys, credit cards, and other essentials so they could be found easily in a crowded tote or briefcase. Reed created a 6-inch-by-4-inch zip-bag expressly for this purpose, adding a looped strap to the pouch so it could hang from a clasp inside a larger Coach bag, or around your wrist. Cleverly, our team named it the "wristlet"—bracelet + wallet + wrist—and we sold it for about $48. Women began taking just their wristlets when they went to the gym, shopping, or out dancing with friends. And they bought multiple wristlets for different occasions. A simple one for walking the dog. A fancier one for a party.

In 2004, wristlets in 75 iterations generated $40 million in sales, which at 4% of our overall revenue was quite impressive for an item at such a low price.

Innovations like the wristlet became new beloved companions, prompting articles like this one from the *Wall Street Journal*, "How Coach Won a

Rich Purse by Inventing New Uses for Bags." The idea of the every-occasion bag for all day and all year round had given way to the notion that you could choose a bag based on your mood and moments. Reed and his team of designers continued to style our bags to be about attitude as well as occasions, encouraging people to keep expanding the role handbags played in their lives.

To stimulate more interest, we implemented tiered pricing, offering products above and below our average-priced bags, which in 2004 was $218. We didn't raise the cost of existing products, or put anything on sale in our Coach stores, which remained a full-priced retailer 365 days a year. Rather, new products were purposely designed and constructed with less costly but still quality fabrics, and in smaller sizes, or with fewer pockets and less hardware. This allowed us to achieve the same operating margins, which is that part of revenue that is retained after accounting for all expenses, including overhead. The slim, $120 Demi Zip bag that hung from your shoulder and tucked under your arm gave stylish but cost-constrained consumers a comfortable way to enter the Coach world.

We went higher-end, too, designing more sophisticated styles that were more costly to make and priced 20% to 30% more. We were delighted as women embraced $300-plus price points for our first evening collection, Madison, some in rich satins, and with embellishments like rhinestone buckles. We used our flagship stores to introduce what we called pinnacle products to the customer who typically bought designer luxury bags for herself, but who came into a Coach store to buy gifts for her colleagues or her kids' teachers. We hoped she'd be intrigued when she saw a fur-trimmed duffle for $698 while shopping for wristlets, and decide to buy it for herself. So as loyal Coach fans traded up, pinnacle products were enticing luxury shoppers to consider Coach for the first time. By year-end, the top 4% or 5% of US households by income who typically bought European luxury brands made up the top 25% of Coach's consumer base.

The more diverse our product mix got, the less we worried about brand ubiquity because our customers were carrying such a wide variety of Coach bags.

Well into our fourth year as a public company, the US branded women's premium bag and accessory category was experiencing an unprecedented level of growth, up more than 20% from the prior year, to about $3.7 billion. Coach was a catalyst for that growth, but there was more at play. In the United States, accessorizing had become a fashion staple, with bags a definitive way to express personal style. The ability to change your entire look with just a bag and a scarf instead of a head-to-toe outfit was also less expensive.

In 2004, our target consumer was buying 3.5 handbags a year, up from 3.1 in 2002, and 2.4 in 2000.

A spate of articles that year had nice things to say. The *Financial Times* explained that Coach had hit the sweet spot between mass and luxury by maintaining the cachet of premium brands at half the price of European "competitors" like Louis Vuitton, Prada, and Gucci. The *Wall Street Journal* observed that Coach had made handbags "the shoes of the 21st century." A *BusinessWeek* article noted that since our IPO our stock was up 900%, and that Coach was now one of the fastest-growing luxury brands in the world. The reporter wrote that I led the company with the passion of an entrepreneur and the thoroughness of a good city bureaucrat, in reference to my city government training. It was an accurate assessment that reflected the blending of magic and logic at play inside Coach.

In fiscal 2004, our sales were up 39% to $1.3 billion.

Our first strategy of staying focused on the product was paying off. Coach had acquired what one of our execs called brand heat, which is hard to build, and must be cared for in a responsible, systematic way. And it wasn't all about product. We were also using our retail stores to drive and nurture that heat.

• • •

Our second core strategy as a public company was expanding our retail stores' footprint and productivity.

Stores had contributed the lion's share of Coach's sales well before we went public. In 2005, our internal surveys revealed that our most recent customers were now visiting our stores about every four weeks. We used the data as a barometer to determine how frequently to flow new products into stores, or how often we rearranged products on tables and shelves. Changing our floor sets at least every month, and weekly during holiday periods, ensured that a store always looked fresh when you came to visit.

A beautiful, well-merchandised store won't reach its full potential without strong salespeople and seasoned store managers. Coach had long hired top retail talent, many recruited by people they knew who worked at Coach and loved it. Coach had among retail's highest retention rates for good reason. Our total compensation was well above the industry's average, in part because we'd been providing health care benefits and annual bonuses to many full- and part-time employees who worked at least 20 hours a week since the early 1990s. These benefits were virtually unheard of for hourly workers.

After our IPO in 2000, the equity grants we gave to many full-time employees—including store associates, office custodians, as well as employees outside the United States—were also a rare thing for a business to do. We awarded additional grants to store managers and other senior employees. To this day, current and former Coach employees tell me that the value of their Coach stock made a material difference in their lives. Sometimes people walk up to me if they see me on the street, or when I visit stores, which I still do, and share how they used that stock for the down payment on a first home, or a vacation home, or to pay for their kid's college, or to go back to school. Valued employees like Dorrett Creary came to the United States from Jamaica, started working in our New York City store in 1998 when she was in her thirties, and rose to more senior management positions. Over the years Dorrett was able to help her family with money from the sale of her Coach stock.

Rewarding workers in ways other companies did not made us a more attractive place to work, but mainly I thought that giving everyone at Coach opportunities to participate in our success was the right thing to do. It's what made success so sweet. That part of Coach's heritage is something I am very proud of.

Our stores were places of hard work but also camaraderie and learning, extensions of our offices' performance family culture. I could walk into a busy store and quickly sense if it was well-run because of the upbeat tempo and energy that were palpable.

Stores were also our most direct link to consumers, so the first thing I did when I entered one was introduce myself to visitors and ask questions based on my assessment of who someone might be. Were you a young fashionista? A busy professional on a lunch break? I might walk around the store with you to get a sense of what you liked and where you were in your Coach journey. A loyalist, or flirting with buying your first Coach bag? I told shoppers that I worked for Coach but not that I was the CEO, so they wouldn't feel intimidated or hold back their opinions. These conversations were like my own mini focus groups.

I also spoke with sales staff, many of whom I'd known for years, and asked them to tell me about their customers. What products were selling? What were people looking for that we didn't have? My final conversations were usually with the store's manager. I wanted to check that they had everything they needed, and I also wanted to determine if what they told me reflected what I had heard from shoppers and staff. Every manager was essentially a small business owner, and I expected them to act as a proprietor would, as shopkeepers. The store was their show to run.

We'd long preferred to build retail talent from within. After the IPO we had no choice but to do this because we were adding new stores so quickly that it was virtually impossible to recruit the level of talent we needed from the outside. Most of our store managers were naturals at sales and dealing with people. The best imbued their teams with enthusiasm, and their leadership positively impacted stores' performance. For a great store manager, no task was too small. They'd take out trash, or arrive early to open, and stay late to close. They had a strong eye for talent so they could hire and promote wisely. They were also clear communicators, willing to learn and listen to feedback. And, like most people who excelled at Coach, they were genuinely nice humans. Many store managers went on to higher positions in the field and corporate.

Dave DeMattei had left Coach after five years transforming our retail stores. Our next head of retail was Mike Tucci, a seasoned merchant who had worked under two of the most consequential shapers of American retail, Ed Finkelstein, a legend at Macy's, and Mickey Drexler at the Gap, where Mike had risen to head of merchandising. He joined Coach in the winter of 2003, when Coach's increasing brand recognition was bringing many more visitors into stores, some who arrived curious but with little intent to purchase.

Thus, there was a real opportunity for our sales associates to convert shoppers into buyers. Mike's mandate was to improve how our stores operated, and he developed three principles that built on many of our longstanding values and rituals.

Mike's first principle was: Measure store productivity more rigorously. What gets measured gets done, or at least attended to, and three main metrics drive how a store performs. One: traffic, which is the number of people who come in. Did traffic rise or fall over time? Traffic is a lagging indicator of our brand's health because it represents the culmination of past connections a consumer has with Coach, from how happy she is with her current Coach bag to how inspired she is by photos of celebrities carrying a Coach bag. Another important measure in addition to traffic is store productivity by conversion—that is, how many of the people who come into a store actually buy something. Our store sales staff can't control traffic, but they can influence conversion. A talented salesperson quickly gets a sense of you as a customer, and her goal is to sell you products you genuinely want. A third key productivity metric is ticket: how much money a single shopper spends per transaction. Ticket is the sum of the products, or units, the customer buys in a single visit. Average units per transaction (UPT) and average daily ticket (ADT) are related metrics. One of the best ways to increase ADT is to increase UPT. A customer probably won't buy two handbags in one visit, but she may buy a handbag and a wristlet.

The combination of these three metrics—traffic, conversion, and ticket—leads to a store's total sales. When comparing sales from a given period—a day, a week, a month, a quarter, a year—to a prior period, the percentage up or down is that holy grail of retail metrics, same-store sales, the most accurate measurement of a retail brand and business's vibrancy.

A well-run retail business not only measures traffic, conversion, ticket, and same-store sales, but combines that data to set and achieve new goals. We knew, for example, that the top 20% of Coach customers at a given time accounted for as much as 80% of sales, so store associates nurtured relationships with our most devoted fans, alerting them to new products before they arrived, which sparked advance purchases. Sometimes I'd visit a store days before a new product hit the floor, and I'd see dozens of reserved, prepurchased bags stacked in the back room awaiting pickup.

Mike, like others on our leadership team, took pride in being able to forecast our business within ridiculous levels of accuracy. As we grew, we needed each store manager to more rigorously track traffic, conversion, and ticket to help us make those projections, and improve their own store's productivity. Mike wanted to drive this practice home at his first store managers' meeting in the summer of 2003.

Coach began holding annual gatherings for our store managers in the fall of 1985, when just six gathered at Manhattan's Barbizon-Plaza Hotel for a single day. We'd upgraded the meetings over the years, of course, holding conferences for multiple days at hotels like the Ritz-Carlton in fun destination cities, and including spa appointments and free Coach products. The event was also about learning, and managers broke into groups that covered teamwork, merchandising, and leadership. We also used the meetings to solicit managers' ideas; after all, they were our direct links to customers. The gatherings were highly anticipated and filled with a lot of joy and camaraderie.

Mike's first-ever managers' conference was a chance for about 350 people to meet Mike, and for Mike to jump-start his mandate to improve store productivity.

"I really love the business. And I really love what we do," he said on stage. "I watch how your stores perform, and I care about your sales." He truly did. "I also care about traffic. I care about conversion. And I care about average ticket."

As he spoke he waved one of the daily reports that he reviewed with his field team each afternoon at 4 p.m. It was rife with lines of yellow highlights to accent the metrics that mattered most.

"Reach under your chairs," Mike said. Every manager did and discovered a yellow highlighter that Mike's team had taped to the bottom of each seat. "You should be doing this too!" he said, hoping he'd made his point. Increased attention to measuring performance, emphasized by Mike well beyond that meeting, contributed to the robust, double-digit same-store sales growth in the years that followed.

Mike's second principle, after measuring store productivity, was a recommitment to customer service, something I was pushing. Early in his tenure, Mike came into my office with multiple agenda items for a status meeting. As he opened his folder I told him we only had one: making Coach as famous for our customer service as we were for our products. I was telling him to go do it, just not how to do it. We discussed it a bit, then he closed his folder and left the room.

Mike launched our Coach Service program in mid-2004. The program had five components that institutionalized many rituals we'd practiced for years. First, the greet. I'd been saying since our first store opened on Madison Avenue that we should treat everyone who came in as if they were guests in our home, starting with a genuine warm welcome. The second component was conversation and engagement. We told associates to replace "May I help you?" with open-ended questions to encourage dialogue and get to know individual shoppers. The third component was the try-on. We encouraged a shopper to hang a bag from her shoulder. Hold it in her hand. Walk around with it. Inspect the inside. This was our chance to show her its versatility and call out the zippered pocket that would safely hold her keys, and the outside pocket positioned to keep her phone accessible but stitched in such a way to make sure it wouldn't pop out. The more knowledgeable a shopper became the more likely she was to go from a curious browser to a happy buyer.

Once she chose to purchase, our sales staff would honor the transaction, the fourth component of Coach Service. The exchange of money for goods was choreographed to convey how much we appreciated you and your business. After we carefully packaged your products, we walked around the table, looked you in the eye, and thanked you as we handed it to you. Today this behavior has become more common in service-oriented stores, but it wasn't as common 20 years ago.

Finally, the fifth element of Coach Service was the post-visit thank you. In addition to thanking customers in the store, our associates followed up with handwritten notes. Again, many associates and managers were already doing this. Our best sales associates might write 20 to 30 letters a day.

The third and final element of Mike's three big operating principles was talent, rewards, and recognition. Since the early 1990s, every Coach employee, including many part-timers in our stores, received a bonus based on the company's annual performance. A cashier could get a check for $2,500, quite meaningful for hourly workers in retail. Now, Mike amped up our rewards program so store associates could earn additional compensation when store teams met performance goals. Anyone who achieved $1 million or more in yearly sales was given additional compensation and a coveted invite to the annual store managers' conference.

Mike's incentives reinforced and elevated the already stellar performance of long-time Coach employees like Fazila Mustaphalli, for whom exceptional customer service came naturally. Fazila joined Coach in 1996 as a cashier and worked full- and part-time for us as her four children grew. She was already a high performer who loved to talk to people, listen to them, and build conversation. She had a genuine passion for the undertaking—a crucial element of magic and logic—which led Fazila to achieve million-dollar-seller status five years in a row.

In addition to our full-priced stores, Mike was also responsible for our 80 Coach factory stores in outlet malls. In 2005 factory store growth outpaced same-store sales growth of our full-priced stores in large part because the discount retail sector was surging.

Customers at Coach factory stores, as they were called in the mid-2000s, were notably different than our customers at our full-priced stores. In fact, there was only 10% overlap. Both had college degrees, usually worked a professional job, and had similar household income. But a factory consumer was about 10 years older, in her mid-to-late forties, and had less discretionary income, often because she had children. She preferred a classic, functional handbag to a more fashionable one. Our factory stores were a way for us to service the brand-conscious discount-oriented shopper. We carefully curated our factory store product assortments to reflect this consumer, but within the guardrails of our brand's touchstones.

Most factory products were made exclusively for that channel by a factory-focused team of designers, merchants, and sourcing professionals. We almost never sold products from full-priced stores in factory stores until a year or more after they left the full-priced store. So if you bought a Soho Leather Satchel at Coach in the Mall at Short Hills, you wouldn't find it for less a few months later at the closest Coach factory store at Woodbury Common. In fact, you might never find it there. And while the factory store ambience was more relaxed, it was no less rigorous, and consistent with our high customer service standards.

Factory and full-priced stores were truly two different sales channels for two different types of Coach consumers.

As I told Wall Street, Coach factory stores were our version of a diffusion brand, a strategy that many apparel brands had employed for years by making lower-cost products with their brand's familiar aesthetic under a recognizable but unique name. Ann Taylor had Ann Taylor Loft. Donna Karan had DKNY. Tommy Hilfiger had Tommy. Old Navy was the Gap's diffusion channel. Because Coach almost never sold its products at off-price retailers like T.J. Maxx, Coach factory was a brand-consistent way to reach a segment of discount consumers, as well as a method to dispense some excess inventory so our full-priced stores never had clearance sales. The only place to buy Coach products at a discount was in a Coach factory store.

Some analysts, investors, and board members had an unfounded belief that our factory business inevitably risked eroding the Coach brand. They worried that lower prices made Coach too accessible and thus ubiquitous, and less special. They didn't trust the data that proved there was low customer overlap. In addition, our research gave no indication that it was diminishing the brand.

Also, discount shopping in the United States was too massive a movement for us to ignore; most premier and some luxury brands like Gucci and Prada had a presence at many of the more than 100 premium factory malls across the country. Factory was simply another way for Coach to be accessible.

From a business perspective, Coach factory would continue to grow our overall sales and profits substantially. Compared to full-priced stores, factory sales volume was considerably higher and operating costs lower, which made for insane productivity levels. As a brand, our integrity was maintained as long as the product assortment stayed distinctive yet consistent with our equities, and as long as the store environment was image-enhancing and its service levels high.

In the fourth quarter of fiscal 2005, Coach's same-store sales rose 22%, with comps at our North American full-priced stores up 13%, while sales at Coach's North American factory stores jumped 34%.

For the full year, Coach's companywide sales in 2005 were $1.7 billion, a 29% leap from 2004.

• • •

We executed our third core strategy of growing our share of the Japanese consumer market by staying true to our winning pricing strategies and constantly fine-tuning execution. Under Ian Bickley as president of Coach Japan, the business grew at a much faster clip than our business as a whole despite Japan's sluggish economy and mature accessories category.

In 2005, Coach Japan had sales of more than $370 million. That same year we bought out Sumitomo's 50% share for $250 million, ending the partnership too soon for Sumitomo but with a lucrative payout and gratitude for its contributions. After almost 17 years in Japan, we finally had 100% ownership of our distribution and operations. I had no regrets about taking our time to reach that milestone because it had freed us to focus on building the brand instead of worrying about the back end of the business.

By fiscal 2007, Coach Japan retail sales reached $480 million, now representing 18% of total Coach sales. Our share of the Japanese market was now 11%, up from just 2% to 3% six years earlier.

Building our Japanese business remained one of our four key strategies because it was such a significant contributor to global sales, and our highest margin channel—even as we improved margins throughout the rest of the business.

• • •

Our fourth core strategy between 2001 and 2007 was driving margins higher.

Coach had among the highest profit margins in the bag space, and higher than any publicly traded apparel or accessory brand in the United States. We had up to 80% gross margins once a product left the facility where it was made. That left us with a lot of room to invest in activities that enhanced the brand, like marketing, and still achieve operating margins over 35%. We were able to get such high gross margins for several reasons.

For one, we were in a category where people were willing to pay a higher price for value.

Internally, we had an efficient global supply chain, with a matrixed organizational structure that ensured people across disciplines had a deep understanding of the supply chain's ecosystem, from product development to raw-material sourcing to manufacturing. Our designers knew that adding or removing any element from a bag increased or decreased its manufacturing cost. If you wanted to add a buckle, you might have to nix a pocket. Designers were in constant contact with our supply chain and finance teams as they mixed and matched the various elements that went into creating a particular bag—different leathers, fabrics, shapes, embellishments, and sizes, to name just a few of the variables they could play with.

At the same time, our production experts remained focused on negotiating the best prices for materials, reducing waste, and finding new ways to simplify the time it would take to make a product, without compromising quality and our labor standards. Coach engineers were in factories every day, watching our partners make bags, so we could reduce the lag time between discovering and fixing problems. This collaborative, rigorous approach to product development—choosing combinations of elements that gave us industry-leading profit margins while appealing to consumers—was, as Reed described it to *Time* magazine, like a big puzzle.

Another key to driving our exceptional gross and operating margins was having a dispersed yet disciplined financial function that understood the product-price calculus, monitored expenses, and engaged in rigorous financial planning.

Mike Devine joined Coach as our chief financial officer right after 9/11. Of course, this was a particularly difficult period, especially for New Yorkers. At the time of the attack, Coach was hosting a group of Japanese executives, who understandably were as shocked as all of us that America was under attack. Luckily, no one from Coach's store in the World Trade Center was injured. I remember commuting to the office the next day via ferry because the GWB was closed. It was as sunny a day as it had been the day prior, and I stood on the deck with hundreds of other commuters in silence, looking at the lower-Manhattan skyline in disbelief. Smoke was still billowing into the air from where the towers once stood. Tears ran down a lot of faces that day, and for weeks to come. If you loved New York, you loved it even more after 9/11.

It was during this period that I first interviewed Mike Devine. He was a disciplined practitioner whose financial acumen was complemented by his commercial savvy. He came to Coach pleased with the rigor and routines we already had in place.

When *BusinessWeek* named Coach number #12 on its annual list of 100 Best Small Companies in 2003, a Wells Fargo analyst told the magazine that "the quality for the dollar spent is unparalleled" at Coach. We were already running a disciplined financial ship when Mike joined us, and he made us even better, because his intent was not so much to reinvent but to improve upon and scale the business. He was also a people person and an effective communicator. Steady and unflappable, Mike was the situational leader we needed in that role, someone who understood the connective tissue of the business, who could adapt to its different personalities.

He built a dispersed team of division CFOs that were embedded in each business unit. They reported both to Mike and to the head of their division. Such dual reporting is not a choice all companies make, as it can rankle the order of things, and not everyone is equipped to toggle well between two bosses. The ones who thrived at Coach were emotionally intelligent, collaborative professionals who found ways to make any awkwardness work.

The matrixed structure let Mike, Keith, and me have our fingers on the daily pulse to better control and forecast our overall business.

Mike never wanted to guess at anything. Like me, he was a curious data junkie, and there was rarely a detail in the business that one or both of us were not aware of. If we got criticized by some for being micromanagers, Mike repeated the corny truism about our industry: retail is detail.

In the main, being so dedicated and involved was a net-positive, allowing us to be precise in projecting margin rates as the company grew in size and complexity. At some point I started calling Mike Mr. Gross Margin, maybe around the time one of the top analysts that followed Coach, Bob Drbul, told *Fortune* that Coach's execution and business planning was in the league of Walmart or Target.

In fiscal 2006, companywide sales surpassed $2 billion, up 23% from the prior year, and we reported gross margins of 77%, a 100-basis-point lift from the prior year, while operating margins rose from 33% to 36%.

We were no longer considered small when we appeared on *BusinessWeek*'s 2006 list of 50 Top Performing US Companies, and ranked #43, having "deftly cultivated the accessible luxury segment," according to the write-up, and "avoided the bargain bin dilution that has plagued brands from Calvin Klein to Tommy Hilfiger."

With Coach now in its 65th year, I pushed for us to continue to act like a small company with large sales by staying hungry, entrepreneurial, and not assuming our size made us invincible, which was easy to forget at times.

Meanwhile, a secular shift was taking place in the United States. Spending on accessories was growing at a much faster clip than overall spending on apparel as women used bags to update their wardrobe in the same way they once bought clothes. Bags were exploding into a highly emotional category, and Coach was credited as a primary catalyst that changed the way women thought about accessories. Our target consumers were now buying four bags a year, up from 2.4 at the beginning of the decade. Our US market share was now 25%.

• • •

Beyond our four strategies, there was another factor that helped propel our growth as well as mitigate risk in the years following the IPO: the addition of a board of directors.

After Sara Lee sold the remainder of its stake in Coach about a year after going public, I was free to build a new board, with me continuing as chairman. The only public-company board I had direct exposure to had been Sara Lee's, and from my perspective its nearly 20 directors made little contribution beyond their fiduciary duties. I vowed back then that if I ever had a chance to create a board, its purpose would be to enhance my performance and that of the leadership team. What I did not want was a board of sycophants, or anyone looking for a seat just to make extra money or fill time.

In my view, a high-performance board was made up of domain experts whose skill sets were additive to the company's existing talent. I wanted seasoned professionals who had experience in operating roles and who knew how to build and lead teams. People who had been around long enough to see how external events like economic slowdowns or regional conflicts can impact businesses and consumer behavior. I also looked for people with conviction and courage to express their views. That's not to say I took all of the board's advice—I had pretty strong conviction myself—but I wanted to hear it all.

It was also important to me that my leadership team respected our directors as credible so they would listen and get the full benefit of the board's counsel.

Boards larger than 10 people can get unwieldy, and from day one I kept Coach's board smaller, to six or seven directors. Because we chose well, that number covered the expertise we needed. Yet even at our size we could still feel cramped when we gathered at the round table in Coach's main conference room. The night before each quarterly board meeting we had dinner together, which was a chance for everyone to get to know and appreciate each other in a relaxed setting, and develop the rapport and camaraderie that led to productive working relationships. Over dinner, we'd have free-flowing conversations about areas of concern and what we wanted to accomplish the next day.

After dispensing with our fiduciary responsibilities, the board often had vibrant discussions around issues facing the company. Where to focus. How to prioritize. Which initiatives to lean into, which to park. Some members of any group inevitably talk more than others, and because I wanted to hear everyone's thoughts I made a point of going around the table and requesting that each director tell the rest of us where they stood on a given topic. It's empowering to be asked your opinion. People could be confrontational at times, with me and with each other, but interactions were for the most part respectful.

Transparency allows a team to get the full benefit of a board, so I encouraged our directors to speak frankly, and to access anyone at Coach at any time. Many CEOs don't want their senior executives talking to board members in private, but I didn't try to manage such interactions. Of course I was always curious, and if they chose to share the nature of their conversation with me, fine. There were times a director might come to our headquarters unbeknownst to me until he or she popped into my office to say hello after chatting with Keith, or Reed, or Andrea, or one of the Mikes. I, too, spent one-on-one time with directors between our quarterly meetings, soliciting their thoughts on any number of issues.

Some board members knew Coach prior to our IPO. Keith Monda remained our supply chain expert. Goldman's Joe Ellis stayed on for a few years, but Sara Lee's CFO and vice chairman, Mike Murphy, stayed with us, heading our audit committee until just before I retired in 2014, despite asking me if he should retire at 70, when many directors leave boards. Mike was too valuable to let go just because of his age. He was knowledgeable and as sharp as ever, had unmatched experience, and was a true gentleman who worked harmoniously with Coach's financial teams.

Irene Miller had helped sell Coach to Sara Lee in 1985. Since then she'd been vice chairman and chief financial officer of Barnes & Noble and headed her own investment firm. She also served as a director for a number of retail companies. Irene was a logical, broad thinker, as well as Coach's target consumer.

Ivan Menezes was a marketing wizard who became CEO at Diageo, the British multinational alcoholic beverage corporation. Like me, Ivan was in the midst of building a global business in a discretionary consumer category, so we had that in common. He was quieter, but when he spoke we all listened.

Gary Loveman was the COO of Las Vegas–based Harrah's Entertainment when he joined the board in 2002, joking with me at the time that he didn't know the difference between a handbag and a handgun. When he became Harrah's CEO a year later, he grew it into the largest casino operator in the world. He had a keen analytical mind, as well as rich insight into customer relationships and building loyalty.

In 2006, Jide Zeitlin joined the board almost 10 years after he helped me shop Coach, then take it public. Jide was the ultimate lateral thinker who had spent a lot of time around boards, and was very good at getting us to see things from a different angle, and coalesce diverging views.

The same year Jide joined us, Susan Kropf also became a director. The president and COO at Avon, Susan understood how to build brands and how to manage a large, dispersed workforce. She was also an avid shopper who loved to walk department stores and share observations about how Coach was faring next to competitors, urging me not to ignore department stores when I insisted that they were an aging channel. To her credit, Susan was relentless, reminding us that the department store accessories floor was the most democratic marketplace for product comparisons because consumers could see different brands side-by-side and no one brand had home-court advantage.

Someone described the Coach board as a unique blend of informality and intensity, which I suppose is also a form of magic and logic. The personal nature of our interactions did not compromise the duty the outside directors felt to the business. In fact, it made us better because we were an assertive group of people who felt comfortable to speak our minds, and disagree.

Despite the board's prodding, I was slower than they wanted me to be when it came to accelerating expansion into China. Acquisitions were also something they occasionally brought up, which I usually shot down, due to my own bias. I felt most comfortable growing the company organically, especially after acquiring and then shuttering Mark Cross, and from my Sara Lee days, when overseeing a portfolio of brands distracted me from the brand I loved most.

One of my big mistakes was not paying enough attention to Susan and others as they warned me about an encroaching competitive threat—a reminder that you can have an A+ board, but it doesn't matter if you don't listen to it when it counts.

• • •

In fiscal 2007, Coach's sales rose 28% to $2.6 billion. Net income jumped 37% to $637 million.

We had also grown the overall accessible luxury market, plus our share of it. That fall Coach completed its 22nd consecutive quarter of at least 20% sales growth.

No one element fueled Coach's momentum during those golden years. If anything, I'd say it was tenacity and commitment to stick to our four-strategy playbook, as well as to things that had been a part of Coach for decades: Our consumer-centric orientation. Our nimble, collaborative, matrixed operating structure. Our performance-family culture. And our brand equities.

In September of 2007, *Fortune* magazine ran an article headlined "Luxury Goes Mass Market," and the reporter made some interesting observations. "Luxury used to mean beautifully crafted, hideously expensive, and unashamedly elitist. . . . For the most part, luxury is no longer reserved for the spoiled rich. Increasingly it's the domain of the global middle class on an ego trip—people from Indiana to India prepared to pay a premium for the thrill of owning something that makes them feel special." Of course, I thought he was too cynical.

He did assert two things I agreed with. One was that luxury products were about creating an emotional rapport between the consumer and the product, which I believe Coach achieved, or we could not have grown. The other was that luxury products were no longer the domain of the wealthy. He even quoted me as saying luxury had been democratized, a twist on the phrase I'd been using to describe Coach since the 1980s. Back then, I'd believed that Coach was a democratized luxury brand because we gave more people access to quality products at more affordable prices. As we grew our presence throughout the 1990s, democratized luxury was still about pricing products people loved at prices they were willing to pay for, and could afford. But it was also about offering consumers more convenient ways to purchase products—wherever they chose to shop. And, throughout the early 2000s, we appealed to an ever more diverse range of personalities and attitudes.

In addition to quality, price, and location, democratized luxury was now about offering a wider array of products so a broader cross section of people could express themselves. Our Ergo patchwork hobo bag could make a 25-year-old smile, while the more classic-inspired Bleecker in rust-colored leather made a working mother with three kids feel like she'd made a wise investment. Coach was now a luxury brand that was more accessible than ever. But were we a legacy brand? All I knew was that we could not rest on our laurels and stand still.

In January 2008, I told investors that the wind had clearly been at Coach's back for years. We even ranked #1 on *BusinessWeek*'s annual list of the Top 50 Best Performing US Companies, based on sales growth and return on invested capital between 2005 and 2007.

What the ranking did not reflect, however, were headwinds that would threaten our pace of growth in the years ahead, including some ongoing problems that I hadn't addressed, and some I didn't even see coming.

CHAPTER 16

Overcoming Adversities, Adapting to Endure

The blending of magic and logic were also at play during periods of crisis, and in the latter part of the 2000s Coach faced several such periods, some self-induced, some external. The most severe was the financial crisis.

"I think something very strange is going on in the world," Mike Tucci said when he called me over a summer weekend in July 2008. "We don't have command of the business like we normally do."

Our sales were all over the place, doing well in some pockets of the country while other regions declined. Metrics we tracked, like traffic and conversion, were inconsistent week to week. Future purchase intent—the percentage of our customers' likelihood to buy another Coach bag—was usually in the high 80s or low 90s, but fell to the mid-70s so unexpectedly that it shocked me, and triggered anxieties that I hadn't felt in years.

Overall consumer spending had been weakening since fall 2007, but it hadn't wreaked too much havoc on our performance.

Now, however, Mike and I were both losing a feel for the business.

Despite these signs of trouble, Coach ended fiscal 2008 with sales up 22% to nearly $3.18 billion. Impressive performance by most measures, but still lower than the year-to-year growth we were used to.

My team and I believed that the slowdown in spending wasn't a blip, and our answer was to put ourselves in the position of people who were being more careful about how they spent money. Rather than in-store markdowns, we doubled down on innovation to create a wider range of bags below $300 that would "wow" people.

We also fast-tracked future designs so products scheduled to debut in 2010 or 2011 would come out in 2009, essentially compressing three years of innovation into 12 to 18 months. New products would include lighter-weight bags with novel details like soft, chic pleating, and hanging charms shaped like our iconic horse-and-carriage. We also introduced a modern variation on our Signature logo, inspired by the 1960s' op art movement that contrasted positive and negative space to create optical illusions. The new OpArt logo platform recast our classic *C* as a thick, sans serif font that when repeated created a modern, abstract pattern.

We could make all these changes in short order because we already had the nimble infrastructure and collaborative know-how to engineer the price points and margins we wanted, without sacrificing design. And because the front and the back end of the business already worked together seamlessly.

We were busy adapting to the economic downturn when the economy fell off a cliff in September 2008 with the abrupt bankruptcy of investment bank Lehman Brothers. It was followed by other banks teetering on the brink of insolvency, and the Dow Jones Industrial Average's largest point drop to date. A devastating economic period followed as millions of people and families lost homes and life savings. Many others who didn't lose everything feared they might. The magnitude and depth of the economic collapse was a shock to individuals and to businesses, especially those that sold discretionary items.

Stores across the country emptied as the economy deteriorated into the most challenging holiday season in my 30 years with Coach. Mike and I walked malls in November and early December and couldn't believe how desolate they were. Most retailers had sale signs in their windows as they heavily discounted merchandise to attract reticent consumers. We deliberately chose not to discount any products at Coach's full-priced retail stores. Instead, we leaned into our 104 US factory stores, where we could drive purchases through already lower prices, as well as additional discounts for a consumer that expected and responded to sales. Traffic, conversion, and ticket at factory stores were up, albeit modestly, which helped buoy our overall performance.

Still, like the economy, Coach's sales also fell off a cliff during the holiday season, when our North American same-store sales for the quarter sank 13%. Unheard of for us.

Consumer malaise continued into 2009 as total spending on bags and accessories in North America dropped more than 10% during the first half of the calendar year, compared to the prior year. There was only so much we could control given the macroeconomic factors at play. More nights than usual I slept fitfully as my mind raced with fears that the economy wouldn't improve, that we would need to lay off many employees, and that the business wouldn't rebound. I could usually go three or four days with only a few hours of sleep, but by Fridays I was spent. Lack of sleep can negatively impact moods and exacerbate stress, so I tried to take power naps and "go under the covers" at home on weekends.

In addition to introducing new products and lowering prices, we pulled every lever we could to protect the business. For instance, we stopped publicly sharing comparable store sales data for full-priced and factory stores in the United States, and instead began to report a single, aggregate metric for all stores in North America. External reporting would now reflect how we ran the company internally—as one brand with one set of equities, and multiple points of distribution. We didn't want investors to interpret a sales drop or rise in one channel, like factory, with bias about the overall health of Coach, and punish the stock. Investors needed to judge Coach on its overall performance and the strength of our brand.

We also initiated the first dividend in Coach's history. This was one of the few times Mike Devine and I differed. Mike believed having cash on hand during such uncertain times was safer than putting a dividend in place. My take was that using the significant cash flow our business model generated to return capital to shareholders when our stock was down sent a clear signal to investors that Coach was healthy, even if the economy wasn't. We did it, and Mike later agreed it was the right move to show just how confident we felt about our future. To drive home that optimism, I also bought a significant number of shares the week in February 2009 when our stock fell to $9, down 70% from its peak at more than $35 just two years earlier.

Overall, our response to the financial crisis was thorough, consumer focused, and swift. We also didn't try to reinvent ourselves out of panic. The core strategies, values, and equities that had served us for so long stayed the same. We adapted them to reflect the new reality, but staying true to our foundation armed us with confidence that no matter how bad things got, we could find our way through it.

Nonetheless, the stress of it all was compounded by other problems, including that competitor I should have seen coming.

• • •

At some point in early 2009, I went to the Roosevelt Field mall in Long Island with a few people from my team to visit one of Coach's most productive stores, and to check out a competing brand's store that had recently opened. We were walking toward Coach's prime location at the mall's 50-yard line when I stopped abruptly at the sight of a bright, glistening, busy new store directly across from ours selling chic leather handbags, spiked-heeled shoes, and women's clothing.

Above the window displays, polished chrome capital letters declared "MICHAEL KORS."

I stood there in disbelief. This was the first time I'd seen the full expression of the Michael Kors brand as a retail concept. It was so well staged with just the right lighting, casting, fixtures, and finishes, that I couldn't help but admit just how big a threat the brand was to Coach—a fact I'd been ignoring, or denying.

Michael Kors the fashion designer had been around for decades, creating what he called "easy glamour" apparel since the early 1980s. He was talented, but his business had its ups and downs. In 1997, LVMH invested in Kors's company about the same time LVMH made a low offer to buy us. Two years later, LVMH acquired one-third of Michael Kors Holdings Ltd., and Michael spent seven years as creative director of LVMH-owned Celine, another French luxury brand, before buying back his ownership with investors and repositioning his brand with lower-priced, ready-to-wear accessories. The business grew, but what really catapulted the brand was Michael's widespread popularity as an irreverent, witty judge on the hit reality series *Project Runway.*

The first Michael Kors lifestyle store opened in 2006 selling handbags, shoes, and clothes, all at accessible prices—Coach prices—that emanated an aspirational, jet-set attitude through slick ads with beautiful people poolside or boarding private planes. The brand's image wasn't for everyone, but for a certain segment it made accessible luxury sexy and fresh, and especially compelling for younger consumers.

Some of my colleagues and board members had been insisting for at least a year that Kors was a rising competitive force Coach needed to keep an eye on. Director Susan Kropf was the most vocal about how Kors was killing it in department stores. Instead of heeding warnings from people I trusted, and listening to my instincts, I wasn't particularly concerned. I'd seen the bags but wasn't impressed because they weren't original, but rather derivative of European luxury brands. Maybe I figured that Kors wasn't dangerous because it wasn't anchored in a distinctive product, like Coach.

What I had no idea about at the time was just how strategic the company had been. In later years, I'd run into Michael Kors's CEO, John Idol, who'd unabashedly thank me for giving him the Coach playbook for Kors to follow. The comment was intended to be flattering but it didn't make me feel good. Not only did Kors adopt Coach's accessory-driven assortments and price points, but it followed our real estate strategy by identifying our best locations and situating their stores as close as possible to ours, like at Roosevelt Field, where I can still see myself standing in disbelief. The Michael Kors store emanated a gleaming, glamourous energy that made Coach look tired. It was so undeniable and upsetting that I called Reed in a frenzy. How had this happened? How had we missed this?

Sometimes, you need to see something to believe it, and it was hard for me and many of us at Coach to imagine that another brand could come close to our success, particularly in such a short period. That was hubris, and I was guilty of ignoring what the data and people I trusted told me about the competitive landscape, which led me to underestimate Michael Kors, and become complacent. The thing about hubris is that you don't realize it's affecting your decisions until the consequences jolt you out of passivity. As for complacency, it's the enemy of innovation and creativity.

Fiscal 2009, which ended in June, was Coach's worst-performing year since going public. Sales were up a paltry 2% to $3.23 billion.

Our new products and lower pricing had yet to counter the drop-off in consumer spending and increased competition, but we stuck to our core strategies. We did, however, slow the number of new US stores to reflect decreased demand. We also continued full steam ahead with our expansion into China. The country still represented a small portion of our total sales, but it was our biggest growth opportunity. We were projecting that by 2013, the premium handbag and accessories market in greater China, Hong Kong, and Macau would exceed $2.5 billion, growing 50% from its current size. We just had to keep positioning Coach as an accessible luxury brand for the middle-class female.

During the summer of 2009, US consumers began to return to stores and we were seeing signs of improvement. Sales at factory stores were robust, and traffic in full-priced stores was inching up. We pinned a lot of hope on a new, happy collection called Poppy that our design and merchandising teams strategically created to offer an attitudinal counter to the economy's gloom and attract millennials. Poppy's playful, vibrant aesthetic was inspired by notebook graffiti, with bright pops of yellow, turquoise, red, orange, or purple that felt raw and spontaneous. On some bags, *Coach* was hand-drawn in bubble letters. Other bags had patterns that overlapped our Signature and OpArt logos. It was a fun, youthful array of bags, wristlets, wallets, jewelry, and shoes that really did put a smile on shoppers' faces, and excited our full-priced store teams.

We launched Poppy after one of our most successful pilots ever, and with a robust "Are you Poppy?" marketing campaign. And with an average bag priced at about $260, Poppy was a great value while delivering high gross margins. If sales continued to go well through fall and the holiday season, Poppy would prove to be a positive inflection point at a time when more than competition and the economy were distractions.

• • •

Back in 2007, Reed had approached me about creating a luxury brand under his name. I wasn't surprised, because we'd discussed it many times. From a business perspective, I believed that expanding Coach's higher-end product assortment made strategic sense. Our pinnacle products were still selling relatively well—we'd yet to truly feel the shift in economic headwinds—and an elevated assortment would be relevant to luxury-minded consumers looking for exclusivity, while counterbalancing our growing factory outlet channel. We could do all that under the Coach name, but I felt that Reed had earned the opportunity to pursue his dream. His talents were instrumental, albeit not alone, in Coach's resurgence and global growth.

I also felt a great deal of loyalty to Reed, and I worried he'd leave Coach if I refused. I wasn't sure I'd be able to find another creative thought partner that I connected with so symbiotically. I also couldn't imagine what Coach would look like without Reed. I had other concerns, too. Reed was widely respected in the industry, but consumers didn't know him, so he lacked a large platform from which to launch a namesake brand. And unlike Coach, a brand under Reed's name would not be based on market research or consumer insights; it would be strictly designer-led, reflecting Reed's point of view, which was influenced by art and interior design. The board supported an initial investment, and as part of the deal we agreed that Reed would divide his time between the two brands, with an understanding that Coach would come first.

Reed was in the midst of developing the Reed Krakoff brand (RK) as the financial crisis took its toll. He and his teams had done a fantastic job developing Poppy, but in hindsight I should have told Reed that the company was in the midst of its own crisis, and that I was sorry but we couldn't allow him to spend even 1% of his time on RK. We needed all hands on deck for the Coach brand. Instead, I chose to muscle through the crisis, the competitive threat, and the development of RK, doing everything we could on all fronts with the resources we had.

When we announced the RK brand in July 2009, we positioned it as a stand-alone lifestyle brand categorized as new American luxury. Ambitious in timeline and scope, it would launch just a year out, and encompass handbags plus ready-to-wear apparel, footwear, and jewelry. The brand would be sold in select premier department stores, as well as Reed Krakoff boutiques in the United States, Japan, and Hong Kong.

Creating commercial products with a distinctive point of view takes an enormous amount of time. That's why most designer brands start small, trial in department stores, learn from error, refine, and build up a clientele. I enabled the RK brand to short-circuit all that through sheer will and resources, moving too fast and overestimating our abilities as a business to create a desirable luxury brand, especially during a recession. Reed also pulled some of our best designers off the Coach brand to support RK, and I did not stop him.

In 2010, the Reed Krakoff brand launched to lukewarm reviews and mediocre sales—disappointing, but we stayed the course. The second RK collection a year later got a more favorable response. While beautiful, the collection didn't resonate with consumers enough to build a viable business. Eventually, Coach stopped funding the RK brand because we didn't see a path to profitability.

In retrospect, I realize that I let my fear of losing Reed blind me to the greater good. The best thing for Coach was not a designer-led brand. I also lost sight of what we were originally trying to solve for, which was reaching more consumers with elevated products. The consequences would be many, but primarily it was an investment that did not pay off, a distraction from our core brand. It would also eventually lead to Reed and a group of investors buying out his label, and Reed leaving Coach. It was an unfortunate way to end the relationship between Reed and Coach, as well as between Reed and me, but it certainly didn't negate the essential role Reed had played in Coach's history, or the memories I had of our journey together.

All of this was going on while the company also addressed a problem that had been a thorn in our side for years.

• • •

Counterfeiting and copying the likeness of Coach bags had been going on since the 1980s, when we threatened or sued more than half a dozen manufacturers for imitating our designs and even the Coach hangtag. In the 1990s, fake Coach products that sold for a fraction of legitimate prices still existed but didn't begin to dilute our sales until after we introduced the distinctive *C*s of Signature in 2001. Some replicas were so spot-on visually that if you were walking down the street and saw one you wouldn't know it was an imitation unless you handled it and felt its cheap make and material.

To address counterfeiting and other legal issues, Keith and I decided Coach needed a business-oriented general counsel.

"You need Todd Kahn," said Felice Schulaner, our no-nonsense head of HR who had left us in 2006 and returned on an interim basis when her replacement did not work out. Thankfully, we listened to Felice.

Todd's father was a Holocaust survivor, and both his parents had immigrated to the United States, where they started an estate jewelry business. Todd worked in the store as a kid, cleaning counters and watching his mom and dad deal with customers. He was the first in his family to go to college, and he went on to law school, then Wall Street, then several general counsel positions, eventually transitioning to operations as the COO for several retail companies. He'd been through complicated acquisitions and restructurings, and he wasn't looking to be a general counsel again when we offered him the role, which was a step back in his career. But as Todd put it, "If you get a chance to play for the Yankees, you don't care what position you play." I was grateful that a lot of talented people felt that way about Coach, especially Todd.

He became our chief legal officer in January 2008, and it took about a nanosecond for him to demonstrate his value to me and to the company. Todd was as emotionally intelligent as he was knowledgeable. If I questioned him on a legal issue, insisting he show me the case law behind his opinion on a given topic, he'd fire back, "Lew, that's not what you pay me for. You pay me for my judgment." He was right, and he became my thought partner on any number of issues. We all came to discover that Todd had many talents well beyond strategic legal expertise. He was a natural leader, and his scope was going to grow significantly over time, to Coach's benefit.

Up to that point Coach had taken a serious but traditional approach to fighting counterfeits. We spent millions of dollars retaining lawyers who brought lawsuits to shut down counterfeiting operations. We educated customs officials so they could stop counterfeits at the US border. We worked with local governments and police departments to orchestrate raids on illegal street vendors. We joined industry consortiums to prevent fraud. But all of that didn't pay off to the extent we needed it to.

Todd's approach was radically different. His Operation Turnlock—the clever name he came up with—had a no-tolerance policy and went after any organization or individual even tangentially involved in the making or distribution of fake Coach products. Not just manufacturers but distributors, too. Even a landlord in Florida whose property was the site of a flea market where multiple counterfeited brands were sold. Not only did we get a monetary judgment in that case, but we were awarded the land, which we sold with a deed that prevented hosting flea markets again.

In a smart move, Todd used intellectual property lawyers who worked on contingency instead of charging by the hour. The strategy was less costly for us.

Todd also went after knockoffs, which, while not as problematic as counterfeits, also created confusion in the marketplace. We filed trade-dress suits against any company, including large retailers, that produced or sold bags close enough to our core equities in shape, material, and hardware that consumers could mistake for a Coach.

Todd made it known that if you copy Coach, we will go after you, and you will pay.

At one point we were launching something like 50 lawsuits a quarter, and getting large monetary judgments. We never collected most of it, but in Operation Turnlock's first three years we brought in some $20 million. Todd likes to recall a business review meeting when I asked him, in part tongue in cheek, what his legal department expected to comp in the coming year.

These years were not all about missteps and fighting fires as Todd pursued counterfeiters, Reed focused on his brand, Michael Kors encroached, and the company navigated the financial crisis. At the same time, another group inside Coach was not so quietly creating a new revenue stream that would give us more control over our financial performance exactly when we needed it, and for many years to come.

• • •

Coach's online presence had been limited to our website, Coach.com, which during the first decade of the 2000s mostly functioned as a digital version of our catalog. "Make the product the hero" had been my directive to our creative teams whose job was to translate to the screen the visceral experience of touching and trying on a bag in a store. A lot of attention went into photography to capture the look and feel of our materials online, but we put much less thought into consumers' digital experience beyond our site. Then, in 2007, the head of our North American retail merchandising group, David Duplantis, made the compelling case that we should.

David had been with Coach since 1998, after helping to start J. Crew's retail division, which followed his four years at the Gap, and seven years at Macy's, where he began his retail career and completed Macy's renowned executive training program. The epitome of Coach smart, David had knowledge and conviction bred from his rich retail experience, and he was a genuinely good person. We all considered David a pleasure to work with, even when he had to ruffle some feathers to get things done.

In 2008, social media sites were still nascent, and luxury brands were figuring out how to navigate the digital landscape. Facebook started in 2004. Twitter launched in 2006. Instagram wouldn't exist until 2010. David knew little about what it actually meant for Coach to have an online presence in the budding age of social media. He did, however, have a keen appreciation that people were beginning to engage with brands differently on digital platforms than they did in brick-and-mortar environments. They talked to each other and shared opinions.

The importance of traditional media coverage of consumer products was declining as a result. Where once a brand like Coach used public relations and guerrilla marketing to try to secure or influence publicity at established magazines and newspapers, the online world had become a free-for-all of individual content creators with no barriers to entry or oversight. Anyone could post product reviews with relative ease and reach an audience. Bloggers were the influencers of the day, with niche platforms that had names like PurseBlog. The most successful bloggers earned millions of followers through the authenticity and originality of their voice. Consumers increasingly followed blogs they admired and trusted, and to get a blogger's attention, a brand had to earn their trust and know their tastes.

The so-called blogosphere and social media sites were digital mediums Coach had yet to tap. David said it was time for us to meet a growing number of younger women where they were increasingly going online, instead of expecting them to come to Coach.com. The last time someone raised their hand to advance Coach's online presence was back in 1997, when our website functioned more like a landing page that didn't process sales. You could look but not buy. I can still remember the leadership meeting with about 100 employees when the head of IT at the time, Tom Britt, stood up and said, "Lew, when are we going to launch e-commerce already?" A roar of applause filled the auditorium, so I said, "I guess we're going to start it as soon as we can." Everyone clapped again. Ten years later, Coach.com had evolved but was still serving as an online catalog that generated only about 2% of companywide sales.

I could have hired someone with social media experience, but I believed David was the natural choice to build out our Global Web and Digital Media

Group. David had two things more important than digital expertise: the curiosity and drive to learn it quickly, and a seasoned understanding of Coach the brand and how we did business. That abundant knowledge and those instincts would take years for someone new to Coach to acquire.

I gave David free rein and ample resources. He embarked by doing just what I did nearly 30 years earlier when I had to start Coach's mail-order business. He sought out experts, most notably a marketing professor at New York University, Scott Galloway, who had a business, Luxury Lab, a think tank for digital innovation, that ranked brands on their digital competence. Coach ranked rather poorly, so David asked Scott for his advice, which Scott offered in his signature no-nonsense style. Wisely, David retained Scott to help us define our strategy, and Coach became one of Scott's first consulting clients.

One thing we had going for us was our database with millions of customers' email addresses and purchase histories. We'd always been intentional about collecting the information of shoppers who came into our stores. Now we got more diligent about tracking consumer behavior online—whether or not they made a purchase—and slicing the data to reveal patterns so we could communicate with consumers in ever more targeted ways, digitally. If we knew which bag styles you bought in the past and how often you bought from us—one a year, every few months—we could email you photos of new products that reflected your tastes with a frequency that didn't bombard you but matched your buying history. Eventually, David developed his group's own advanced analytics team to more deeply parse online buying behavior.

We also experimented with digital mediums beyond Coach.com, first by posting our own product videos on YouTube. In 2008 we joined Facebook, then Twitter in 2009, making Coach one of the first higher-end fashion brands to have a social media presence. For the first time we were talking to our customers publicly and giving them more opportunities to talk to each other about Coach, uncensored. Some people inside Coach were uncomfortable, worried we might open some Pandora's box. True, we lacked control over the conversation, but I had enough confidence in people's perception of the Coach brand that I wasn't worried the dialogue would hurt us. Plus, I was watching my kids come of age in the digital world and was fascinated that someone in the privacy of their home could send a message and instantaneously reach so many humans at once. I believed digital was changing not just how people shopped, but how their opinions were shaped about all sorts of things. It was a huge opportunity for Coach.

Our first major social and marketing initiative, Design Your Own Tote, went viral and got more than 3,200 entries and 6.5 million impressions. We chose three winners, flew them to New York, and made limited-edition versions of their totes.

Our consumer insights told us that women shopping online were particularly interested in blogger fashion trends. David's team was creative and strategic in how they engaged top bloggers like Emily Weiss, a former fashion-magazine editor whose popular blog *Into the Gloss* would evolve into the disruptive beauty brand Glossier. Coach was known as the first luxury handbag brand to enlist influential bloggers to write about new products, and to include them in our marketing campaigns. We embraced Emily and others as partners, treating them like magazine editors, with respect. We also made sure that the products we asked them to showcase reflected their voice. Matching the right bag with the right blogger could bring a product to life in a way we could not, "completing the Coach story," as David liked to say.

In 2009, we brought a few bloggers to Coach's offices, where we filmed them chatting about our holiday products. We used the conversation as part of our online marketing campaign, which got a lot of attention and sparked sales. That same year we flew bloggers from around the country and overseas to our New York offices to get an inside preview of future collections. I spent some time with them, and I was so impressed with the sophistication and savvy of this younger entrepreneurial set. They knew exactly what they were doing.

Another successful program was the Guest Blogger feature on our website that each month spotlighted someone who'd supported one of our products. Visitors to the Guest Blogger page were more likely to buy something than people who just came to Coach.com but didn't visit the page.

We were also less surgical in our approach. When Poppy launched in 2010, we used social to build buzz, hoping to organically engage 100 bloggers. Ultimately, more than 800 touted Poppy to some degree.

To measure the financial impact of our social media efforts we came up with a calculus that correlated online activity with online traffic and sales. This was harder to do with in-store activity, aside from anecdotally. What we did know was that Coach.com served as an invaluable browsing destination that people pre-shopped before visiting a store in person. They'd print out a picture of the product they liked from the site and bring it into the store with intent to buy.

We were learning never to rely on just one social channel with one message, but to apply consistent, customized messaging for each digital medium.

We were also students of other companies' online strategies, and we adapted some techniques. One proved a game changer for our overall business. Websites like Rue La La and the Gilt Groupe were known for conducting flash sales, making select merchandise available at reduced prices for a limited time. We decided to try it, but within the guardrails of our brand.

Coach factory stores were the primary place to find discounted Coach products, and our full-price and discount Coach shoppers remained distinct segments with very little overlap. We had to maintain these two distinctions online. Our approach was to create invitation-only online flash sales just for Coach factory-store visitors. Because this consumer was willing to drive a decent distance to an outlet mall to get a Coach, our online flash sales offered a huge convenience factor that saved her hours of travel and the cost of gas. The attraction of flash sales to this Coach consumer could not be understated.

We tested various flash tactics, like limiting or expanding the number of products available, or letting the sale last a few hours instead of a few days, or requiring reservations instead of drop-ins. We managed the online experience so carefully that eventually we could closely forecast how much revenue each flash experience would generate based on the mix of product, length of time, nature of attendees, and even the season.

The introduction of invitation-only flash sales gave Coach access to a large, untapped, on-demand revenue stream. By blending the right products with the right customers with the right timing, we could quickly achieve predictable revenue generation. In fact, engaging the discount-oriented, online consumer via a well-planned flash sale enabled us to drive profitable growth exactly when we needed it most. It allowed us to counterbalance negative effects from the financial crisis, the rise of Michael Kors, and the distraction of the RK brand. This was a major unlock.

There was, of course, a now-familiar chorus of people worried that we risked degrading the brand as online factory sales accelerated. But our research and experience reassured us that we could further grow revenue from the discount shopper without diluting Coach's brand integrity.

For me, the immediacy of being able to track views and clicks and know within hours if we had a hit product was lightyears away from where I'd started. Back in the early 1980s, I was mailing catalogs to addresses I'd resurrected from dusty shoeboxes and had to wait at least a week for the first orders to be mailed back.

Our strategy to reach a qualified, targeted audience in authentic and relevant ways paid off. By 2011, we had 2.3 million Facebook fans and 300,000 Twitter followers, impressive stats at the time. Coach also was recognized as one of the first luxury brands to find success creating a global digital presence, and one of the earliest to adopt social media practices into our business model. We had e-commerce sites in three countries, and informational sites in 14 more. Coach's digital channel was now our single largest store in the world, and it was growing at significant double digits. It was also our most important marketing tool.

Like most things at Coach, the success of our digital platform and channel was not an accident. Looking back, I see that it was the blend of elements so intrinsic to Coach that allowed digital to flourish: The immersive curiosity that propelled David to learn about e-commerce. My belief in an online channel's importance to the greater good of the business facilitated the necessary buy-in and collaboration from other group leaders. Bold imagination and lateral thinking allowed us to seek out new ideas and experiment with out-of-the-box strategies, like flash sales, which we executed with our usual rigor. Our measure-and-modify, test-and-learn culture bred insights to inform our decisions so we could adapt our site and strategies to maximize results.

The fact that our digital channel used so many elements that had informed Coach's growth over the prior three decades was proof that blending magic and logic was an approach that continued to transcend time and trends.

In fiscal 2010, sales in the US bag and accessory category resumed growth, rising 3% to 5%, to about $8.3 billion. During the same period, Coach's North American bag and accessory sales rose 10% across all channels, and 18% in our own stores.

All told, fiscal 2010—which had one extra week compared to 2009—was a rebound year for us as Coach's global sales jumped 12% to $3.6 billion while net income rose 18%, to $735 million. Excluding the extra week of revenue still gave us a hearty 10% year-over-year bump.

The financial crisis was like other periods of economic upheaval in that it had short- as well as long-term effects on consumer behavior. Post-recession, people were still price sensitive, and many weren't going back to previous spending levels. Coach adapted, continuing to sell more bags priced between $200 and $300, a new sweet spot. We designed new iterations of the wildly popular Poppy, supported by attention-grabbing marketing that drew people, especially more millennials, into stores. Traffic and conversion were up at our factory stores, too.

Sticking to our pricing, merchandising, and expansion strategies maintained our momentum.

It helped, of course, that our business in China was also growing. By mid-2010, revenues there were more than $100 million, and we had 41 locations, primarily in second- and third-tier cities, plus 10 locations in Hong Kong and two in Macau. Stores open more than a year were comping double digits.

Consumer confidence continued to improve. In June 2010, we interviewed 5,100 active Coach users, and 30% felt that the economy was getting better, compared to just 8% a year prior. Our customers also told us that their intention to buy Coach over the next 12 months had dramatically increased. That 2010 holiday season was exceptional, with an extra boost by Oprah picking our patent leather Sophia satchel, in crimson or camel, as one of her favorite things. It all boded well as Coach entered our 70th year.

• • •

In 2011, the year Coach turned 70, sales surpassed $4 billion for the first time in our history. A dollar invested in Coach at the IPO in 2000 was worth about $30 in September 2011. For comparison, a dollar invested in the S&P 500 over the same period would be worth about 98 cents.

That fall, to celebrate our 70th year, *Women's Wear Daily* dedicated a 50-page issue to chronicling Coach's Journey "from Local Leather Shop to Global Fashion Powerhouse." The articles and congratulatory ads saluted the brand as a trailblazer of classic, incomparable American style and quality craftsmanship, and celebrated seven decades of milestones: Miles and

Lillian's ownership. Bonnie Cashin's whimsy. My arrival in 1979, when Coach had $6 million in sales. Our first catalog. Our first store. The sale to Sara Lee. Our retail expansion and product extensions. Reed's creative vision. The IPO. Our iconic styles and launch of collections like Hamptons, Signature, and Poppy. Coach's popularity in Japan, where we were still the number-two brand. Our fits and starts in Europe. Our rapid adoption in China. Even our industry-leading digital channel. All in all, the overview was nostalgic and optimistic, but far from complete.

Missing were the names of so many other people past and present who'd made those and other milestones even possible. In my own mind's eye I could still see Myer working closely with craftspeople on our factory floor, and Mr. Leather visiting tanneries. There's Maxine leading a meeting, and Mary Grace poring over computer printouts, looking for stories the numbers told. I see Gary Dembart on his first day at Coach in his Timberland boots, and the Tarica brothers, Jim and Larry, welcoming me to their showroom. I see Arun's feisty smile. Occasionally, I still heard his voice in my ear.

Photos sprinkled throughout the issue brought the past back to life. One showed the inside of our first store in 1981 on a busy weekend day near the holidays. The cramped space is packed with more than two dozen customers standing shoulder-to-shoulder in winter coats as they wait in line to check out, or look over the wall of leather bags lined up like library books. I'm standing behind the register wearing a beige sweater-vest over a white shirt, my sleeves rolled up, as I look down to handwrite a receipt.

The scene in the photo seems like a lifetime ago but also feels like yesterday. It's cliché to say that so much had changed yet much was still the same, but for Coach I think that rang true, from our natural glovetanned leather to the language I still used. I told *Women's Wear Daily* that the way we run our business in 2011 is a combination of magic and logic.

"The magic is the touch and feel of great design and great positioning, and the logic is the rigor and discipline of using knowledge to help make informed decisions. The people on the creative side use a great deal of logic, and the people on the business side use a great deal of magic." The result was a product that's "aspirational for some consumers, classic for those who wanted well-made bags that would endure, and stylish for those who wanted bags relevant for the season . . . we're offering consumers accessible luxury products that are innovative and relevant at a good price. Standing behind a product, you can build lasting franchises."

At 70, was Coach a legacy brand?

I wasn't yet in a position to say.

The thing about legacies in general is that even when we do everything in our power to shape them, they're ultimately out of our control. Legacies are formed by what endures, so we can't know the legacy of a brand, or a company, or even a person until long after we've stopped trying to shape it. I'd been at Coach 32 years, and I had a few more to go. All I could do in these remaining years was continue to control what I could, including how I responded to what I could not control, and be grateful for it all.

EPILOGUE

Legacy

It's just before Thanksgiving in 2023, and I'm driving to Coach's offices to cohost the annual luncheon honoring exceptional employees at the director level and below. When Felice started the tradition 20 years earlier it was called the Chairman's Award, but after I retired from Coach in 2014 it was renamed the Lew Awards. Attending the event is a highlight of my post-Coach years.

Coach's headquarters now resides in a towering glass building not far from where our 12-story loft building once stood. One of my final decisions prior to leaving was relocating the company to Hudson Yards, the massive, multi-use neighborhood that today spans the city's former West Side railyards. We made a deal with real estate developer Steve Ross for Coach to become Hudson Yards' first corporate tenant. It's an urban, open campus that sits on the edge of the High Line and keeps Coach in the hub of Manhattan, where it all began.

I walk into the lobby, where the focal point is a wall of glass-encased shelves that showcase dozens of vintage Coach bags in a rainbow of silhouettes. The slouchy Duffle Sac. The sturdy Stewardess bag. The everyday City bag. The Legacy Zip. Hero products on display.

I sign in as a visitor, and at the elevator bank I see a few familiar faces of people who were working for Coach when I was still CEO.

By the time I left in 2014, Coach's sales had reached $5 billion and the North American market for premium handbags and accessories—a market that Coach helped define—topped $11 billion. I had chosen a successor, and we did a phased transition, but once I left, I left. I knew that I wouldn't agree with all of the decisions the incoming leadership would make, so I didn't even want to sit on the board. My shadow was extremely long, and I couldn't risk it overshadowing the new team. I also wasn't sure I could bear not steering a company I'd led for so long. Maybe I finally understood why Miles walked out the door the day we sold to Sara Lee. Coach and I each needed a clean break. I would watch Coach evolve from a distance, in ways I could not foresee but that future leaders and employees would envision and bring to life. It's why I love days like today, because I get to experience the energy of people who are so passionately committed to the business and the brand.

I step into an elevator that whisks me up to the 17th floor so I can say hello to Coach's creative director, Stuart Vevers. He joined in 2013, after Reed left. Stuart is a visionary talent with a down-to-earth soul and a cool, playful sophistication. We'd recruited him away from LVMH, where he was chief designer and creative officer for luxury brand Loewe. It was such a coup that to evade detection from his employer we flew Stuart from Madrid to New York on a private plane the night before the public announcement. People love working with Stuart. His calm confidence has earned him a loyal following. I marvel at how he and his team continue to boldly reimagine the brand with collections that stay true to Coach's heritage of authenticity, while resonating with a new generation. Their wildly popular Tabby Collection adds a little glamour to Coach bags from the 1970s. Nostalgia-chic, Stuart calls it. A breakout sub-brand called Coachtopia fuses fashion with sustainability for a fun collection of bags, clothes, and other accessories made from recycled Coach leather, fabric scraps, and renewable materials. Stuart's interpretation of modern luxury is about prioritizing the personal over perfection. He believes a bag that is loved and worn has more appeal than something that's pristine. It's a philosophy that's spot on for Gen Z, and reminiscent of the authenticity that made Coach's bags so beloved in its early years.

It's the people that I miss most about Coach, but I have no regrets about stepping away when I did.

It helped that I had a plan for what came next.

• • •

A few years before I retired, my son, Sam, and I had been talking about forming a family office to invest in early-stage businesses. Sam had worked on

Wall Street for many years, and was a confident, quick thinker as well as an inquisitive, incisive decision-maker. He was also a good judge of opportunities, as well as people's character. And, like all my kids, he easily cultivated lasting relationships. We'd always communicated in a straightforward, respectful manner, so I could envision us as business partners. Plus, we enjoyed each other's company. The two of us had tested the waters prior to my Coach retirement, working with and investing in a few early-stage consumer brands. This gave us confidence to go ahead with our plans. We were joined by my son-in-law, Ernest Odinec, who had a background in investment management, was extremely smart, and brought rigor to financial analysis. Ern also had a keen appreciation for what was required to move businesses forward. His soft-spoken nature balanced the high energy Sam and I could bring into a room.

The three of us formed the Benvolio Group—named after our family's beloved labradoodle. My longtime, irreplaceable assistant Pat Cherry joined us, too. In 2014 we all moved into office space overlooking Central Park.

After I officially left Coach, my days quickly filled with back-to-back meetings. I didn't even take much of a break in between the two roles, aside from a five-day beach vacation with Bobbie. In retrospect I should have stayed away longer, but I feared that having down time would leave me feeling purposeless, even lost. So to avoid any chance of that, I immediately immersed myself in my new, full-time venture.

Benvolio's mission is to invest in early-stage, disruptive consumer-facing brands, and add value where we can. I love coming into our Benvolio offices. I still have that entrepreneurial spirit, and my role has allowed me to learn about industries I knew little or nothing about after a lifetime steeped in the accessories business. Beverages. Health and wellness. Consumer tech. Most of our investments are passive, but for several we have been more active advisors. I spend much of my time talking with company founders and their teams about their vision, their strategies, their products, their people, and how to best lead.

In addition to how to manage their companies, we occasionally discuss how to manage their own emotional well-being. Running a business is stressful at all stages. I know a lot about that, of course, and I often share my own attempts to navigate the emotional tolls that manifest from my fear of failure and drive for excellence. People are often surprised, but also relieved, to know that someone who built a successful business still struggles with fears and doubts.

Not until a few years into Benvolio, though, did I realize just how much my drive and fear could still grip me.

Early on we invested in a retail concept that I was especially enthused about. A few years in, we increased Benvolio's stake to a degree that allowed us to have significant influence, and a more operational role. We were so bullish on the potential that we brought in outside investors for the first time, including people I knew professionally. I began to spend about one-third of my time on the business, which added to my already full plate. I was prepared to help guide it, but I wasn't looking to be a CEO again, so we needed to find the right leader to work with us. After a few false starts, we recruited a very senior person with industry experience who seemed ideal. She came in with a lot of energy and was well liked, but it quickly became clear to us that she didn't lead as we expected, and as time passed the company didn't perform as we projected. Of course, I felt compelled to do everything I could to change the trajectory, but the CEO we'd hired—and chose not to replace for a variety of reasons—wasn't collaborative or coachable. There were other issues, too, and I found myself watching problems I was unable to fix stack up as my ability to influence decisions diminished.

In the past, my anxiety tended to spike when I had little or no control over the outcome of an endeavor or situation that I truly cared about. What also triggered me this time were the consequences for others—primarily people who trusted me to invest alongside us that stood to lose money. And if the business went under, thousands of loyal customers would be disappointed. Many talented, dedicated staffers would be out of jobs. I ruminated endlessly about the situation, unable to compartmentalize. Distraught, I couldn't sleep. My bandwidth narrowed and my energy flattened. Feeling so powerless to stop what I feared would be a trainwreck even made me question my self-worth.

I had stopped seeing my therapist regularly, so I reached out and scheduled more routine visits to try to work through everything weighing me down. Bobbie and my kids knew what I was going through, and they reassured me that my value as a person was not wrapped up in this singular event—or for that matter any singular event. Or any one business. No one thing ever defines us. Even when we know this to be true, it's easy to get so caught up in our emotions that we lose sight of reality.

It had been years since my circumstances had triggered a depressive episode, and it was clear that I still had more to learn about how to manage my mental health, even at this stage of my life and work.

Subsequent conversations with my family, close friends, and therapist helped me see that I could proactively take control of an uncontrollable situation by either avoiding working with certain types of individuals, like hardwired narcissists, or removing myself when I had little or no opportunity to influence outcomes. It was incumbent on me to recognize this pattern and stop it before it took hold of my psyche. I didn't need absolute control; I just couldn't tolerate not having any when it was warranted. Caring for myself meant honoring this aspect of my human nature.

I was as surprised as anyone that I could still descend into such a dark place, but just as the manifestations of my fear and drive influenced me at Coach, they also influenced me at Benvolio. Most of us bring our full selves to our jobs; in turn, we take our full selves with us when we leave.

Without Coach, Lew was still Lew.

An entrepreneur's path is full of ups and downs. Seeing impassioned founders try to turn their ideas into businesses has given me an even greater appreciation for just how hard it is to do. No one person, or strategy, or product is ever solely responsible for a brand's rise. This applies to all businesses—including Coach today.

• • •

After chatting with Stuart at Coach's headquarters, I make my way to the workshop, where sample products are still made by hand, as well as with laser cutters and 3D printers. The room is bustling. Its director, Massimiliano Arbo, greets me wearing a white lab jacket and a warm, wide grin. Massimo, as everyone calls him, was born in Florence, joined Coach as a pattern cutter in 1997, and is as gifted at managing people as he is a craftsman.

A small group of employees is touring the workshop for a requisite class on how Coach products are made, and I say hello. Lauren Grunberg is a VP in product development who joined Coach in 2003, "back when we all had phones on our desks." She tells the group, "Lew used to leave us voice messages called broadcast bulletins, where he talked about the season's bags and how they were selling. If you wanted to make a call, you first had to listen to his broadcast bulletin." She laughs at the memory. I'd forgotten about that. "I loved that we heard directly from you," she says to me. "You brought everyone along for the journey, and made it feel personal." That's nice for me to hear.

Carrie Shigetomi, an SVP who also works in product development, recalls attending my business review meetings after she joined Coach in 2006. "We really had to be on our game," she says. "One time, you asked me why the bags in our new Legacy Collection were so heavy." After the meeting, she took the bags apart to find out. "It really made me think about how all the components of each bag contributed to its weight."

Someone else recalls how I used to walk around the office and knew everybody's name. "You made people feel seen and heard and important." I thank them for sharing their memories.

It's nearing noon and I head to the sunlit atrium where about 100 people are milling about. I say more hellos, including to Todd Kahn, who has been Coach's CEO since 2020. I always knew our lawyer-turned-leader was destined for much bigger things than going after counterfeiters. Todd is Coach's third CEO since I left, and under his leadership Coach is experiencing a renaissance. He's a well-respected leader doing a remarkable job, and I consider him a keeper of Coach's culture, as well as a beloved friend.

Round tables are set for an elegant lunch, and we take our seats as Todd introduces me.

"Our legacy of excellence starts with Lew," he says. I think to myself, *It's a legacy that really starts with Miles,* then I look around and realize that most of the people here weren't even born when I met Miles following my serendipitous taxi ride with Mel Herman, whose words jump-started my Coach journey. *I have a childhood friend that runs a small pocketbook company who's looking for a successor.*

Todd continues, "Lew grew Coach through multiple iterations, and reimaginations, and creativity. He is what motivates us. He is what inspires us. He is why I came to Coach." I'm touched by the praise. I get up and say a few words, not nearly as eloquently.

"I'm not sure where to begin," I admit, so I make a few remarks about what Coach was like when we had just $6 million in sales. "Our entire company had about 95 employees. We had space at 516 West 34th Street, where 20,000 square feet was a manufacturing floor, and the floor directly below it was a warehouse, shipping room, and showroom." I want people to appreciate our roots. "We have come a long way," I say.

After I share a few more thoughts, each awardee walks to the front of the room to accept their award as a colleague describes why they were nominated. I'm struck by how many of their traits have been core to Coach for decades.

Alexander Knox, a senior designer, is lauded for being an extreme collaborator.

Emma Lindberg is a photo producer who is able to balance different perspectives.

Melissa Ruggiero in product development stays open to possibilities.

Katie Leccese, a buying manager, creates inclusive environments.

Karen Reid in allocation always goes above and beyond.

Angelina Hazzouri in merchandising uses focus groups and surveys to understand Gen Z consumers—and inform innovation using magic and logic.

And designer Ken Pan makes everyone around him feel like they are part of something big, and he is committed to upholding the company's legacy.

After the ceremony, we take a group photo before I say goodbye and head uptown to the apartment where Bobbie and I now live.

On the way, I think about that word *legacy.* What it means for Coach and for me.

Giving decades of your time and energy to your work can make it hard to separate your professional legacy from your personal one. What was my legacy at Coach? It certainly isn't something that can be measured. A legacy only exists in the mind. It's what we believe to be true.

At Coach, I believe my fear and drive inspired elements of magic and logic, forging a culture that unleashed countless people's talents so they could realize their own potential to achieve some pretty remarkable accomplishments: Expanding a beloved American brand in the 1980s. Reinventing it in the 1990s. Growing it exponentially in the early 2000s. And, in the years that followed, overcoming crisis and other challenges to emerge as the strong, growing company it is now, one that continues a heritage of delighting people with products that serve many purposes and personalities. Whether you worked for Coach or owned a Coach bag, you, too, are part of the story.

When I think about my personal legacy, the answers come to me as emotions more than words. Feelings of gratitude for my mother and the future she envisioned for me. Respect for my father's work ethic. The connectedness I feel to my sister Claire, to longtime friends, and to former colleagues and mentors whose influences have lasted well beyond our years together.

Mostly, though, I'm filled with unconditional love for Bobbie and our kids. The family I came home to after my long days at Coach was a source of joy and strength. Their well-being is my highest priority, and almost everything Bobbie and I did as parents revolved around instilling Tamara, Sam, and Alana with foundational values to prepare them for life. Each has chosen a path paved with education and friendship, and work that is true to their individual passions and talents. They are thriving adults, raising their own children. We see each other often, and each makes me a better version of myself. Alana's energetic spirit uplifts me. Tamara's wisdom centers me. Sam likes to remind me that life is about special moments, not the daily slog, or even the endgame. I can use the reminder. I no longer work Fridays and weekends, and I leave the office at a reasonable hour Mondays through Thursdays to spend more time with Bobbie. This overdue balance has helped me feel more content, which I have also come to understand is a quieter version of success.

With Coach in my rearview mirror, a sense of pride and gratitude comes over me as I look forward to spending another Thanksgiving with my family. No bag man could ask for more.

ACKNOWLEDGMENTS

Writing this book was more challenging, illuminating, and rewarding than I ever anticipated, and there are many people to thank.

Foremost, my wife, Bobbie. Nothing on these pages or during our 50 years together would have been possible without your love, wisdom, and partnership.

It was my children, Tamara, Sam, and Alana, who urged me to write about my own story as well as Coach's, especially my emotional struggles. My kids understood that those experiences would resonate with many professionals. I'm so glad they encouraged me to be more personal. There is a real, sincere willingness among younger generations to understand themselves, and find ways to navigate their own emotional well-being as they progress through their careers. It's my hope that sharing some of my challenges and coping tools will be meaningful to people at all stages of their lives.

Reflecting on my past decisions and behaviors for this book helped me better understand the arc of my own life and Coach's journey. I could not have gotten there if it wasn't for my writing partner, Joanne Gordon. She compelled me to dive deeper than I thought was possible in understanding the forces that drive me both positively and negatively. Due to her curiosity, empathy, and investigative skills, Joanne came to truly understand me and became an expert on Coach. During hundreds of hours of conversations, we developed a natural and easy working relationship. We share similar values and I am honored to consider her a lifelong friend.

Joanne and I also want to thank everyone who shared their time and memories. Between us we spoke with more than 75 people whose expertise and candid recollections let us capture history with more depth and accuracy.

I also came to appreciate that it takes visionaries to bring a book to market. Our editor, Melinda Merino at Harvard Business Review Press, believed from our first conversation that Coach's story was worth telling. I'm thankful that she reintroduced me to Joanne, who wrote the *Forbes* article about Coach in 2001. Joanne and I are both grateful for Melinda's wise editorial guidance and thoughtful observations as we shared drafts. HBRP's anonymous readers and seasoned editorial board also made the book better. The design, production, and marketing teams were true partners, especially Stephani Finks and Allison Peter, as well as Sally Ashworth, Sue Boshers, Macaulay Campbell, Julie Devoll, Lindsey Dietrich, Ed Domina, Rick Emanuel, Bill Gallagher, David Goehring, Alexandra Kephart, Jon Shipley, and Felicia Sinusas.

Thanks to my literary agent, Jim Levine, for his pragmatism and seasoned, steady hand.

So many people at Coach, past and present, also contributed to the book. From the outset, Todd Kahn, Coach's CEO, supported my efforts to preserve the history of a brand we both love. Creative Director Stuart Vevers and his talented colleagues captured Coach's essence with a magnificent jacket and insert pages that tell a visual story. For your time and expertise, a special thanks to Michelle Kapp, Erin Kurpiewski, Chelsea Cowan, Louis Minuto, Alanna Hernando, Christine Faulkner, Chris Apichai, Travis Lindhorst, Jeremy Freed, David Gormly, Heather Calugaru, Hooman Pishdad, Camille Watson, and Abby Deering, as well as archivist Ryan Bollwerk for his ongoing assistance as we researched Coach's bag history. And thanks to the marketing and communications team, Amanda Garcia Santana and Brooke Hudson.

Preeti Wali seamlessly stepped in to oversee and advise on production and marketing elements, and became an invaluable part of the book team. Sarah Greenberg's timely transcriptions and Julie Tate's fact-checking assistance helped ensure accuracy. Mark Fortier, Margaret Rogalski, and Mike Taylor's energy and experience helped amplify the book's themes.

Thanks to friends and family who read excerpts and offered insights along the way, including Alan and Marilyn Berkowitz, Dan Doctoroff, Bob Roth, and Francine Della Badia.

A special thanks to my daughter Alana who led the final read-through, offering ideas that made the book better.

In addition to my Benvolio Group partners, Sam and Ern, the incomparable Pat Cherry, Rachel Tamburelli, and Anne Dessaint assisted in countless ways. You all make it a pleasure to come to work every day.

I am also grateful for the many, many years of unconditional love and support that I received from Bobbie's parents, Elaine and Robe.

Finally, to my eight grandchildren—Ella Odinec, Arianna Odinec, Noah Odinec, Gabriel Frankfort, Waverly Frankfort, Sienna Frankfort Spector, Eli Frankfort Spector, and Indigo Frankfort—thank you for the joy you each bring to our family, and for inspiring me to capture history for you and for future generations.

INDEX

ABOUT THE AUTHOR

Lew Frankfort is Chairman Emeritus of Coach, Inc. He joined Coach in 1979 and served as Chairman and CEO from 1985 through 2014. During his 35 years with Coach, Lew built the small leather goods company into a $5 billion global accessories and lifestyle brand and was recognized multiple times by *Barron's* as one of the "30 Most Respected CEOs around the World," and by *Institutional Investor* as one of the "Best CEOs in America." After retiring from Coach, Lew cofounded Benvolio Group, an investment firm that focuses on early-stage disruptive consumer brands, including several where he advises and mentors senior leaders. Lew spent the first 10 years of his career in New York City government, with the last three restoring the city's Head Start and day care programs as the Commissioner of the Agency for Child Development. He grew up in the Bronx and attended Hunter College and Columbia Business School. He and his wife Bobbie live in New York City, where they are active supporters of education and the arts. They have three children, eight grandchildren, and two beloved labradoodles.